POSTCARD HISTORY SERIES

# *South Carolina Postcards*
## *Volume I*

# *Charleston, Berkeley, and Dorchester Counties*

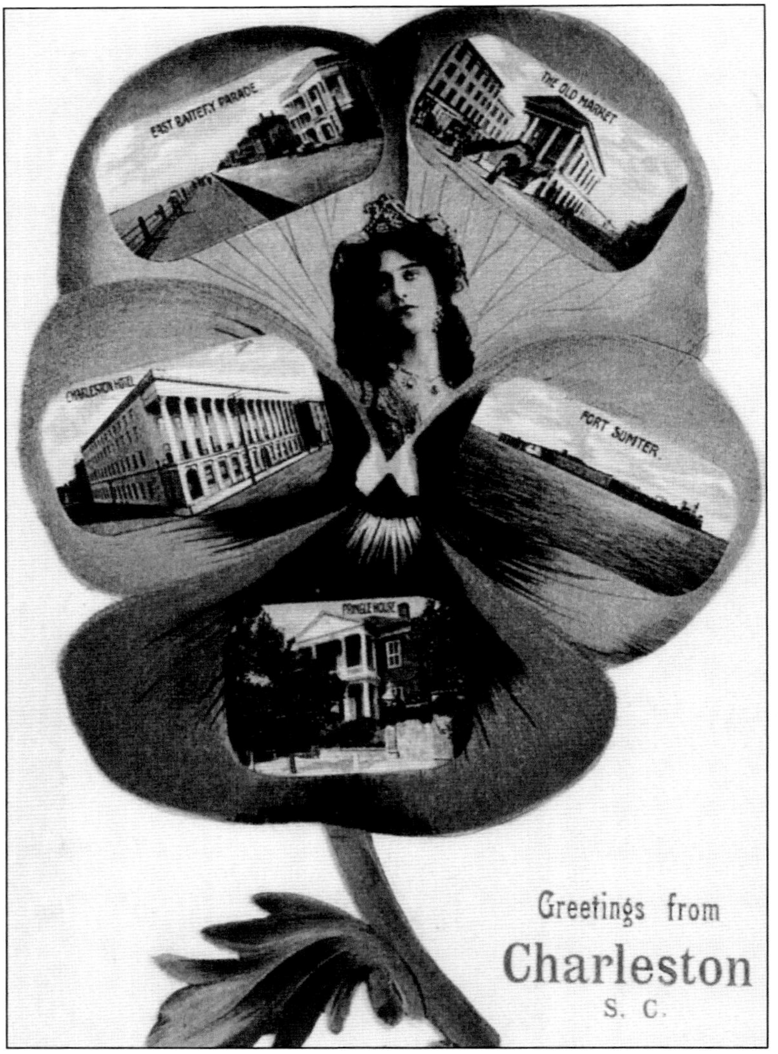


GREETINGS FROM CHARLESTON, S.C. (Color Lithography, [Kosmos Co., Halberstadt, Germany]; Paul C. Koeber, #7502, New York, NY, importer; *c.* 1907.) This stylized photo montage, with its photographs of local landmarks and tourist attractions, is the Charleston version of a design widely used on urban picture postcards of this period. All but one of the five standard attractions portrayed here may still be seen by any visitor to Charleston. The Charleston Hotel no longer exists.

*On the Cover*: CENTRAL MARKET AND THE BUZZARDS, CHARLESTON, S.C. (Color Lithography, Detroit Publishing Co., #11533, Detroit, MI; *c.* 1907.) The tradition of the presence of turkey buzzards, or "Charleston Eagles," on the streets and rooftops of the Old Market, or Central Market, is a long one, deriving from their practice of scavenging meat scraps thrown into the streets from the butchers' stalls. George C. Rogers Jr., in *Charleston in the Age of the Pinckneys* (1969), reveals that when the Duke of Saxe-Weimar visited Charleston in 1826, he noticed a number of buzzards sitting on the roof of the market houses and later wrote: "They are not only suffered as very useful animals, but there is a price of five dollars for the killing of one of these birds." Rogers goes on to observe that "the presence of the buzzards and a certain smell were proof that this was not entirely paradise."

POSTCARD HISTORY SERIES

# South Carolina Postcards
## Volume I

# Charleston, Berkeley, and Dorchester Counties

Howard Woody and Thomas L. Johnson

ARCADIA
PUBLISHING

ISBN 978-0-7385-8233-7

Published by Arcadia Publishing
Charleston, South Carolina

Printed in the United States of America

Library of Congress Catalog Card Number: Applied for

For all general information contact Arcadia Publishing at:
Telephone 843-853-2070
Fax 843-853-0044
E-mail sales@arcadiapublishing.com
For customer service and orders:
Toll-Free 1-888-313-2665

Visit us on the Internet at www.arcadiapublishing.com

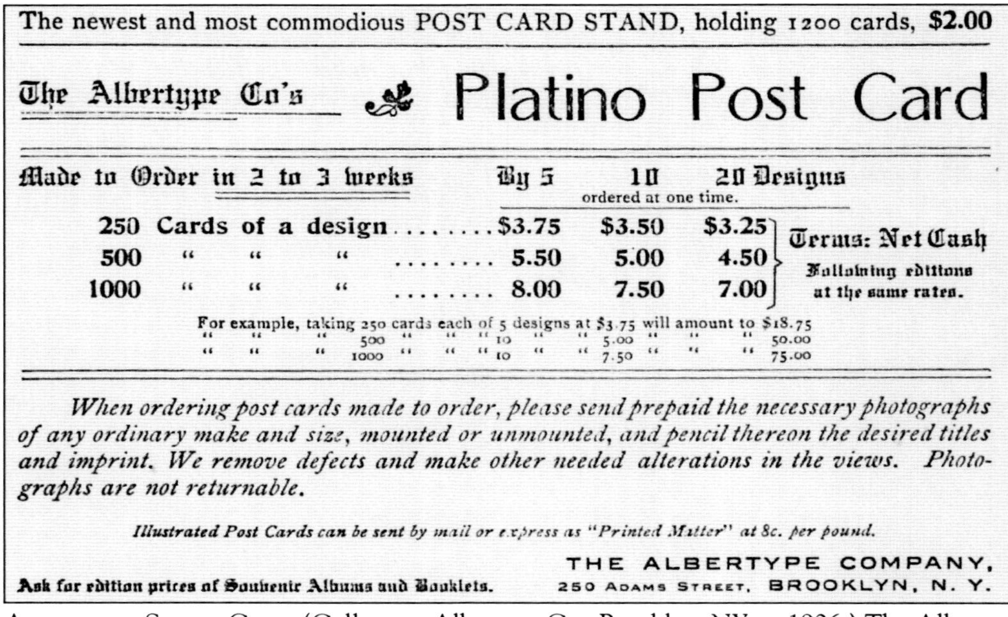
The newest and most commodious POST CARD STAND, holding 1200 cards, **$2.00**

The Albertype Co's Platino Post Card

**Made to Order in 2 to 3 weeks**

| | By 5 | 10 | 20 Designs ordered at one time. | |
|---|---|---|---|---|
| 250 Cards of a design | $3.75 | $3.50 | $3.25 | Terms: Net Cash |
| 500 " " " | 5.50 | 5.00 | 4.50 | Following editions |
| 1000 " " " | 8.00 | 7.50 | 7.00 | at the same rates. |

For example, taking 250 cards each of 5 designs at $3.75 will amount to $18.75
" " " 500 " " " 10 " " 5.00 " " " 50.00
" " " 1000 " " " 10 " " 7.50 " " " 75.00

*When ordering post cards made to order, please send prepaid the necessary photographs of any ordinary make and size, mounted or unmounted, and pencil thereon the desired titles and imprint. We remove defects and make other needed alterations in the views. Photographs are not returnable.*

*Illustrated Post Cards can be sent by mail or express as "Printed Matter" at 8c. per pound.*

Ask for edition prices of Souvenir Albums and Booklets.

THE ALBERTYPE COMPANY,
250 ADAMS STREET, BROOKLYN, N. Y.

ADVERTISING SAMPLE CARD. (Collotype, Albertype Co., Brooklyn, NY; *c.* 1906.) The Albertype Company began around 1872 as a producer of souvenir picture books and later shifted into full-time postcard production when it obtained the rights to Joseph Albert's collotype process. This monochrome photogelatin process—using a light-sensitive solution of gelatin, potassium bichromate, and ammonia—creates a thin surface film of fine granular particles which precludes the use of halftone screens and permits sharp, accurate details. Postcard-size negatives eliminated enlargement problems, and unwanted details were painted out on the negatives to clean up the final image. Stenciled, hand-colored, or watercolor tints were used when color was requested. Albertype, the earliest national postcard printer and the producer of Clyde Line cards, sent its jobbers along coastal shipping routes and distributed its Pioneer and Private Mailing Cards and later issues in most Atlantic ports and major cities.

# Contents

# Acknowledgments

This book has resulted in great part from the interest and efforts of numerous persons who generously assisted the editors in practical ways. In particular we wish to thank Allen H. Stokes and Beth Bilderback at the South Caroliniana Library, University of South Carolina. Other key people in Columbia who loaned cards and offered information and advice were Paul Jeter III and Harvey Teal. In Charleston the essential persons were Mary Giles at the Charleston Museum; William K. Finley, Katherine Fleming, and Dale Rosengarten of Special Collections at the Robert Scott Small Library, College of Charleston; Alex Moore at the South Carolina Historical Society; Solomon Breibart of the Kahal Kadosh Beth Elohim Archives; Joe Holleman, collector and researcher; and Theodore Aiken, on behalf of the Aiken family. David Rison and Barbara Hill shared their research expertise on Dorchester County. William R. Erwin Jr. and Janie C. Morris of Special Collections, Duke University, provided access to the Michael Francis Blake Collection there and facilitated its use in this project. In addition to the South Caroliniana Library, these archives also permitted the appearance of their postcards here: the Charleston Museum, the South Carolina Historical Society, the Beth Elohim Collection at the College of Charleston, and the Hampton County Historical Museum.

Private collectors in Charleston, Berkeley, and Dorchester Counties who allowed valuable items to be included in the book are: Leah R. Barkowitz, Kenneth A. Dandridge, Myrta Hall, Joe Holleman, Robert J. Karrer, Maurine J. LeCato, Ronald Ramsey, Rabbi William Rosenthall, and Dwight H. Stuckey. And these collectors in other areas loaned their postcards: Davie Beard, Mary M. Bishop, Phriness E. Cox, Paul L. Howle, Martha D. Greenway, W. Ashby ("Bubba") McElveen, and Nyles Rowell.

We especially want to express our gratitude to Kirsty Sutton (group publishing manager) and Sarah Maineri (senior editor) at Arcadia, for their firm but patient guidance through the maze of book production.

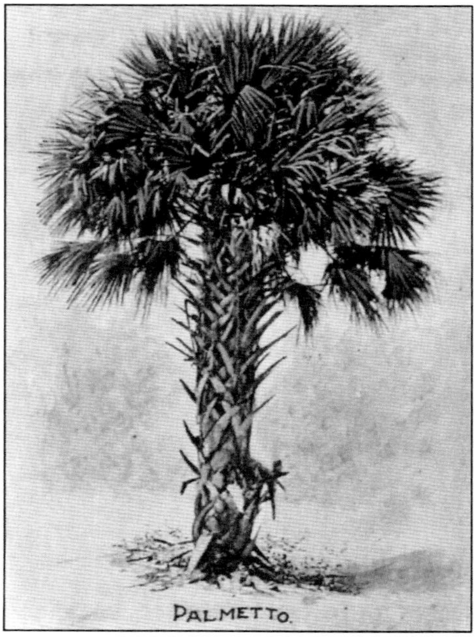


GREETINGS FROM CHARLESTON, PALMETTO. (Collotype, Albertype Co., Brooklyn, NY; 1898–1900.) The postmark on this card "From Irma" is 1902—one of the earliest in the collection. It is not surprising that a single palmetto tree should be among the first motifs to appear on postcards from Charleston. The title of an essay published by William Gilmore Simms in *Harper's New Monthly Magazine* for June 1857 is "Charleston, The Palmetto City."

# INTRODUCTION

Tucked away in the August 1901 issue of *The Exposition*, the monthly magazine which began publication in 1900 in the interest of promoting the South Carolina Inter-State and West Indian Exposition of 1901–1902, is a brief notice that the Ways and Means Committee had "in course of preparation, to place on sale early in August, 'private mailing cards,' descriptive of the Exposition and the vicinity of Charleston." The announcement went on to say that the cards would be on sale at several book stores and that they would prove "interesting souvenirs for mailing both at home and abroad."

This rare allusion to the postcard in South Carolina does suggest something of the significance of the little mass-produced pictorial cards which were beginning to play an essential part in America's habits of communication. Although the Lipman's Postal Card was patented in 1861—as a private postal card for advertisements or messages that needed an adhesive postage stamp—and an initial governmental "Correspondenz Karte" [correspondence card] bearing an imprinted stamp had been introduced in Austria on October 1, 1869, for short unenclosed messages, they could not become the popular means of communication which they would become in America until federal legislation of May 19, 1898, authorized the United States Post Office to permit private companies to publish them for use with a postage stamp. Of course, governmental postal cards were then and still are being produced and used; however, that act—combined with the rural free delivery program inaugurated on October 1, 1896—allowed postcards without stamps to be cheaply made and mailed to any destination, near or far. The commercial potential of manufacturing a "souvenir" mailing card which bore an attractive image as well as space for a message opened the publishing floodgates. Many millions of cards were issued, often by domestic and foreign companies determined to produce, even in huge quantities, images of the highest quality. The phenomenon in America of the ubiquitous picture postcard was the happy result of the merging of sophisticated advancements in the art and science of photography with the federal bureaucracy's decisions relating to mass communications. The insatiable card-collecting proclivity of the public further fueled the growth of the industry.

One of the principal objects of this book, as it will be of the other volumes proposed in this statewide series, is to focus upon the superlatively produced images of South Carolina that emerged on the picture postcard from 1898 to 1912, the period which students of the genre agree was its golden era. Many of these were the work of printers in Western Europe, especially in Germany, who began publishing "postal cards" for resort merchants as an advertising medium to attract new patrons. These artistically rendered items evolved into photographic view-cards which, like their predecessors, spread throughout Europe, Great Britain, the United States, and distant colonies.

Key among the German exporting view-card printers were Stengel and Company of Dresden and Knackstedt and Nather of Hamburg. In Great Britain the principal exporters were Raphael Tuck and Sons, London, who sub-contracted much of their view-card work to Louis Glaser of Leipzig and Valentine and Sons of Dundee, Scotland. In America the two early, nationally established view-card printers were the Albertype Company of Brooklyn and the Detroit Publishing Company. This book begins with Albertype's pioneer (pre-1898) issues, the only postcards of this era distributed in South Carolina, and goes on to focus briefly on those produced to capitalize upon the South Carolina Inter-State and West Indian Exposition, since this was the most ambitious event of its kind held in the state to that time.

The book, then, is also intended as a specimen study of national and international postcard history applied to the local scene. Many of the samples included here represent the excellence of the early publishers and are accompanied by information of particular interest to the postcard specialist. In this way, the project is a conscious, purposeful celebration of the centennial anniversary of the initial United States Postal Act authorizing and regulating the use of postcards. A title line under each item includes the title of the image, a code number, the process (whether color lithography, collotype, halftone, photoengraving, or photoprint [real photo]), the manufacturing company, the publisher and/or distributor, the circulation date (when known), and the name of the photographer (if known). In some cases, the abbreviation *cp.* has been used to indicate a copyright date. In numerous instances the date is an estimate (indicated with c. in the text) based upon a knowledge of the chronological evolution of postal and printing styles and of the word usage on the backs of the cards.

For historic reasons beyond those relating to the postcard, however, the authors have determined that for South Carolina, the term *golden era* needs to include the years up to 1930—even though all that was happening in the state was far from "golden." But the period was one which embraced huge changes in the "New South" experience of Charleston and vicinity before the severe downturn of the Depression. Principal among these were the impact of World War I and the burgeoning of the twin industries of military development and tourism. At this point—from 1913 to 1930—the quality of the picture postcard is less important than what it reveals about the period, the place, and its people. The traveling jobbers of the early years, who had been trained by the publishers to be skilled professional photographers, had done their work very well: they had established an industry-wide standard of excellence. But even poorly made "real photos" and inferior, quickly produced local postcards can tell an unusual or important story. Viewers will find that, throughout the book, some of the most technically modest and imperfect pictures are the most revealing ones.

Of course, it is the desire of the authors that the book serve the educational purpose of an illustrated history, as it reflects the entire social, cultural, architectural, economic, and military experience of a place and its people during a particular time. Presented here are the structures, past and present, which residents erected to live and work in—the town houses, the country dwellings, stores, government buildings, police headquarters, firehouses, barracks, and tents. We see the places where people worshiped, went to school, and sought diversion: the churches, schools, lodges, hotels, museums, parks, fairgrounds, beach pavilions, golf links, and carousels. We catch glimpses of the means of transportation to all these places: the ships, wagons, railroads, and early automobiles.

More importantly, the people themselves are presented at work and at play: thronging the streets, loading the ships, minding the cotton wagons, fighting fires, planting crops, tending the store, performing military drills, swimming at the beach, eating a leisurely meal—posing for the camera, or not posing at all. Here are the styles of the day—in dress and in illustration and printing design. And here are the human stereotypes and the class distinctions as well as the breaking of these stereotypes and distinctions; the encounter between the antique and the new, between the young and the old. Here is the look of wartime and of peace; and the region's sometimes stark, sometimes lush, mellowed beauty—always the beauty.

In addition to acting as yet another historical record of Charleston, Berkeley, and Dorchester Counties, this book may also function as something of a modern guidebook, with material arranged in such a way as to be useful on either a walking or driving tour of the area. It also can be used as a sample book of Charleston photographers, with identifiable works by half a dozen of the city's major commercial picture-takers or studios of the day, including the works of two African-American photographers—Garfield Joyce and Michael Francis Blake. Especially interesting and valuable are the few studio portraits of individuals and families which have turned up in this format and are here presented.

This project represents an intense search and review of over one hundred thousand South Carolina-related pictorial postcards over the course of several years, both in the state and far beyond. While many millions of South Carolina cards may have been printed, mailed, and enjoyed during the thirty-year period beginning one hundred years ago, only a small number of them have been located. Some of the rural areas, in particular, have yielded disappointingly few cards. Many, of course, have been lost forever. On the other hand, unique, unanticipated postcards are being discovered every month, about one-third of which can be considered rare, one-of-a-kind items. A large number of the postcards seen here have been acquired for and by the photographic archive at the University of South Carolina's South Caroliniana Library, where they are available to other researchers. Some were already in the collections there. Others were reproduced from master copies located in a variety of repositories, as well as in private hands.

We have tried to be both inclusive and imaginative in our selection of images used in this volume and to be accurate and informative in the caption material. Bibliographical references in the latter are for those who wish to corroborate information or pursue further research into the subject of a particular picture. Possible errors in both judgment and fact in these regards are the responsibility of the authors, and in no way reflect upon the good offices of those who have so graciously assisted us in our endeavors.

Whether the viewer or reader merely peruses *South Carolina Postcards, The Golden Era: 1898–1930 Volume 1: Charleston, Berkeley, and Dorchester Counties* as one more regional picture book with some interesting old images in it, or consults it as a serious volume on the history of the postcard locally applied, or views it as an illustrated textbook on Charleston and her neighbors, or even uses the work as an architectural guidebook to the "Palmetto City," we hope that it may somehow prove to be truly diverting and enlightening, revealing and delightful.

Thomas L. Johnson
Howard Woody

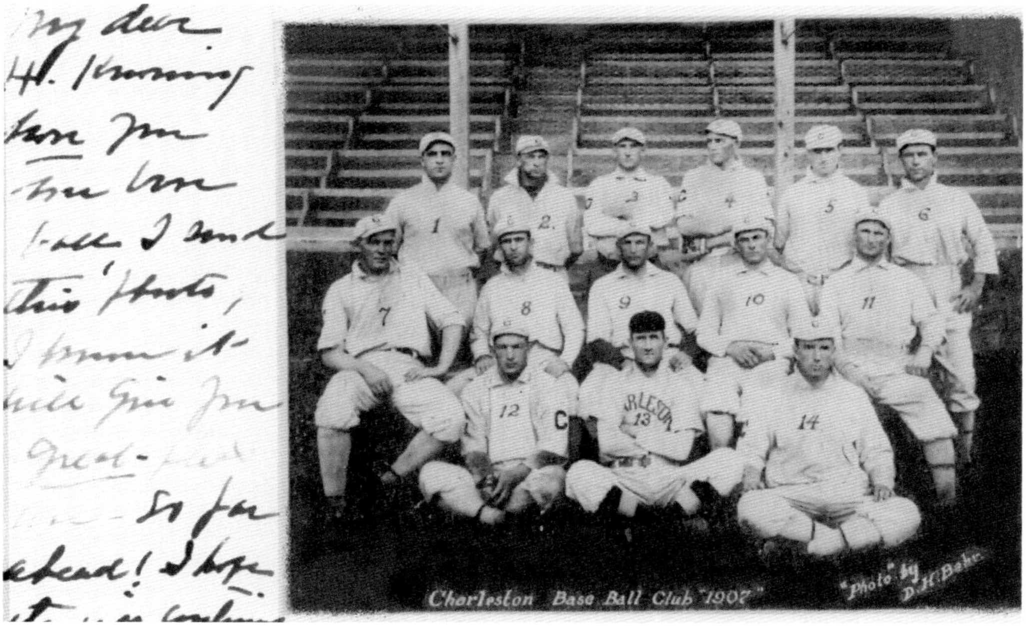


CHARLESTON BASE BALL CLUB "1907." The Charleston Gulls baseball club was a member of the South Atlantic (Sally) League along with Columbia, Augusta, Macon, Savannah, and Jacksonville. The regular players listed by position were Johnson and Wilkinson, first base; Schippy, second base; Markley and Reddick, short stop; Griffin, third base; Evers and Reisenger, catcher; Meany, right field; Mullin, center field; Raftery, left field; Foster, Paige, and Raymond, pitchers; and Matthews, manager. On July 14, 1907, the Charleston team was in first place with 47 wins and 32 losses. Tom Raftery was the Gulls leading batter with a .287 average. The team portrait was made by D.H. Bahr.

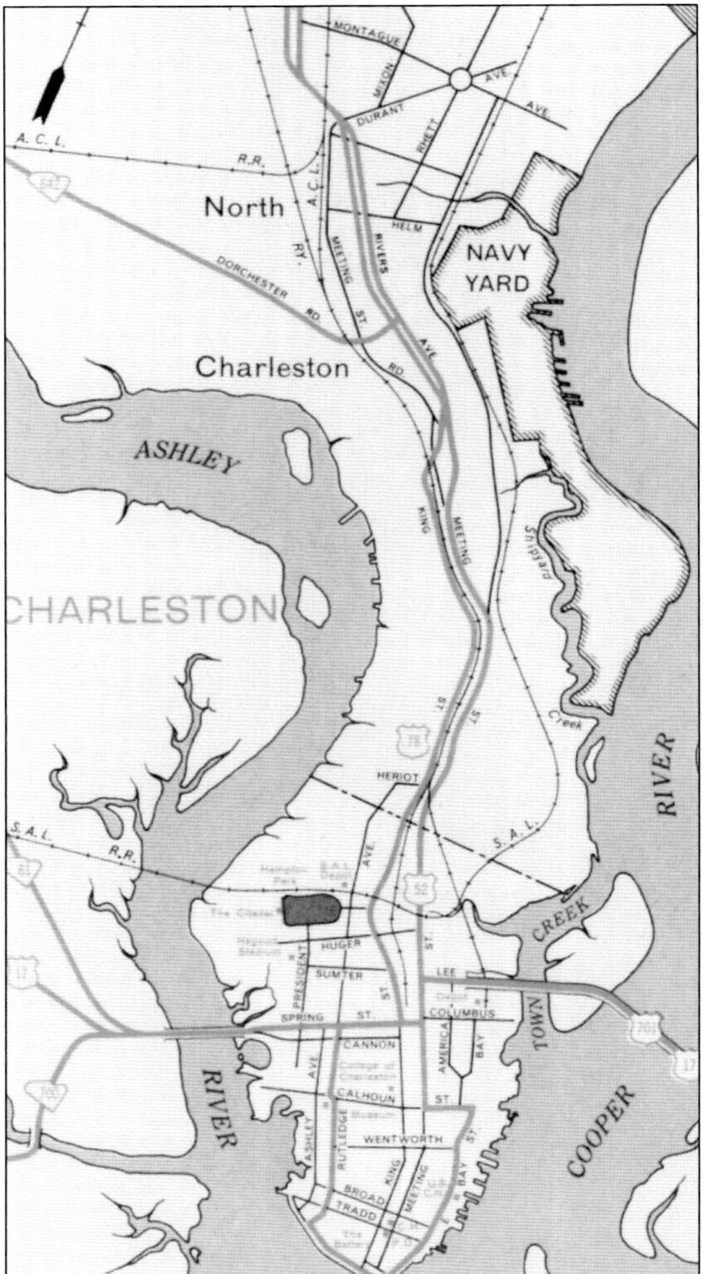


MAP OF THE CITY OF CHARLESTON AND VICINITY. Although of a later vintage (1951), this little Charleston insert—among the first such appearances on the early South Carolina State Highway Department road maps—provides an overall view of the city's peninsula in its relation to the rivers and the surrounding land masses. It also shows the location of the Navy Yard, the railroad lines, and some of the city's principal streets and attractions.

On p. 114 is a regional map indicating the location of such Charleston County communities as Mt. Pleasant, Moultrieville (on Sullivan's Island), Meggett, and Edisto Island.

# One

# CHARLESTON COUNTY

Each section of Charleston County is represented here—from McClellanville to the north, Edisto to the south, and Meggett in the west. However, readers will find many more views of Charleston and its immediate surroundings than of any other locale. This can be explained by the simple fact that the city itself in its many dimensions has been portrayed on the picture postcard more frequently than any other part of the tri-county area. Furthermore, as General C. Irvine Walker remarked in a speech at the Fort Sumter Hotel in 1924, "Standing where you do now, there are more points of historic interest within 5 miles of you than within 5 miles of any other spot in America." As the interested viewer turns this page, the words of the late Samuel Gaillard Stoney (1891–1968) can as well be invoked here as in his own book *This Is Charleston* (1944): "If you use these photographs properly, you will find that however they fail otherwise, they help to tell the story of Charleston as no words could; and that, after all, is what illustrations are supposed to do."

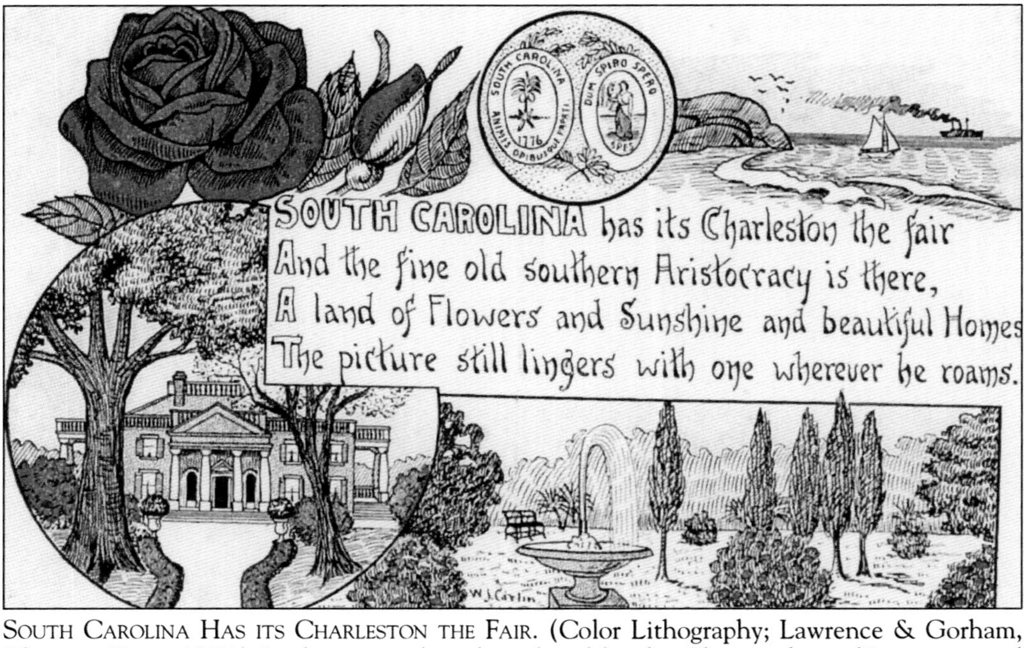


SOUTH CAROLINA HAS ITS CHARLESTON THE FAIR. (Color Lithography; Lawrence & Gorham, Chicago, IL; c. 1907.) In this unusual card produced by the Chicago firm of Lawrence and Gorham, romantic line drawings and sentimental verse proclaim South Carolina as "a land of Flowers and Sunshine and beautiful Homes" and in first-line prominence, home to "Charleston the Fair." This company, a producer of diverse mass-produced generic cards, made hundreds with similar stock verses and images for states and cities across the nation.

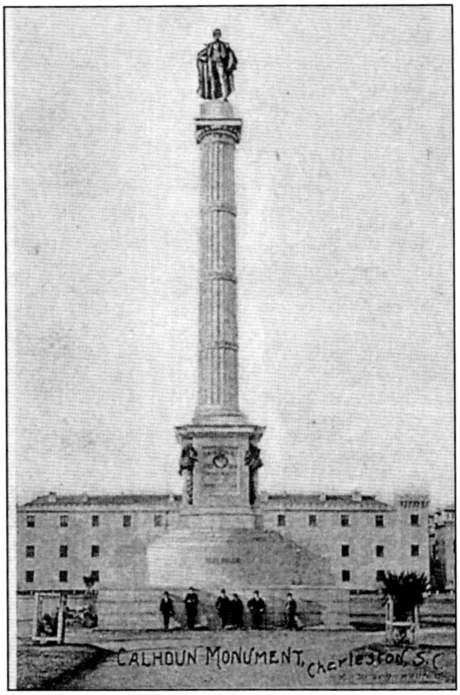


CALHOUN MONUMENT, CHARLESTON, S.C. (Collotype, 3½" X 5½", Albertype Co., Brooklyn, NY; *c.* 1898.) The three cultural groups of people associated with Charleston and its environs from its beginning—Native Americans, African Americans, and European settlers—along with the racial stereotyping which characterized some of the earliest postcards from the period, are portrayed on the four "Pioneer" cards on these two pages. The ubiquitous presence of statesman John C. Calhoun (1782–1850) towers over Marion Square in the statue by the popular Scottish-born sculptor John Massey Rhind (1860–1936), to the left, which was erected by the Calhoun Association in 1895. This is the only unblemished example of this card that has been found, and none of these limited-edition Pioneer cards have been located recently. The image here is actually a 2"-wide, vertical picture on the left side, with a 3-1/2"-wide message space on the right. The caption is placed in this blank space.

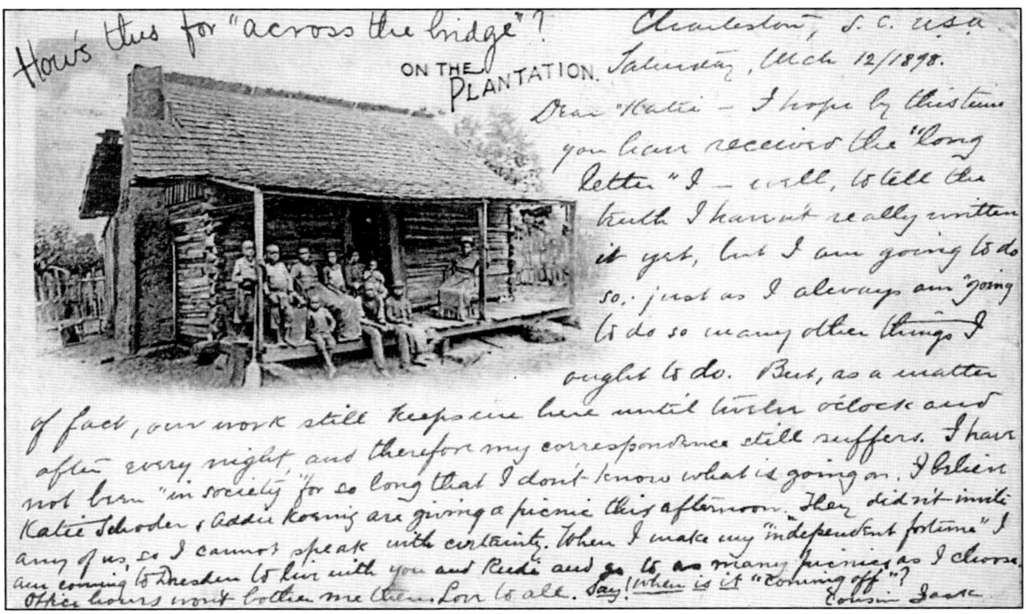


ON THE PLANTATION. (Collotype, Albertype Co., Brooklyn, NY; 1898.) This Pioneer "souvenir card" of a Lowcountry plantation scene, geared to the market for quaintness and local color and mailed from Charleston in 1898, reveals conditions "across the bridge." Pioneer cards—the few cards produced before the initial "postcard" Act of Congress, May 19, 1898—often had a small image with blank space for a short note. The Albertype series probably contained eight or ten cards. Many images were reprinted on the officially sanctioned "Private Mailing Card" of the succeeding era—July 1, 1898, to December 24, 1901—with some reissued after that.

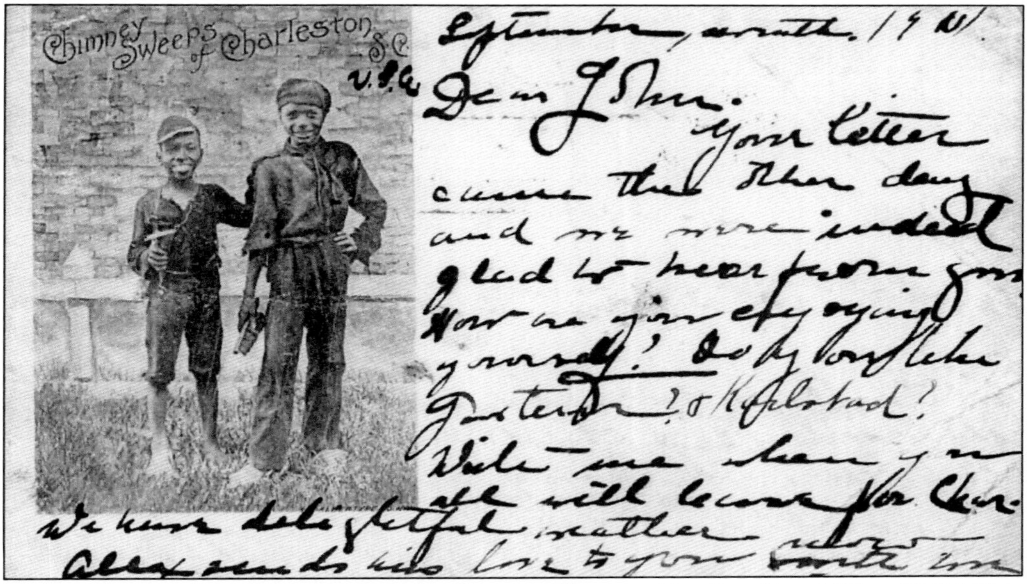


CHIMNEY SWEEPS OF CHARLESTON, S.C. (Collotype, Albertype Co., Brooklyn, NY; *c.* 1900.) This early, "picturesque" miniature of two young black chimney sweeps—a Private Mailing Card—is postmarked September 8, 1901; however, it resembles the earlier Pioneer card style and was likely first issued then. Initial South Carolina Pioneers, produced by a single national company, were only issued in the Charleston area. Only one of this issue has been found.

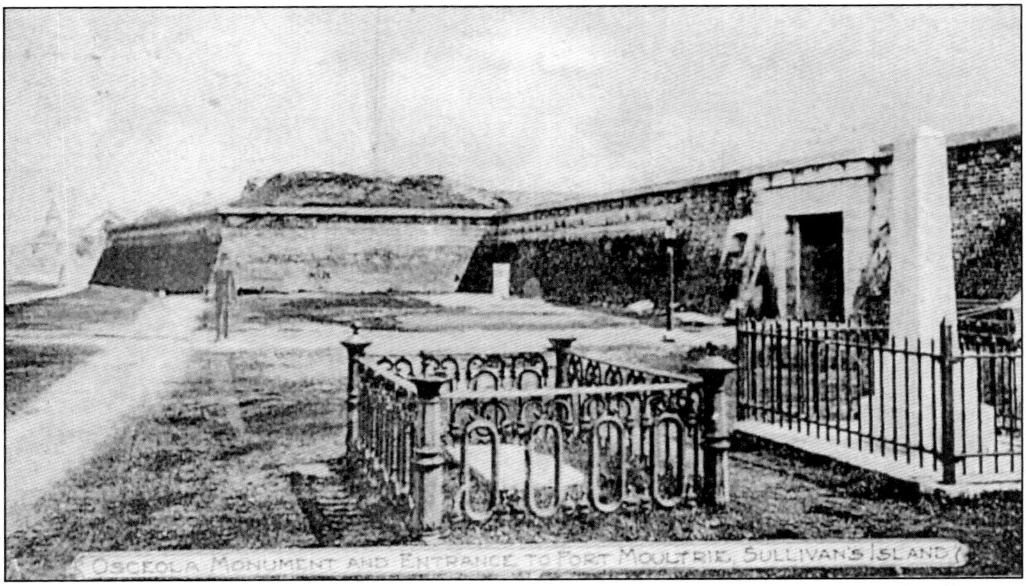


OSCEOLA MONUMENT AND ENTRANCE TO FORT MOULTRIE, SULLIVAN'S ISLAND. (Collotype, Albertype Co., Brooklyn, NY; *c.* 1900.) The story of South Carolina and the Native American, whose presence lives on in the bloodlines of many families and in the lore and language of place, has often been one of treachery, sadness, and decimation. On January 1, 1838, Osceola, chief of the Seminoles, with a party of a hundred warriors and eighty-two women and children, was brought to Fort Moultrie. By the end of the month he had died. His grave lies at the foot of the north wall of the fort, west of the entrance. This was probably a Pioneer reprint card.

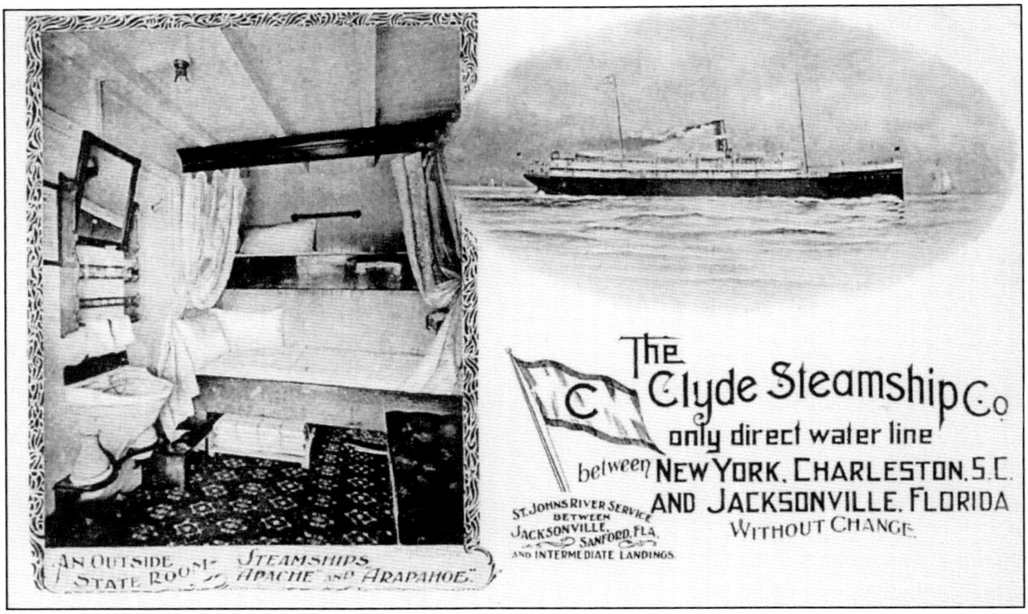


AN OUTSIDE STATE ROOM, STEAMSHIPS *APACHE* AND *ARAPAHOE*. (Collotype, Albertype Co., Brooklyn, NY; c. 1900.) Charleston, wrote John Martin Hammond in 1916, was a very good destination for a sea trip from the north: "One may leave New York by the Clyde Line and have a pleasant coasting voyage here, a trip about as long as the passage to Bermuda and fully as enjoyable in its taste of sea air." This Private Mailing Card featuring a photograph of an outside stateroom shows the comfortable accommodations aboard such ships as the *Apache* and *Arapahoe*. Albertype printed a set of views showing the modern facilities of these ships.

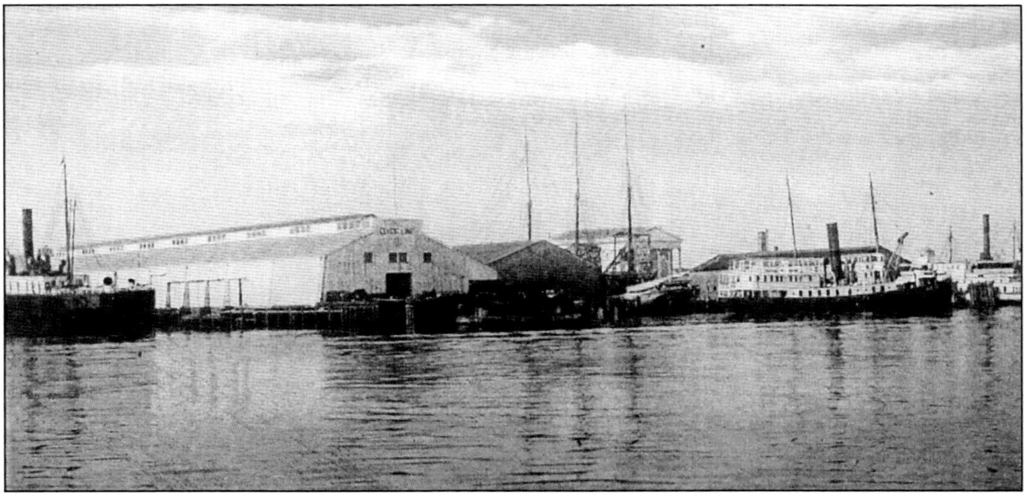

NEW CLYDE LINE DOCKS, CHARLESTON, S.C. (Color Lithography, Curt Teich Co., #A-49178, Chicago, IL; c. 1912.) From the time the first steamship engaged in coastal traffic put into Charleston in 1870, the Clyde Line figured preeminently in the conduct of the old clipper business, with Charleston a regular port of call between New York and Jacksonville. The William A. Clyde Company advertised "Frequent Sailings" and "Unexcelled Cuisine." This view of the docks would have greeted the passenger arriving at the company's terminal at Vendue Range on one of the Clyde Line ships.

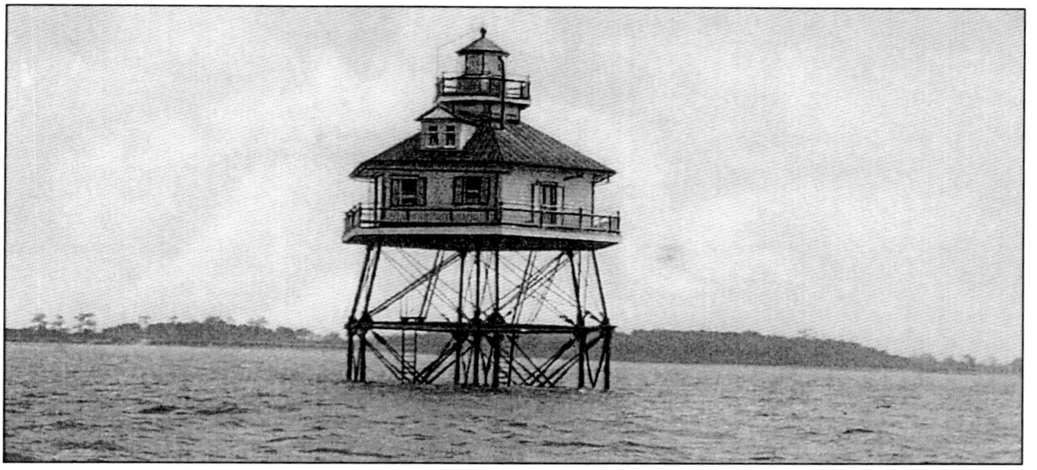

AN ELEVATED LIGHT HOUSE. (Color Lithography, Detroit Publishing Co., #13507, Detroit, MI; *c.* 1907.) Fort Ripley was the name of this little six-sided structure which could once be seen near the edge of the shoal called the Middle Ground, located between Fort Sumter and East Battery. Built by the federal government in 1878, it took its name from a small fortification constructed in 1862 for the defense of Charleston and then abandoned after the war. "The Fort Ripley of romance," Katherine D.M. Simons would write in 1930, "is now one of Charleston Harbor's minor lights. Its bell sounds every ten seconds; it shows a fixed red lamp; and it is catalogued in the Local Light List as 'No. 1988: Fort Ripley Shoal.'" The Fort Ripley Light was demolished in 1932. Only one example of this card has been found.

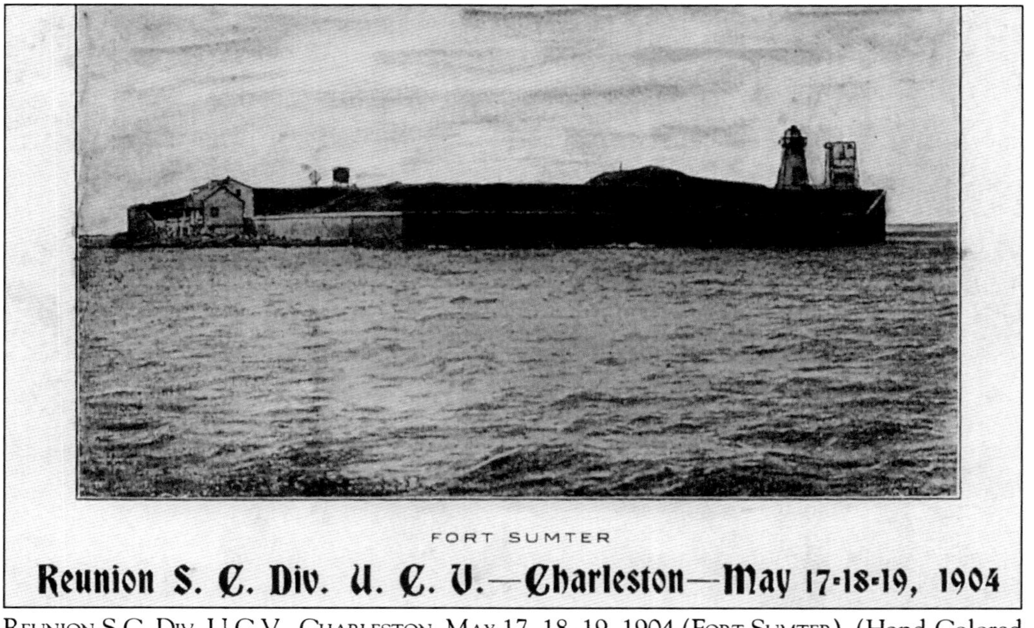


REUNION S.C. DIV. U.C.V., CHARLESTON, MAY 17–18–19, 1904 (FORT SUMTER). (Hand-Colored Halftone; 1904.) The first shot of the War Between the States was fired upon Fort Sumter in Charleston Harbor on April 12, 1861. An image of the fort on a mass mail-out card would have had predictable appeal to members of the South Carolina Division of the United Confederate Veterans who were being reminded to come to their reunion scheduled for May 17–19, 1904. This card, only found once, was produced by a local printer.

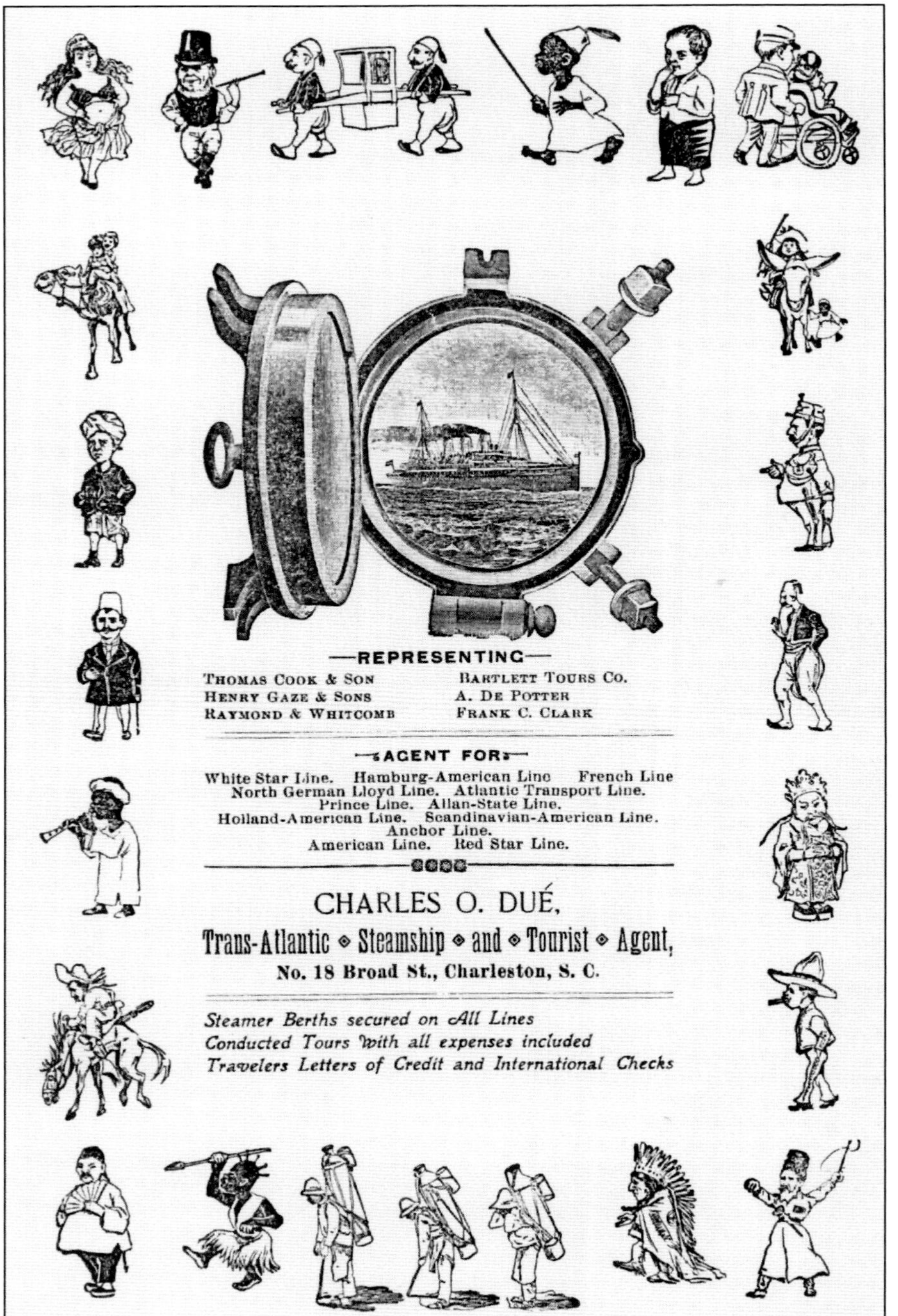


NORTH GERMAN LLOYD MAIL CARD. (Color Lithography, 9" X 6", Gray Lithographic Co., NY, NY; cp. 1899.) The North German LLoyd Line issued this oversized "mail card" which advertised the services of Charles O. Dué as a travel agent. It also appeared as a full-page advertisement in Waldo's 1902 Charleston *City Directory*, apparently Dué's first year in a line of work which would engage him at least through 1914. This limited-issue card has only been found in one collection.

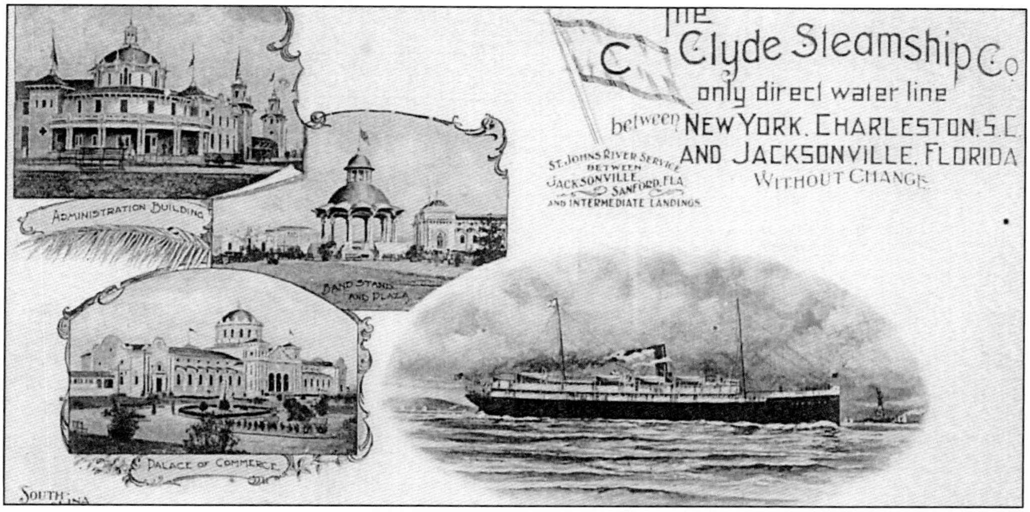


SOUTH CAROLINA I.S. & W.I., CHARLESTON, S.C. (Set 2: 4 to 6 cards; Collotype, Albertype Co., Brooklyn, NY; 1901.) The Clyde Steamship Company issued a limited-set of Private Mailing Cards promoting the South Carolina Inter-State and West Indian Exposition, which was held in Charleston from December 1901 to May 1902. As the city's major inaugural event of the new century, the exposition was "projected to show the industrial development and vast resources of the Southern States and the natural products of the West Indies, and to bring to the attention of the people of the United States the fact that Charleston is the natural and the best port through which to reach the West Indian and South American Countries." Featured on this card are images of the Administration Building, the bandstand and plaza, and the Palace of Commerce. These cards are occasionally seen and usually expensive.

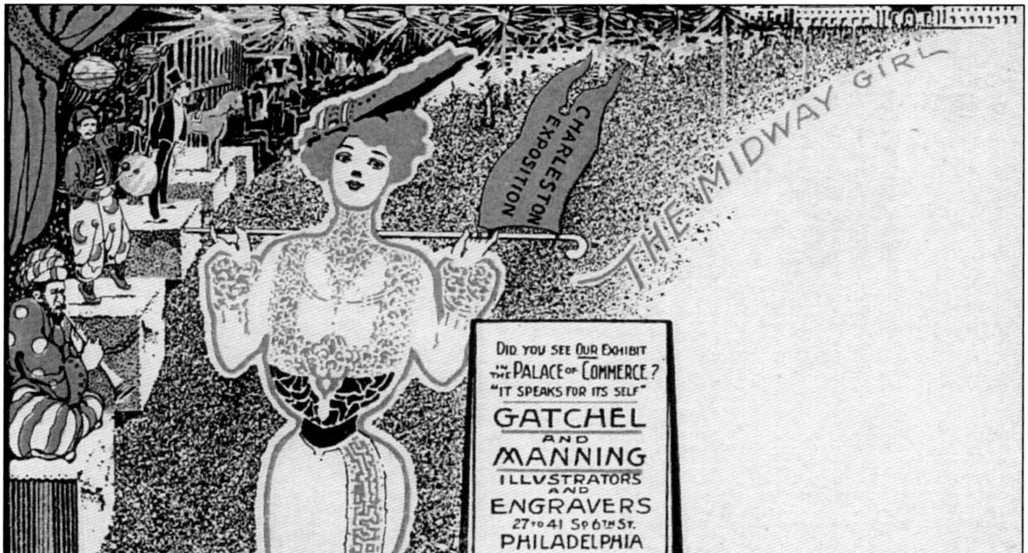


MIDWAY GIRL, CHARLESTON EXPOSITION. (Color Lithography, Gatchel and Manning, Philadelphia, PA; 1902.) This highly stylized "Charleston Exposition Postal Card" advertised the services of the Philadelphia engraving firm of Gatchel and Manning, who exhibited in the Palace of Commerce at the exposition. They designed and printed special advertising cards for merchants, resorts, and expositions. Only a few examples have been uncovered.

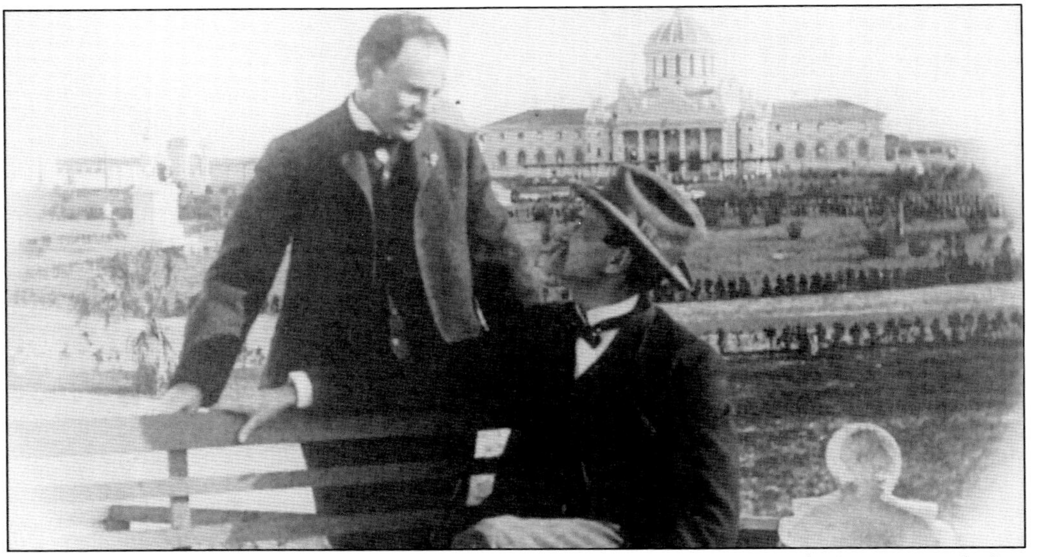

[PORTRAIT OF AUGUST KOHN AND JAMES C. HEMPHILL.] (Photoprint; 1902). Appropriately but informally portrayed in front of the exposition's most imposing building, the Cotton Palace, which held the place of honor in its Court of Palaces, were two of the state's most powerful men and most vocal proponents of the exhibition. On the left is journalist and businessman August Kohn (1868–1930), Columbia correspondent for the *News and Courier* (1892–1917) and secretary of the commission. On the right is James C. Hemphill (1850–1927), editor of the *News and Courier* (1889–1910), a member of the "public-spirited and indefatigable Board of Directors," and the untiring manager of promotion and publicity for the exposition.

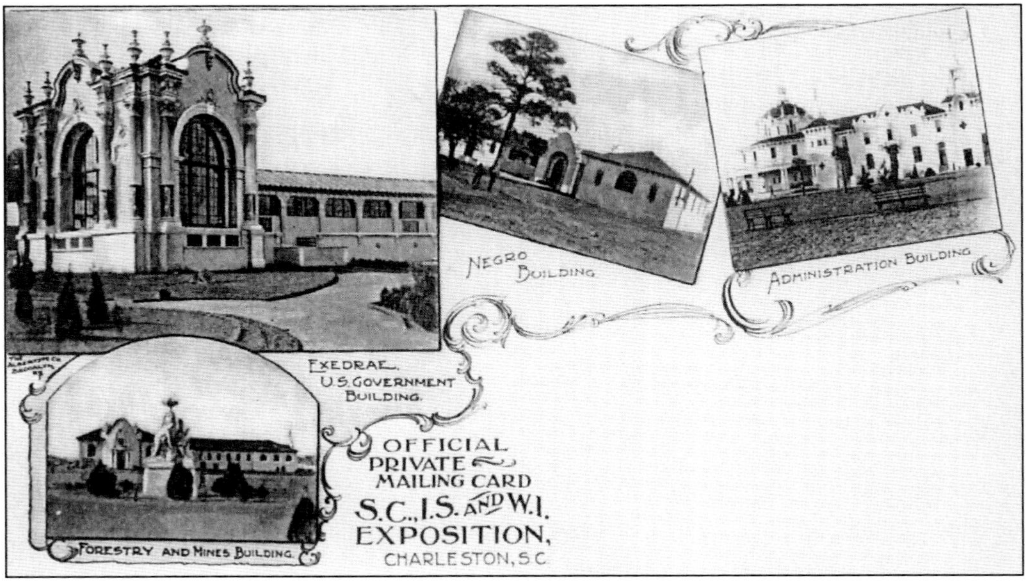


OFFICIAL PRIVATE MAILING CARD, S.C.I.S. & W.I. EXPOSITION, CHARLESTON, S.C., (Set 1: 10 cards; Collotype, Albertype Co., Brooklyn, NY; cp. 1902.) The Albertype Company of Brooklyn produced an official set of ten Private Mailing Cards for the exposition. This one featured photographs of the Forestry and Mines Building, the Federal U.S. Government Building, the Negro Building, and the Administration Building.

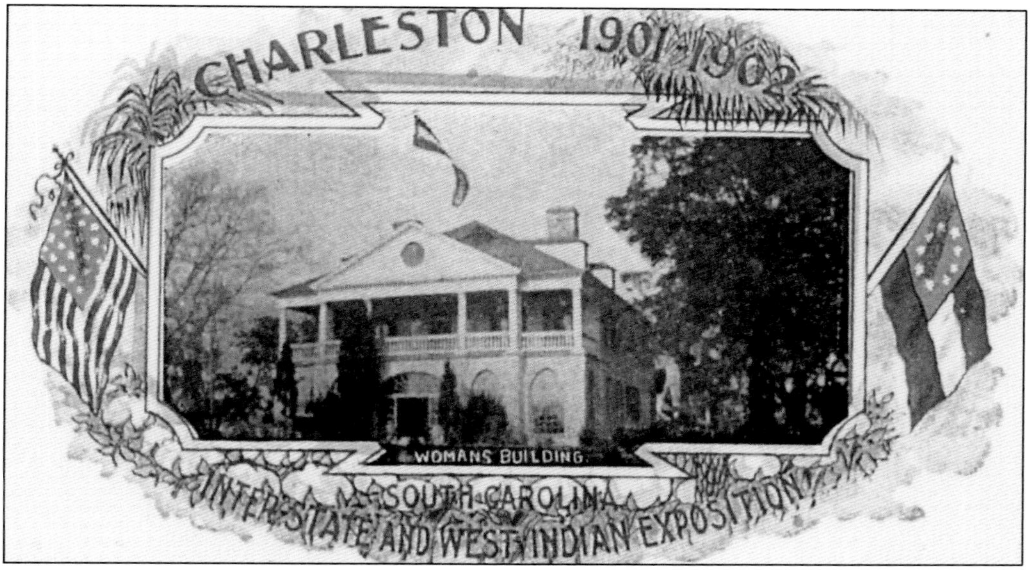


SOUTH CAROLINA INTER-STATE AND WEST INDIAN EXPOSITION, [WOMAN'S BUILDING], CHARLESTON, 1901–1902. (Set 3: five or more cards; Halftone & Color Lithography, $3\frac{3}{10}$" X $5\frac{5}{10}$", 1901.) A colorful patriotic motif frames this card depicting the Woman's Building, a newly renovated Colonial home known as the Lowndes House which existed on the Ashley River farm loaned by Captain Frederick W. Wagener for the use of the exposition. The events and activities at this site were supervised by the Daughters of the American Revolution and the Colonial Dames, who provided a "cool, inviting place for women and children." Mothers could leave "their little ones" in the nursery here while they took in the sights. Here, too, "the mighty who came to Charleston in battalions during the exposition . . . always found good cheer," and many of the exposition's entertainments were presented in its assembly hall. These limited-issue cards are seldom found.

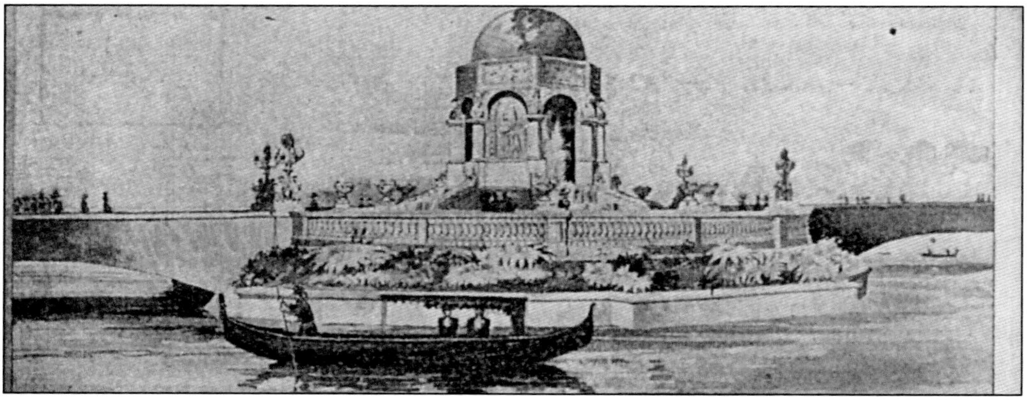

THE SOUTH CAROLINA INTER-STATE AND WEST INDIAN EXPOSITION, CHARLESTON, S.C., [ELECTRICAL ISLAND]. (Set 4: six or more cards; Halftone & Color Lithography, $3\frac{3}{10}$" X $5\frac{5}{10}$", [Lucas & Richardson Co., Charleston, SC]; c. 1901.) This view of Electrical Island, only featured in this limited-production set of exposition cards, probably was produced by Charleston's own Lucas and Richardson. The images were copied from architectural renderings that were framed by solid pale green, blue, or yellow backgrounds indicating at least several reissues of the set. This may have been one of the pre-exposition Private Mailing Cards referred to in the August 1901 issue of *The Exposition* as being offered for sale in local bookstores.

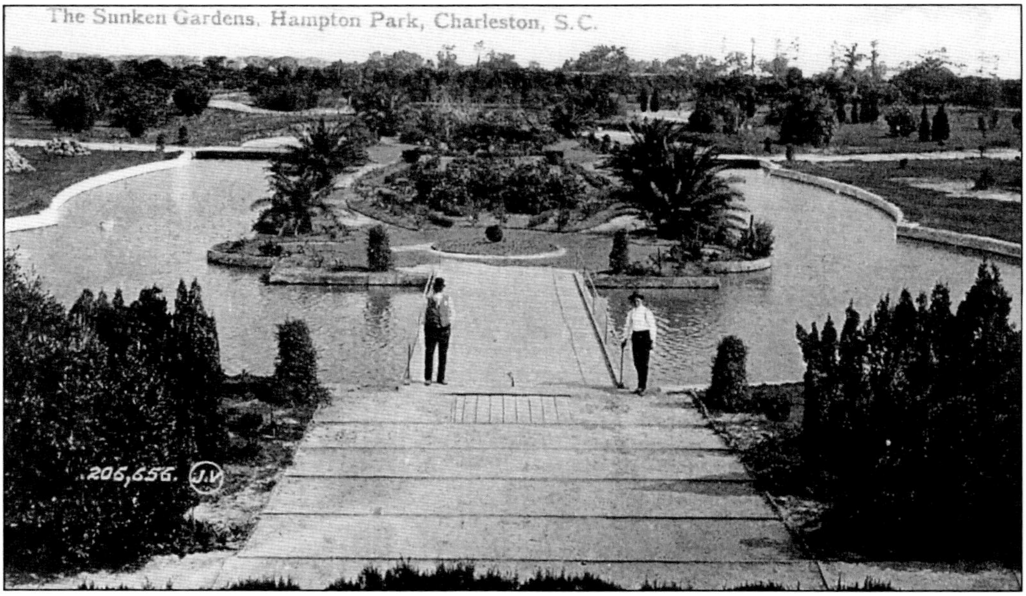


THE SUNKEN GARDENS, HAMPTON PARK, CHARLESTON, S.C. (Color Lithography, Valentine and Sons Publishing Co., #206, 656, Dundee, Scotland; *c.* 1910.) In the last line of "A Short Story of the South Carolina Inter-State and West Indian Exposition" (*Year Book*, 1902), J.C. Hemphill reveals that the site of the "Art Section" of the exposition had been bought by the City of Charleston and would be converted into a permanent park "as an enduring memorial" to the exposition. Named Hampton Park for the Confederate general who died in 1902, it was notable for the profuse beauty of its azaleas and seasonal flower beds.

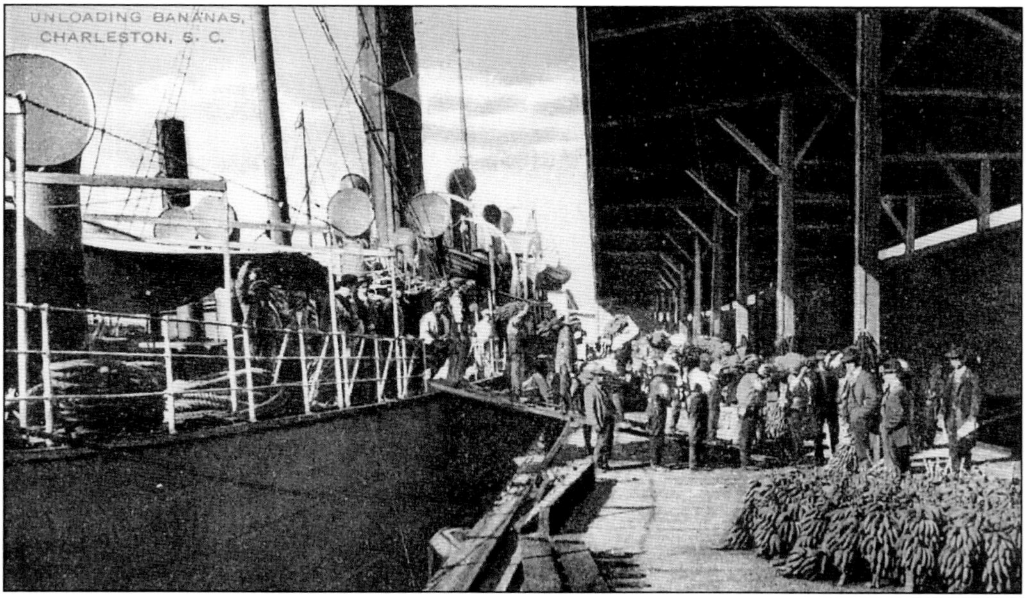


UNLOADING BANANAS, CHARLESTON, S.C. (Color Lithography, [Trenkler & Co., Leipzig, Germany]; *c.* 1908.) One of the significant practical results of the exposition was the decision by the United Fruit Company to locate in Charleston. By 1910 this company had weekly sailings to and from West Indian and Central American ports.

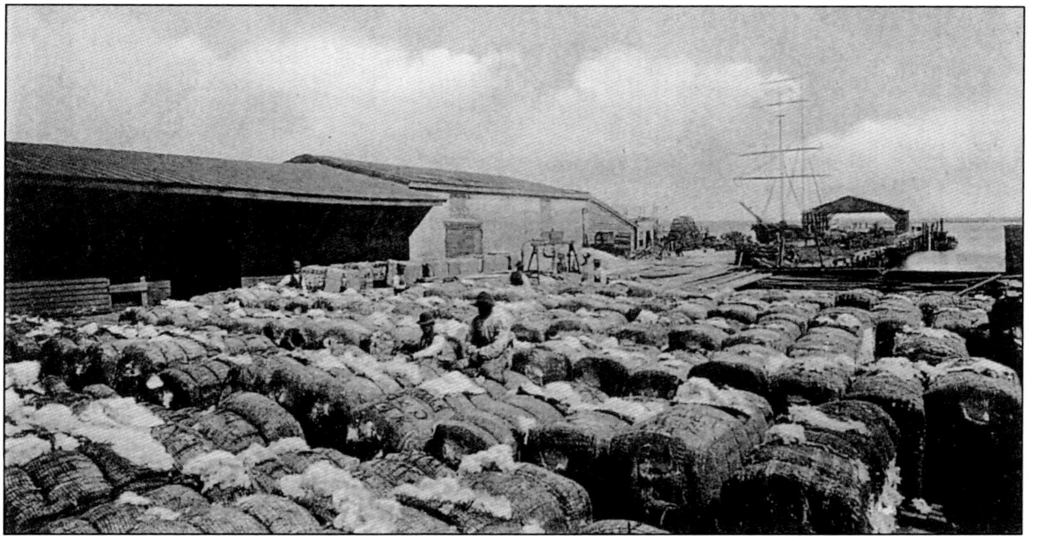

WHARF SCENE (COTTON) CHARLESTON, S.C. (Collotype, [Trenkler & Co., #80866, Leipzig, Germany]; Lange, B.L. Schwalbach & Co., Exporters; American Historical Art Publishers, NY; c. 1908.) In the 1901 publication *Charleston and Vicinity—Illustrated,* published to promote the exposition, the claim was made, simply, that "Charleston will be not only the principal export point for this State's [cotton] production, but also for all the Southern States, as it is the most direct shipping point to European nations. The city has the very best of facilities for receiving and shipping cotton, while the insurance here is as low as anywhere in the country."

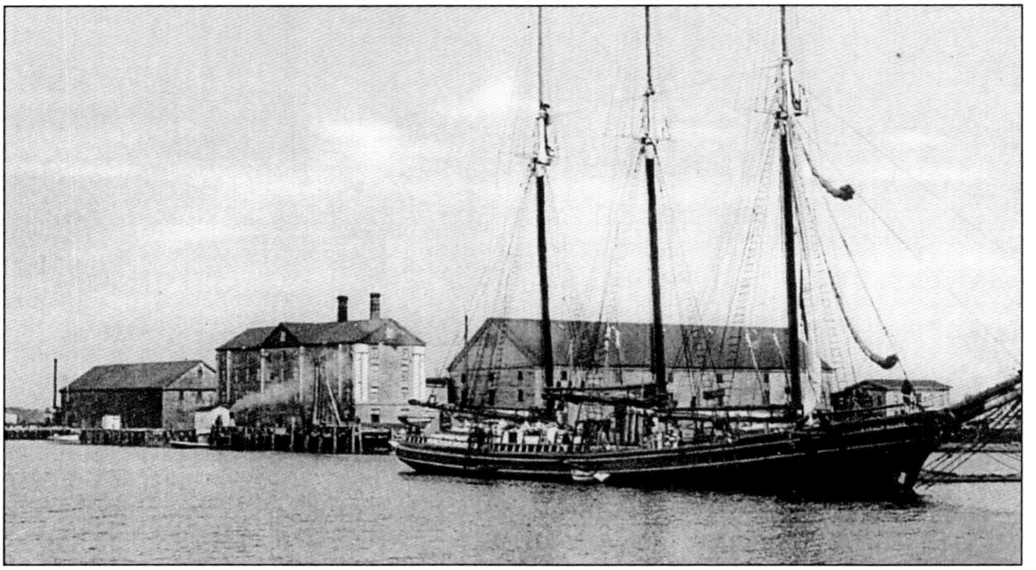

WEST POINT RICE MILLS, CHARLESTON, S.C. (Color Lithography, Detroit Publishing Co., #11548, Detroit, MI; cp. 1907.) Rice was still being processed at the West Point Mill when this picture was made in 1907. The three-masted schooner *Warner Moore* may be loaded with rice for shipment abroad. Constructed in 1860, the mill ceased operations in 1927, was subsequently restored, and presently anchors the Marina Complex as an office building. It is the only remaining mill structure in the city of Charleston, and in 1995 it was listed on the National Register of Historic Places.

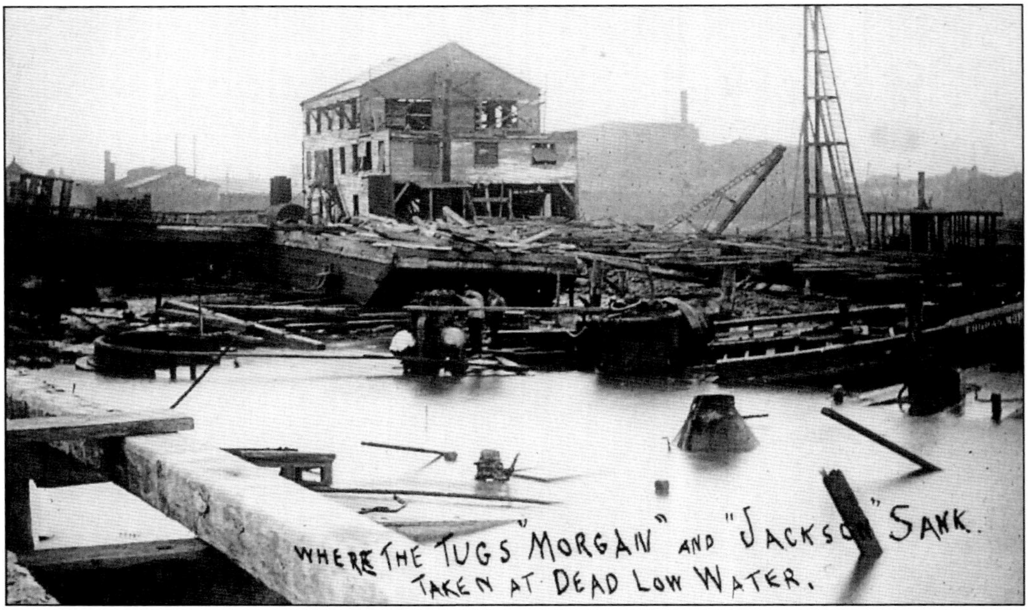


WHERE THE TUGS *MORGAN* AND *JACKSON* SANK. TAKEN AT DEAD LOW WATER. (Photoprint; 1911.) The cards on these two pages illustrate the magnitude of the Great Storm of 1911 and the destruction it wrought upon Charleston. They also document the marketability of the "disaster card." Frequently the most dynamic, interesting images of a subject have been found on photoprint postcards that were often taken spontaneously at a critical moment. Such cards go beyond the rigid uniformity of images offered by the national postcard jobbers.

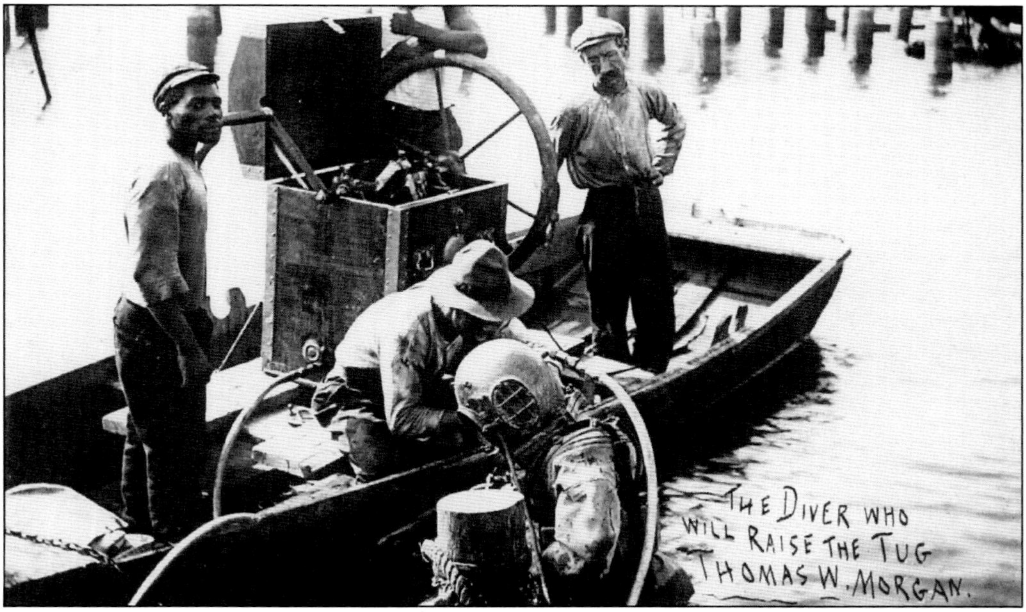


THE DIVER WHO WILL RAISE THE TUG *THOMAS W. MORGAN*. (Photoprint; 1911.) In the hurricane which struck Charleston in late August 1911, winds reached velocities of 106 miles per hour and the tide rose 5 feet over its average level to 13.3 feet. Not until August 12, 1940, would another hurricane strike the city with such force.

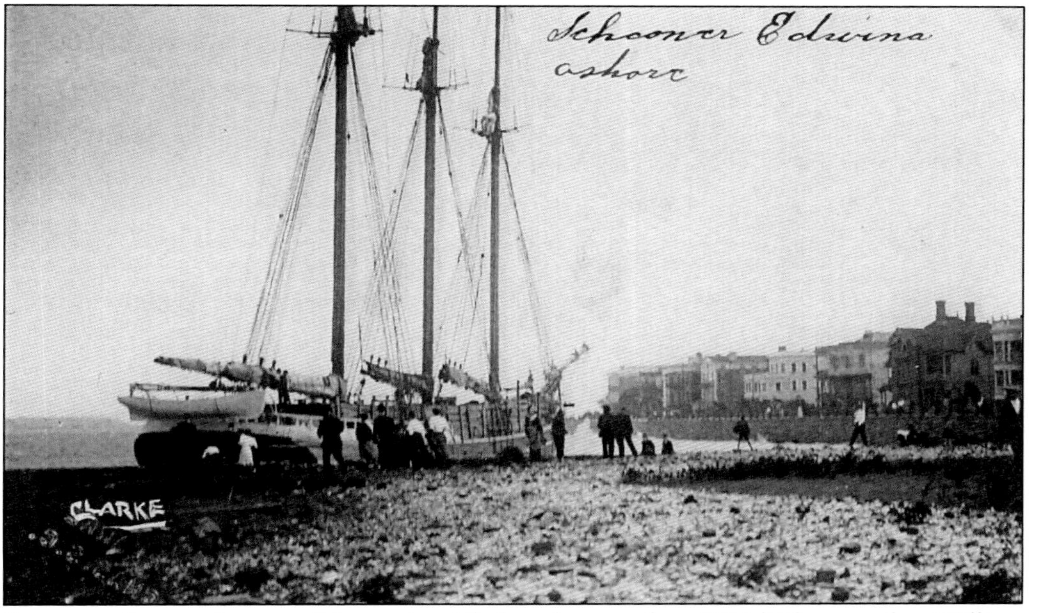


SCHOONER *EDWINA* ASHORE. (Photoprint; Clarke, photographer; 1911.) Photographer William D. Clarke produced this postcard of the schooner *Edwina* marooned in front of East Battery, again presumably after the hurricane of 1911. The Scottish-born Clarke enjoyed a long career in Charleston, at least from 1894 to 1923, and for a period served as a city alderman. At the time this picture was made, his studio was located at 301 King Street.

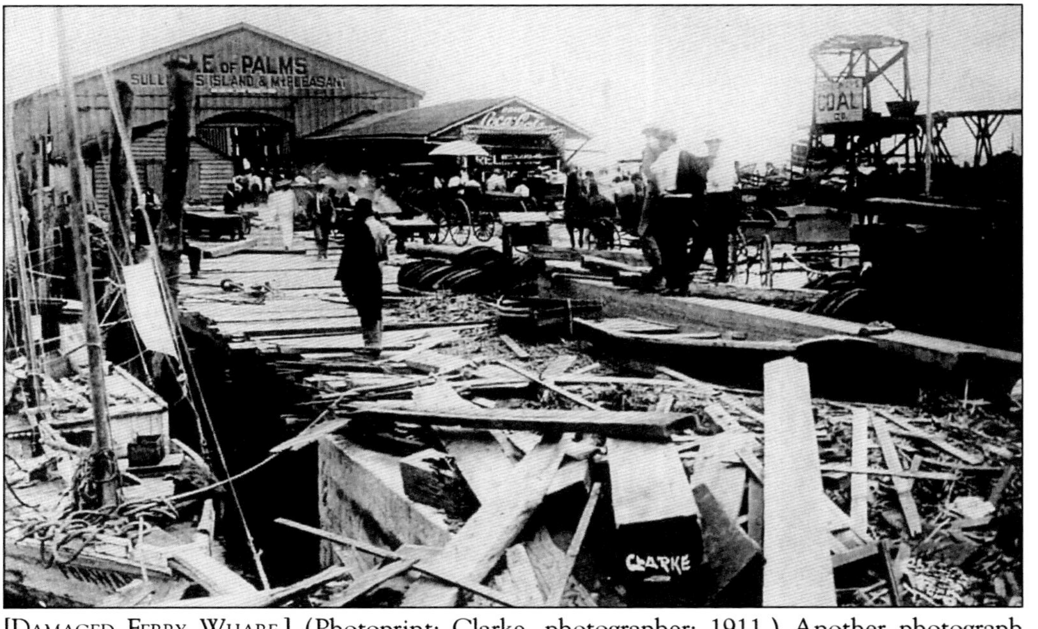


[DAMAGED FERRY WHARF.] (Photoprint; Clarke, photographer; 1911.) Another photograph marketed as a postcard by Clarke captures the damage inflicted by the 1911 hurricane on the Charleston end of the Isle of Palms ferry wharf. The name of the photographer is more often found on photoprints than on printing-press cards. Over fifty views of this disaster were taken and are found in archival and private collections and are occasionally sold by dealers.

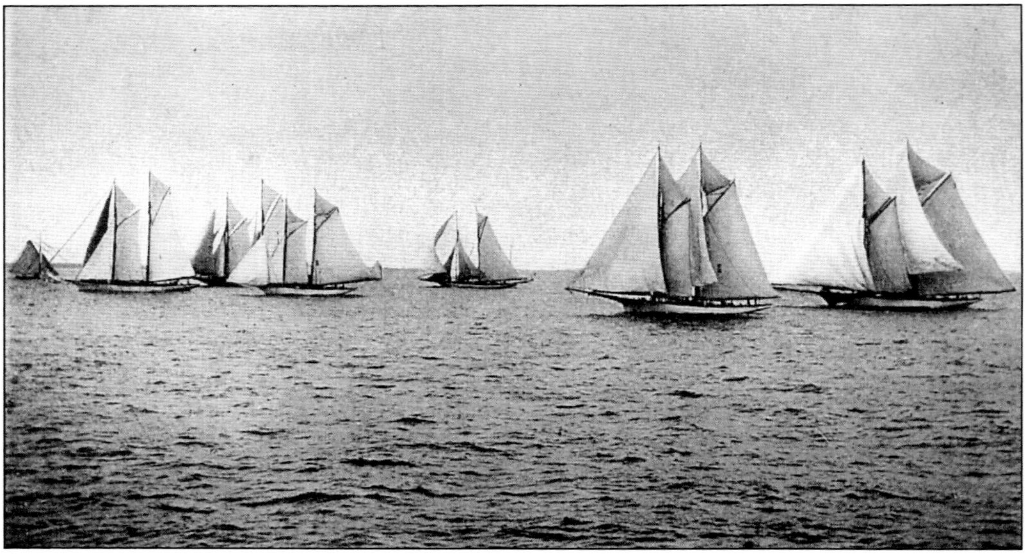

A YACHTING SCENE, CHARLESTON, S.C. (Color Lithography, [Trenkler Co., Leipzig, Germany]; Owens Bros.-Hillson Co., #1016A, Boston, MA, importer; c. 1906.) Yachting has always been an important part of Charleston's recreational scene. The claim has long been made that the harbor was one of the finest in America and that the waters in the vicinity were perfect for sailing. During the boating season, the Carolina Yacht Club sponsored regattas between the different classes of yachts owned by its members. It is possible that this card was a generic image widely used wherever yachting was popular.

CHARLESTON, S.C., PANORAMIC VIEW CAROLINA YACHT CLUB AND SHAMROCK TERRACE. (Halftone, 3 1/2" X 11", Haines Photo Co., #3, Conneaut, OH; c. 1915.) This panoramic view of the Carolina Yacht Club (p.25, to the right) includes at the left a portion of the East Battery. W. Hugh

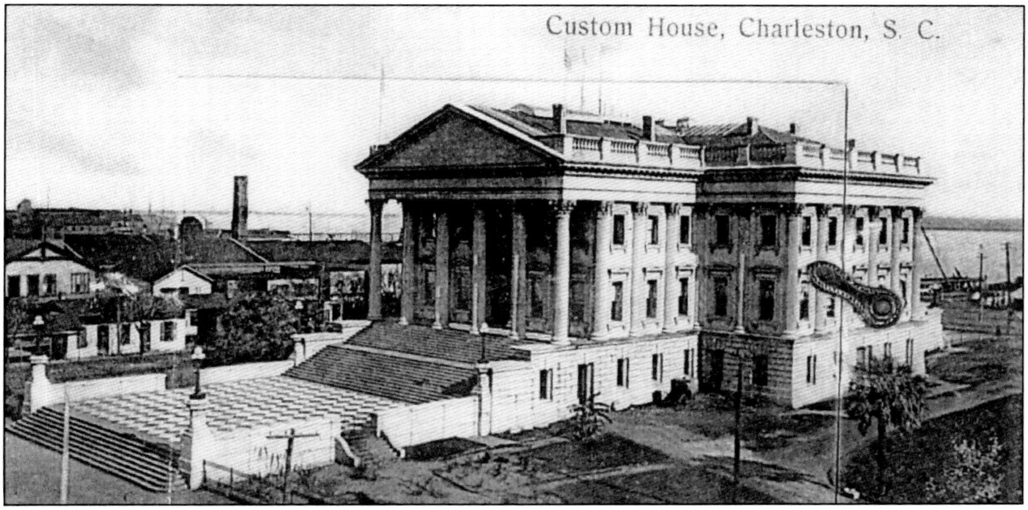


CUSTOM HOUSE, CHARLESTON, S.C. (Collotype, [Knackstedt and Nather Co., Hamburg, Germany]; Rotograph Co., #12572a, New York, NY, importer; cp. 1905.) Construction of the United States Custom House, 200 East Bay Street at Market, was begun in 1849 and completed with federal funds in 1879. A Roman-Corinthian structure of white marble, the front and back facades still make an impression upon visitors viewing the building for the first time from either land or sea. The clasp to the right on this novelty card turns to release a folded unit containing twelve miniature, high-quality black-and-white views of other city landmarks. Manufactured on thick paperboard, this particular "souvenir mail card" is postmarked December 23, 1906.

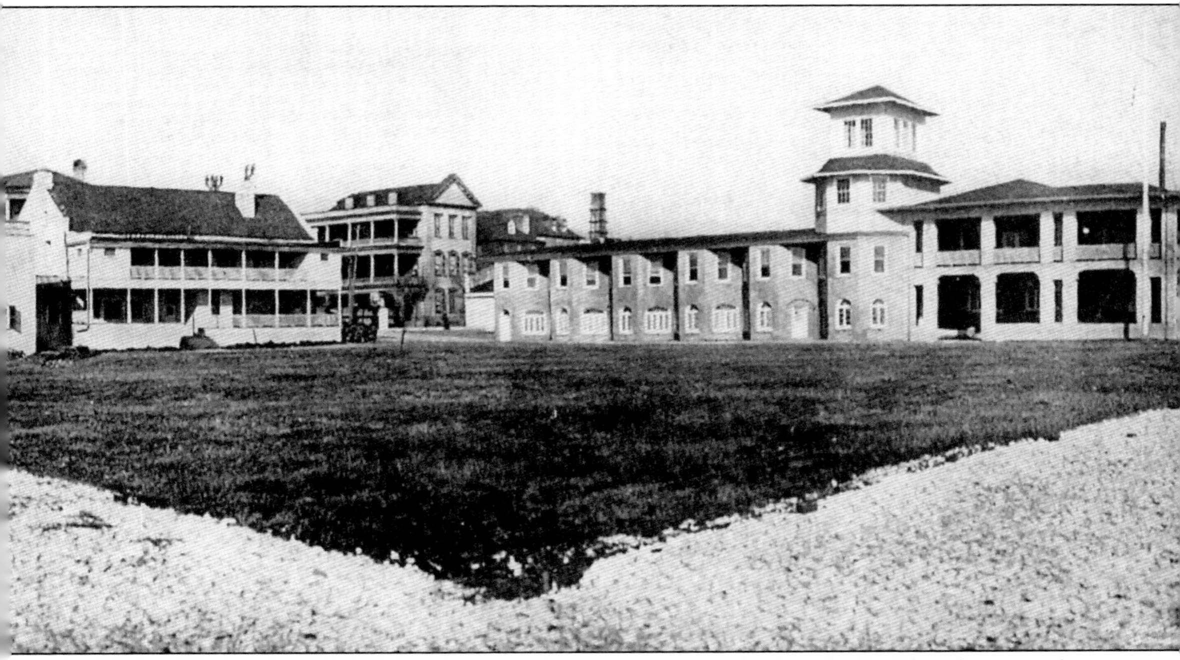

Harkey Jr., in his book *Greetings from Charleston* (1994), reveals that the building housing the yacht club was constructed in the 1830s as offices for agents selling cotton to Northern and English buyers. The club itself was organized in 1883.

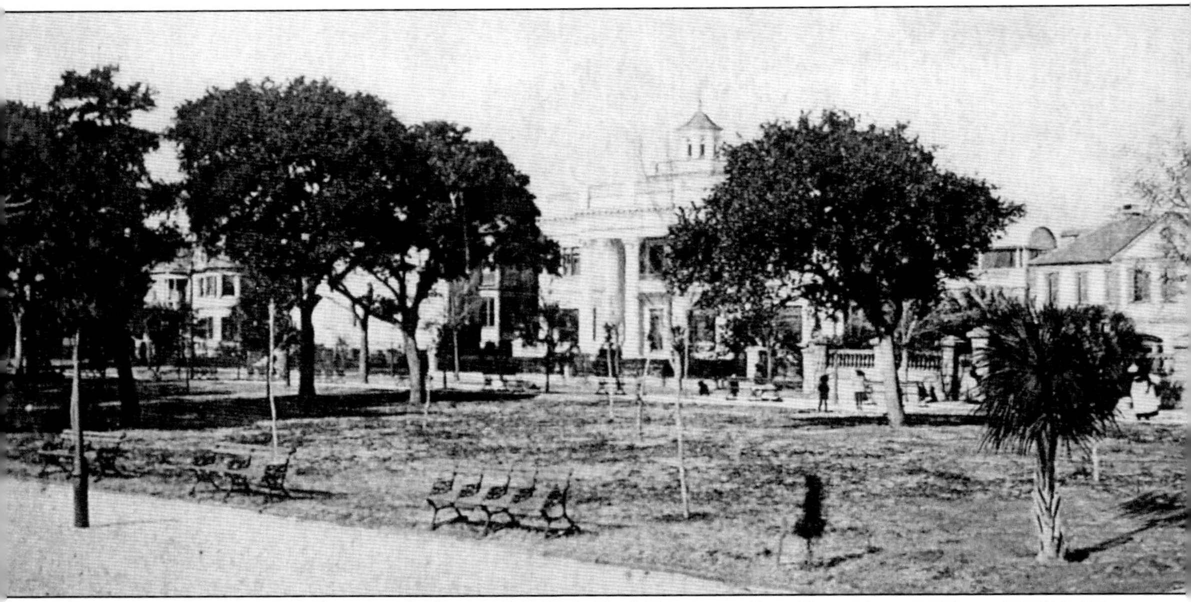

THE BATTERY. (Collotype, foldout $3\frac{1}{2}$" X 11", Albertype Co., Brooklyn, NY; *c.* 1905.) The Battery (White Point Gardens) has been a major Charleston landmark and one of its principal showplaces since the nineteenth century. The name "Battery" probably refers to the period during the War of 1812 when fifteen cannons were placed along the seawall in anticipation of an attack from British ships. Situated at the southeast corner of the city where the Ashley and Cooper Rivers come together to form Charleston Harbor, the expanse of some one hundred acres with its "splendidly kept lawns and the handsome water oaks" makes "a very attractive foreground for some of the more pretentious residences" (as stated in a 1910 tourist booklet). Seen here are the Louis deSaussure House, at 1 East Battery, built in the 1850s (on the right); and the Chicago Exposition-style Andrew Simonds House (1893), at 4 South Battery, which

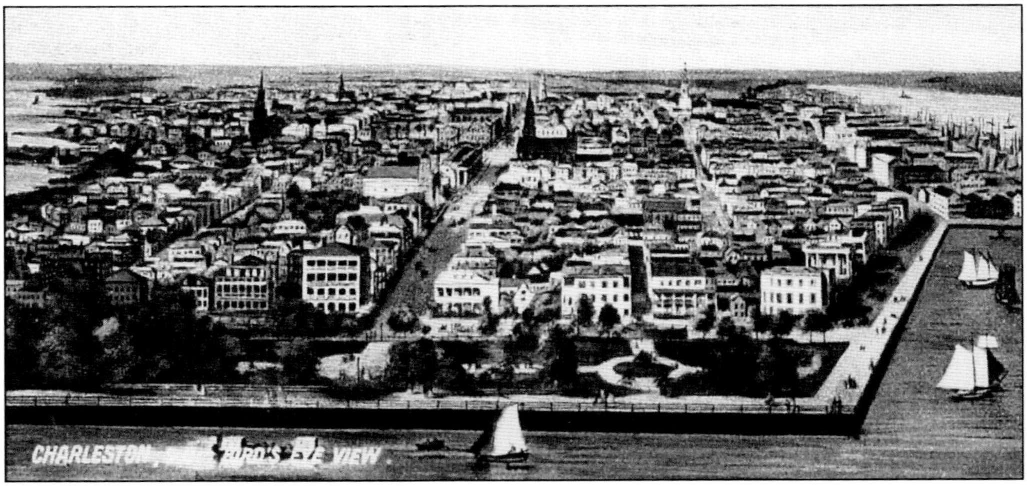


CHARLESTON, S.C., BIRD'S EYE VIEW. (Color Lithography, $3\frac{1}{2}$" X $5\frac{7}{10}$", [Rosenblatt Lithograph Institute, #202,827, Frankfurt, Germany]; *c.* 1908.) This famous bird's eye view of Charleston provides not only a good overall perspective of the East and South Batteries, but also visual evidence for the claim made on the reverse side that Charleston "has nine miles of water front facing a spacious harbor."

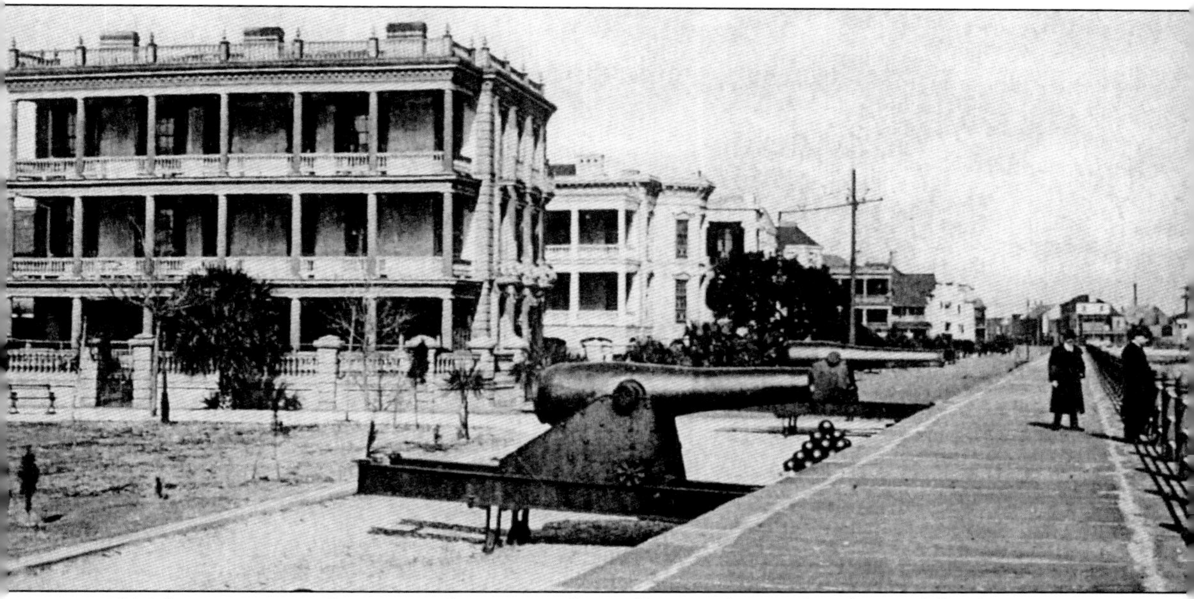

in 1910 became an exclusive inn known as the Villa Margherita (in the middle distance to the left). The park's monuments and weapons serve as reminders of the region's and nation's various achievements and conflicts. On January 10, 1905, when he formally presented a silver punch bowl to the cruiser *Charleston*, Mayor R.G. Rhett referred to the Battery as a taste of "earthly paradise" and explained why it was one of only four scenes of the city engraved upon the bowl: "That Battery is our choicest spot for the best of recreations."

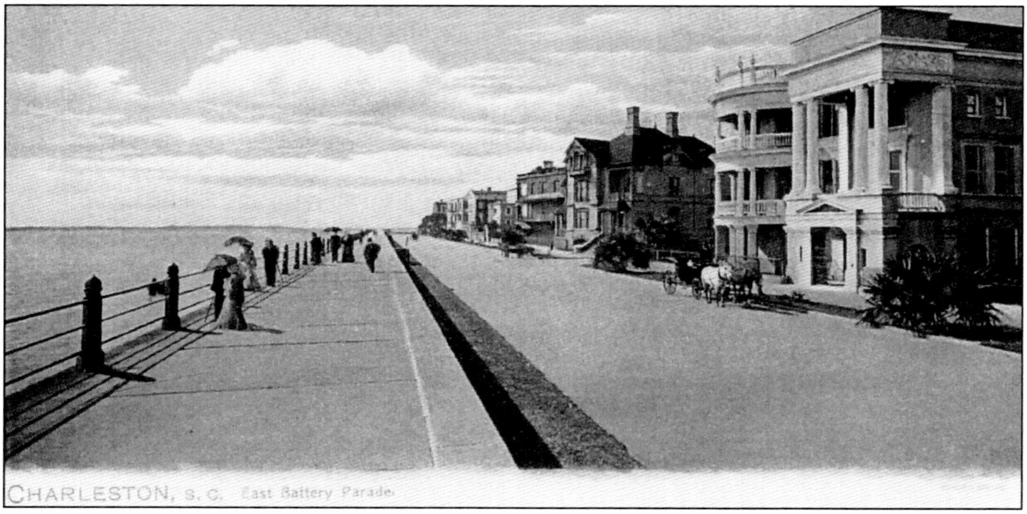


CHARLESTON, S.C., EAST BATTERY PARADE. (Color Lithography, 3½" X 5½", [Louis Glaser Co., Leipzig, Germany]; Raphael Tuck & Sons, #1046, London, Great Britain; *c.* 1906.) "East Battery," according to a 1911 Atlantic Coast Line Railroad tourist booklet, was the general term for Charleston's "splendid" 1,500-foot-long seawall and the subject of the claim that "no more beautiful drive and promenade can be found in the country." In the far distance here (middle of card) are two of the East Battery homes which Samuel Gaillard Stoney lists as architecturally valuable: the Edmonston-Alston House (1838), 21 East Battery; and the William Ravenel House (1845), 13 East Battery (*This is Charleston*, 1944).

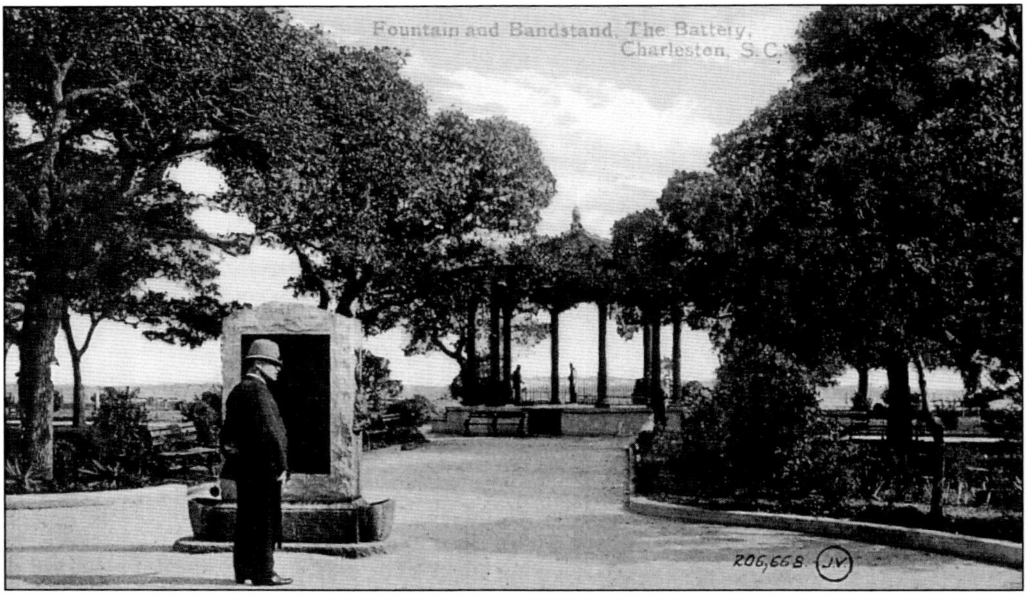


FOUNTAIN AND BANDSTAND, THE BATTERY, CHARLESTON, S.C. (Color Lithography, 3½" X 5½", Valentine & Sons, #206, 668, Dundee, Scotland; *c.* 1907.) A policeman is silhouetted against the *Hunley* monument in this unusual picture taken in Battery Park. The *Hunley* was the submarine which was lost on February 17, 1864, after it had successfully sunk the Federal blockader *Housatonic*. The 8-foot granite monument honoring the Confederates who manned the first torpedo boats and submarines, 1863–1865, was dedicated on May 8, 1899. The concert inaugurating the use of the octagonal Williams Music Pavilion, center, was held June 28, 1907. It had been a gift to the city from Mrs. Martha Williams Carrington in memory of her mother.

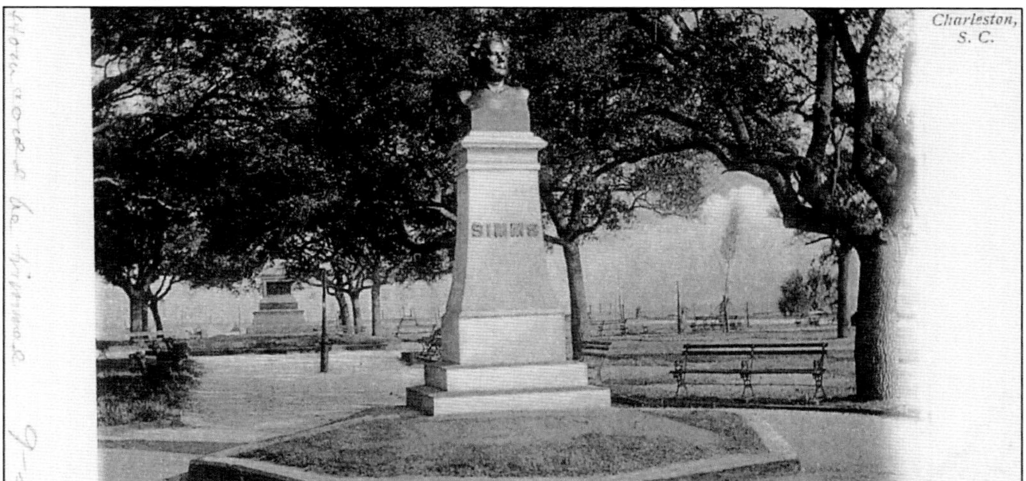


SIMM'S [SIC] MONUMENT, CHARLESTON, S.C. (Collotype, 3½" X 5½", [Trenkler & Co., #80860, Leipzig, Germany]; Lange, B.L. Schwalbach & Co., exporter; American Historical Art Publishers, NY, importer; *c.* 1908.) New York sculptor J.Q.A. Ward's heroic bronze bust mounted upon a pedestal of Fairfield granite bearing the single word "Simms" was unveiled in White Point Gardens on June 11, 1879. It had been less than a decade since the death of the state's best-known nineteenth-century author, William Gilmore Simms (1806–1870).

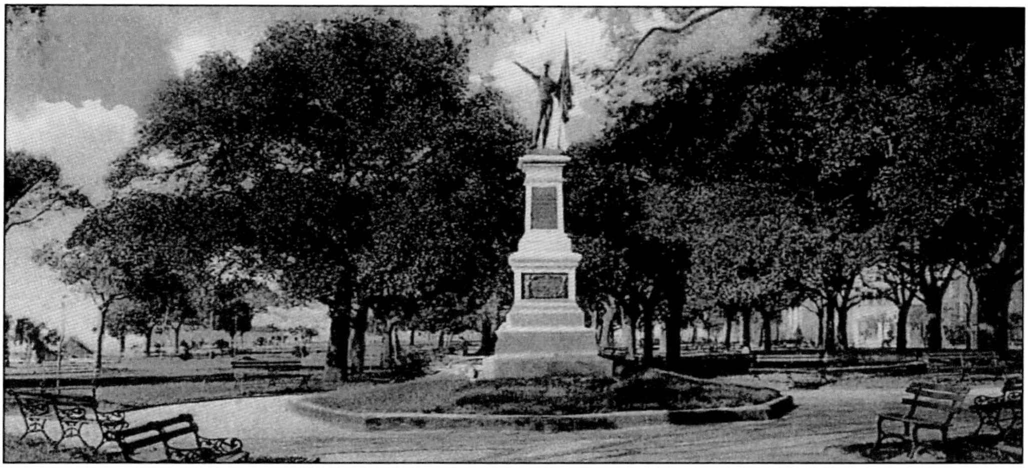

To the Defenders of Fort Moultrie, Charleston, S.C. (Color Lithography, 3½" X 5½", [Knackstedt and Nather Co., Hamburg, Germany]; Rotograph Co., #12579, New York, NY importer; cp. 1905.) "During the Revolution," Albert Simons and Samuel Lapham Jr. wrote in their book *The Early Architecture of Charleston* (1927), "Charleston became one of the chief points of the war-zone." One of the city's numerous Revolutionary War monuments was erected in Battery Park by the Palmetto Guard in 1876, honoring those who defended Fort Moultrie against an attack by the British a century earlier—and especially Sergeant William Jasper's heroic retrieval of the fallen flag.

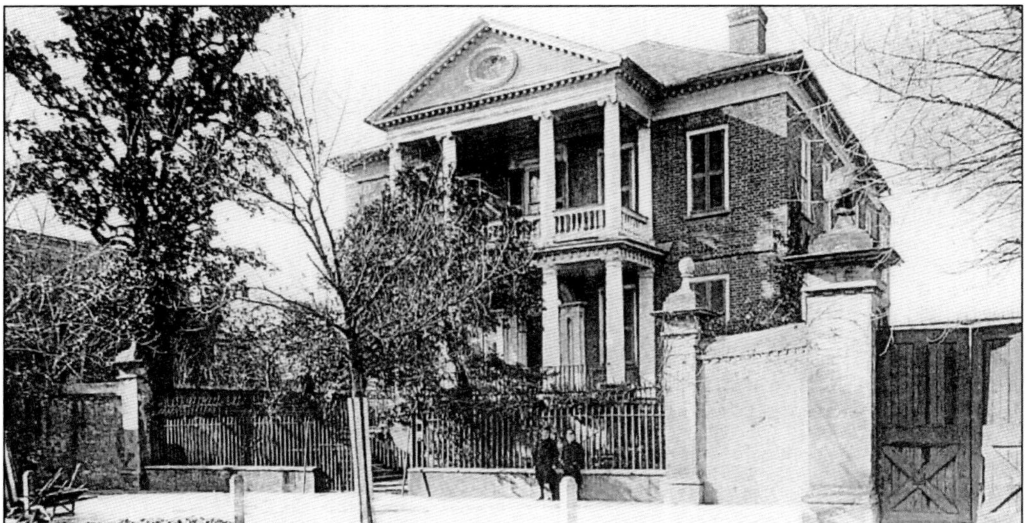

Brewton Mansion, British Headquarters, 1781/82, Charleston, S.C. (Collotype, 3½" X 5½", [Knackstedt and Nather Co., Hamburg, Germany]; Rotograph Co., #A 12580, New York, NY, importer; 1905.) The Brewton (Pringle) House, 27 King Street, built by Miles Brewton about 1765, served as British headquarters during the Revolutionary occupation of the city, 1781–82. One of the oldest houses in Charleston, it has long been considered one of the best preserved and most elegant specimens of Colonial architecture. Preservationist Susan Frost Pringle (1873–1960) was born and died here.

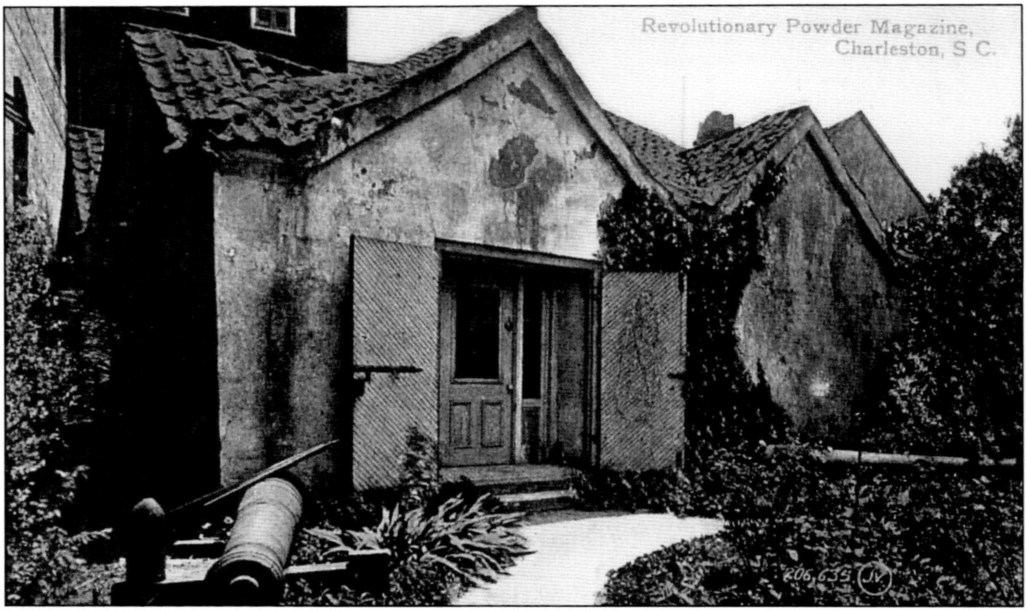


REVOLUTIONARY POWDER MAGAZINE, CHARLESTON, S.C. (Color Lithography, Valentine & Sons, #206, 635, Dundee, Scotland; *c.* 1907.) The Powder Magazine at 81 Cumberland Street was used to store gun-powder and munitions from as early as 1703 until after the American Revolution. Originally built of brick covered with tabby (a primitive type of concrete composed chiefly of crushed oyster shells), the eight-gabled, tile-roofed storehouse is the oldest public building still standing in the Carolinas. In 1993 it was slated for $400,000 worth of repairs.

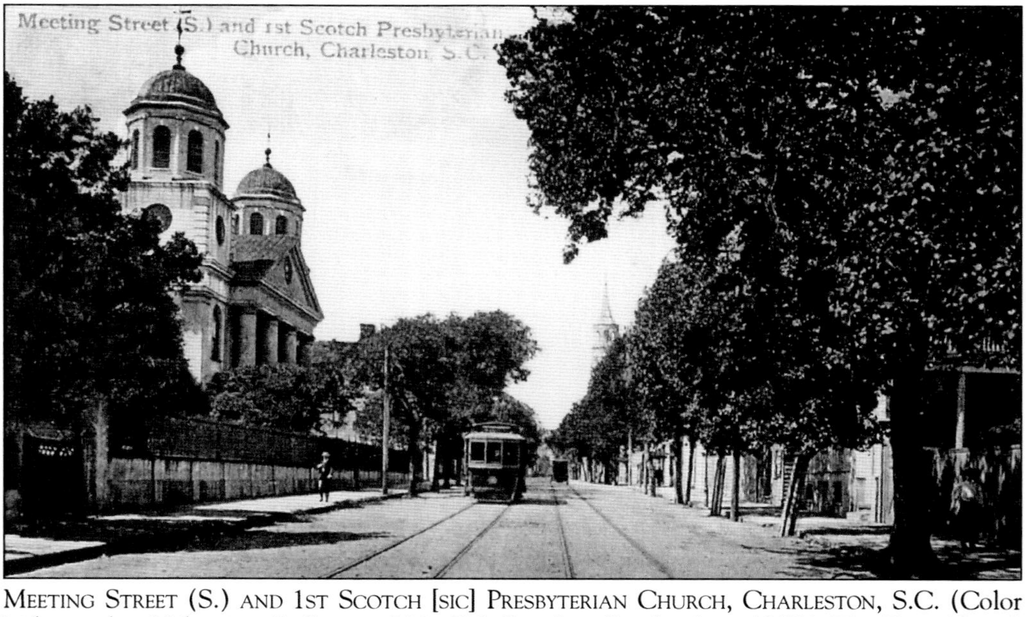


MEETING STREET (S.) AND 1ST SCOTCH [SIC] PRESBYTERIAN CHURCH, CHARLESTON, S.C. (Color Lithography, Valentine & Sons, #206, 636, Dundee, Scotland; *c.* 1907.) The First (Scots) Presbyterian Church, 53 Meeting Street, shown at the left on this card, is distinguished architecturally by the two towers flanking its four-column portico. The fifth-oldest church building in Charleston, it was erected in 1814, replacing an earlier structure on the site.

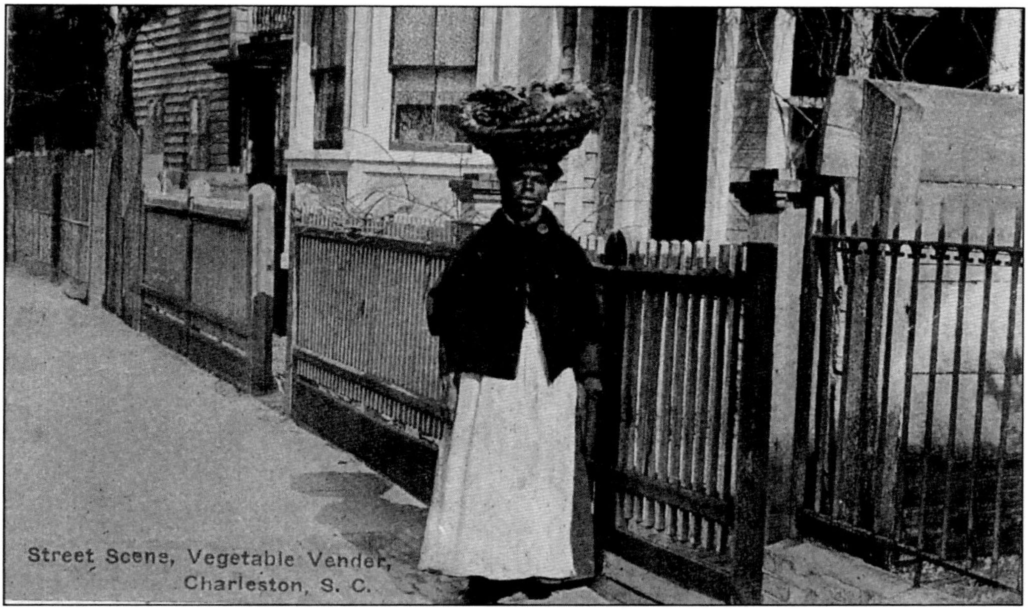


STREET SCENE, VEGETABLE VENDOR, CHARLESTON, S.C. (Color Lithography, [McGown-Silsby Lithographic Co., New York, NY]; 1915.) Charleston street vendors, men and women, have been among the most photographed and photogenic local subjects, embodying a rich part of the city's unique ethnic, linguistic, and commercial heritage.

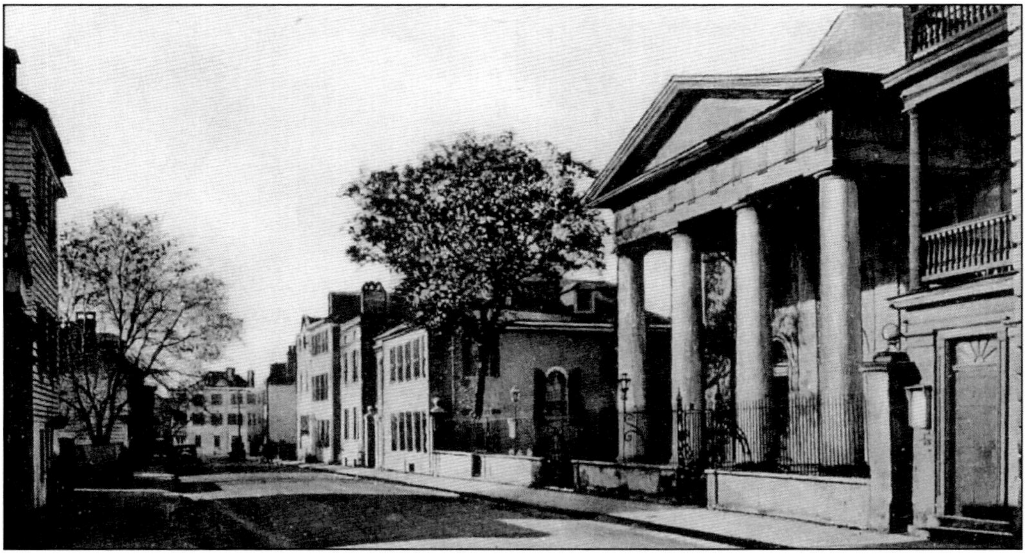

OLD CHURCH STREET SOUTH AND OLD FIRST BAPTIST CHURCH ORGANIZED 1683, CHARLESTON, S.C. (Collotype, Albertype Co., Brooklyn, NY; *c.* 1925.) First Baptist Church, 61 Church Street, has been called "the mother church of Southern Baptists." The late Charleston architect Albert Simons identified the sanctuary as one of the three principal works in the city designed by native-born Robert Mills (1718–1855). Mills, who was a chief American exponent of Greek Revival architecture, identified this church as "the best specimen of correct taste in Architecture of the modern buildings in this city. It is purely Greek in its style, simply grand in its proportions, and beautiful in its detail."

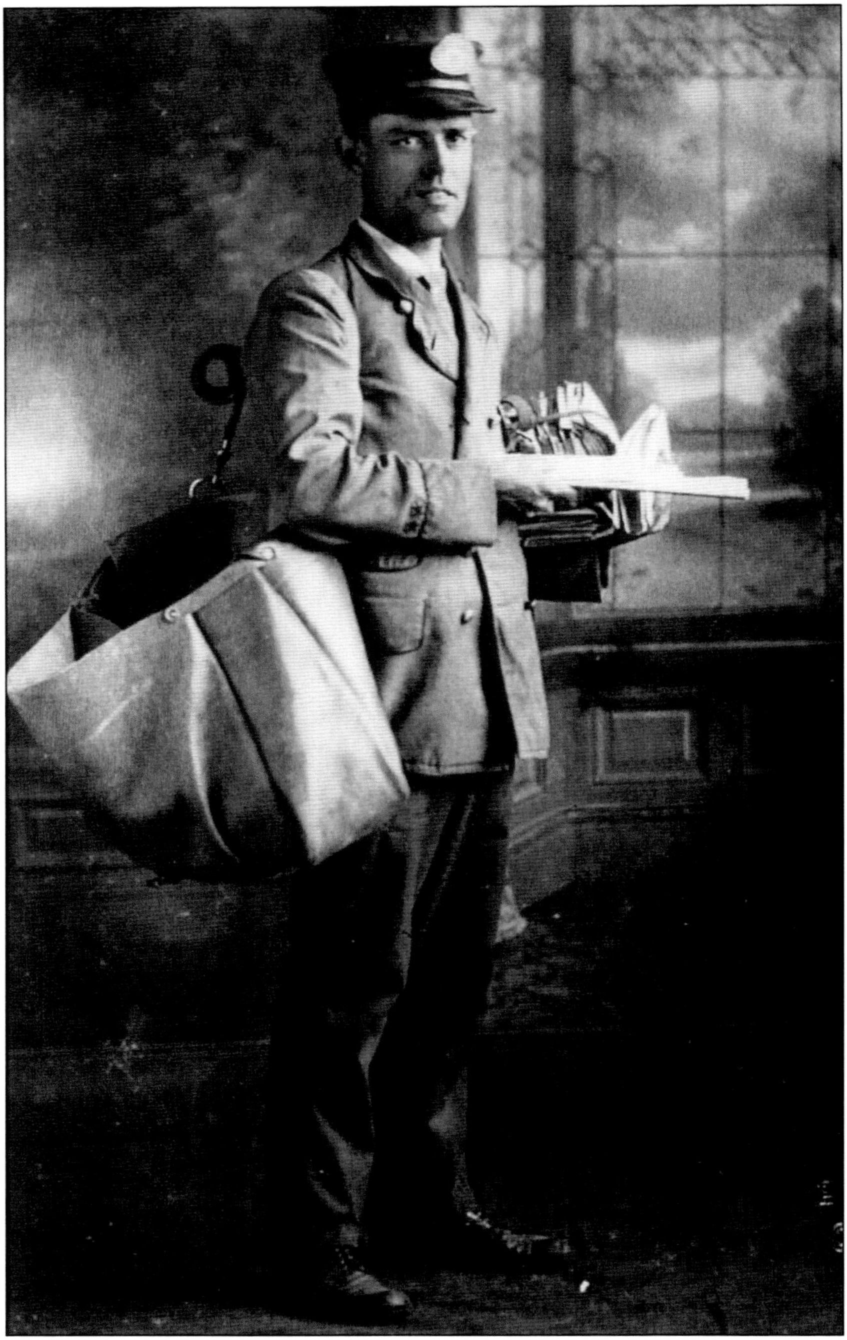

[PORTRAIT OF A POSTMAN.] (Photoprint; *c.* 1915.) This portrait of an unidentified Charleston mail carrier illustrates the breadth of pictorial matter found on postcards from the era, as well as the high quality of work often achieved in the genre by local photographers. An embossed logo at the lower right indicates that this card was made at the Clarke Studio. During the Christmas season, postmen often purchased generic seasonal cards or had portrait cards made to distribute along their routes to thank residents for their Christmas gifts.

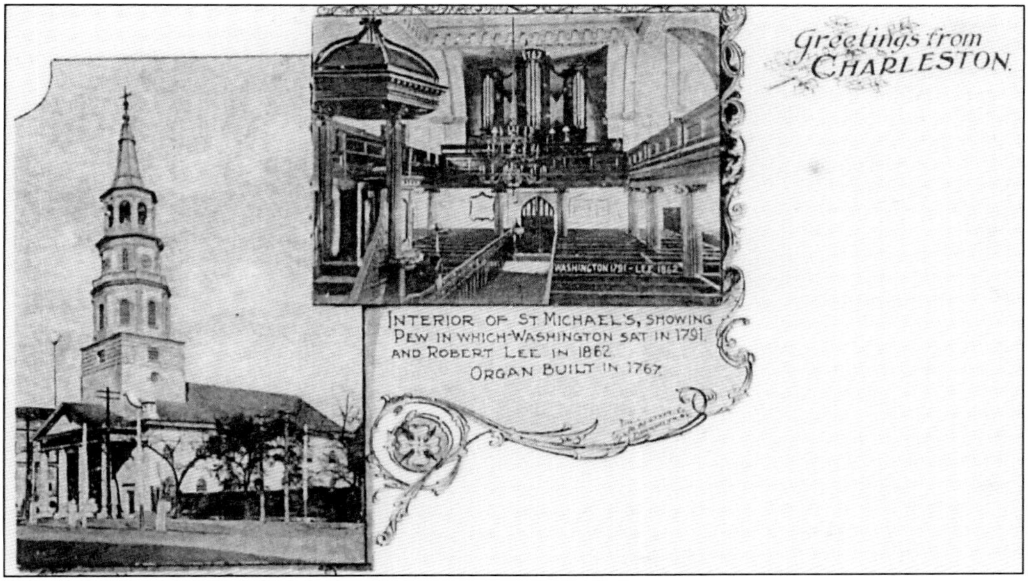


GREETINGS FROM CHARLESTON, ST. MICHAEL'S CHURCH, CHARLESTON. (Collotype, Albertype Co., #25, Brooklyn, NY; *c.* 1903.) St. Michael's Episcopal Church, 80 Meeting Street, is situated at the southeast corner of the intersection of Broad and Meeting Streets, at what has been called the "Four Corners of Law." This early card features both exterior and interior views of the sanctuary which was begun in 1752, making it the oldest church building in Charleston. It has been spoken of as the most historic church in South Carolina, or even in the South.

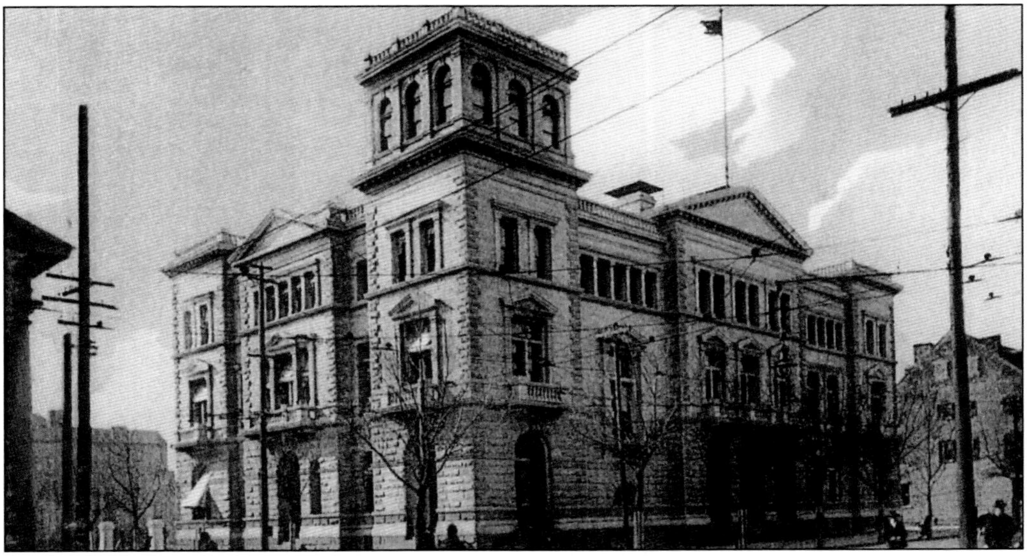

POST OFFICE, CHARLESTON, S.C. (Color Lithography, [Knackstedt and Nather Co., Hamburg, Germany]; Rotograph Co., #G 12581, New York, NY, importer; cp. 1905.) By January 1910, five years after this photograph of it had been copyrighted, the increase in business at the "new" post office and federal courthouse was so great that there was a call for an enlargement of the building. A massive square granite edifice erected in 1896 at the southwest corner of Broad and Meeting, it was the largest in South Carolina and lauded as "the most completely appointed postal establishment in the South, and the best kept public building withal."

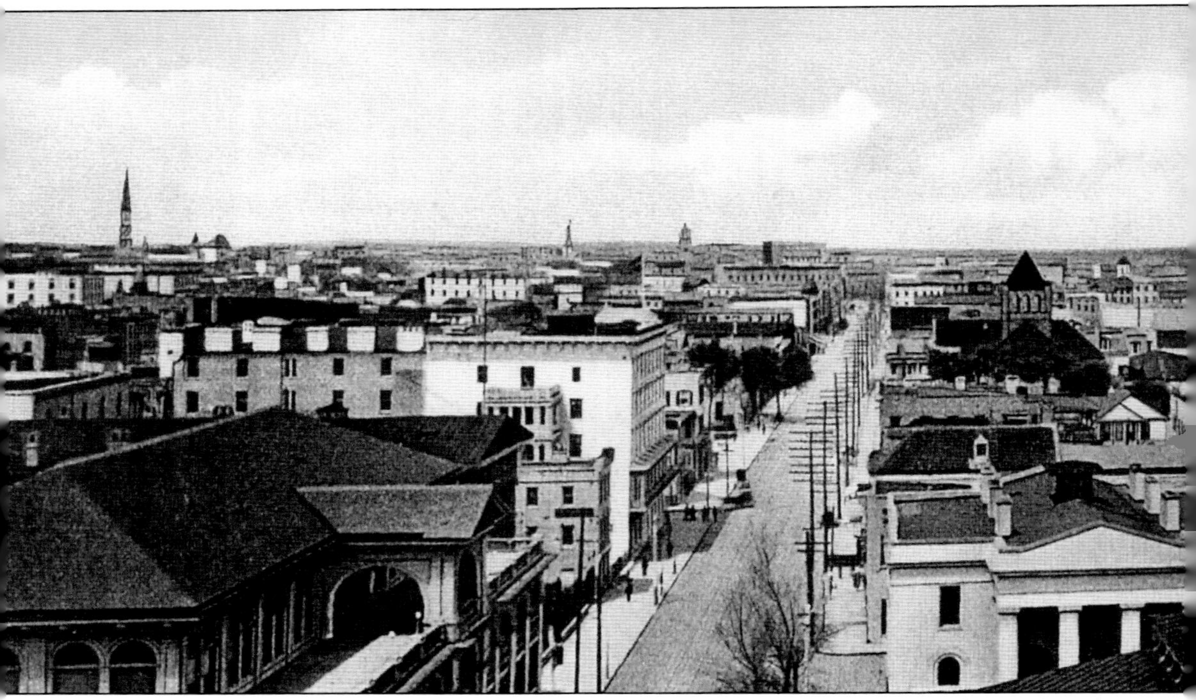

CHARLESTON S.C. FROM ST. MICHAEL'S CHURCH, CHARLESTON, S.C. (Color Lithography, 5 1/2" X 11", [Rosenblatt Lithographic Institute, #202617, Frankfurt, Germany]; *c.* 1908.) This panoramic view from the tower of St. Michael's Church looks up Meeting Street, in the center,

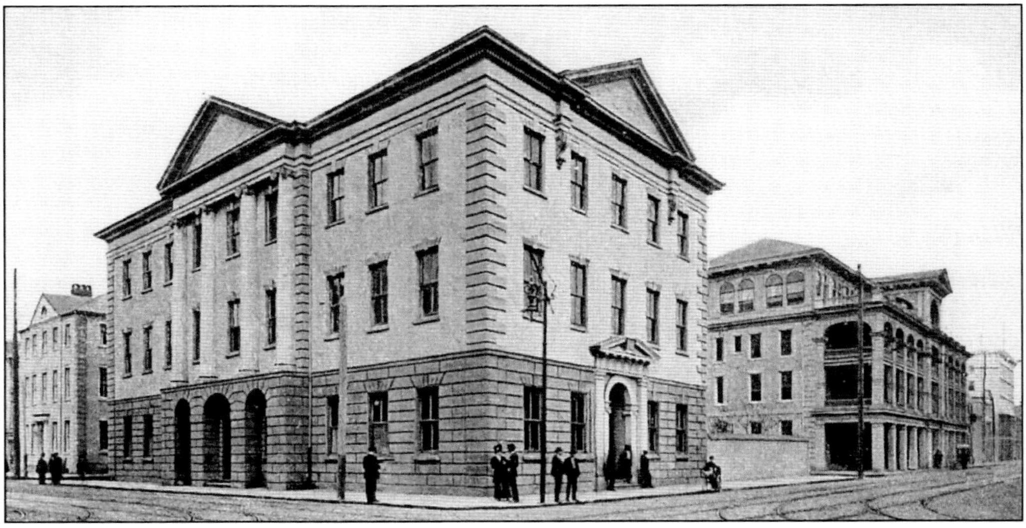

CHARLESTON, S.C., OLD COUNTY COURT HOUSE. (Color Lithography, [Louis Glaser Co., Leipzig, Germany]; Hugh C. Leighton, #26334, Portland, ME, importer; *c.* 1907.) The old Charleston County Court House, on the northeast corner of Broad and Meeting, was erected between 1788 and 1792 upon the foundations, and utilizing some of the exterior walls, of South Carolina's Colonial Statehouse, which burned in 1788. Described by Charles Fraser as "one of the best proportioned buildings in Charleston," it underwent a $650,000 renovation in 1969 and further rehabilitation after Hurricane Hugo, 1989.

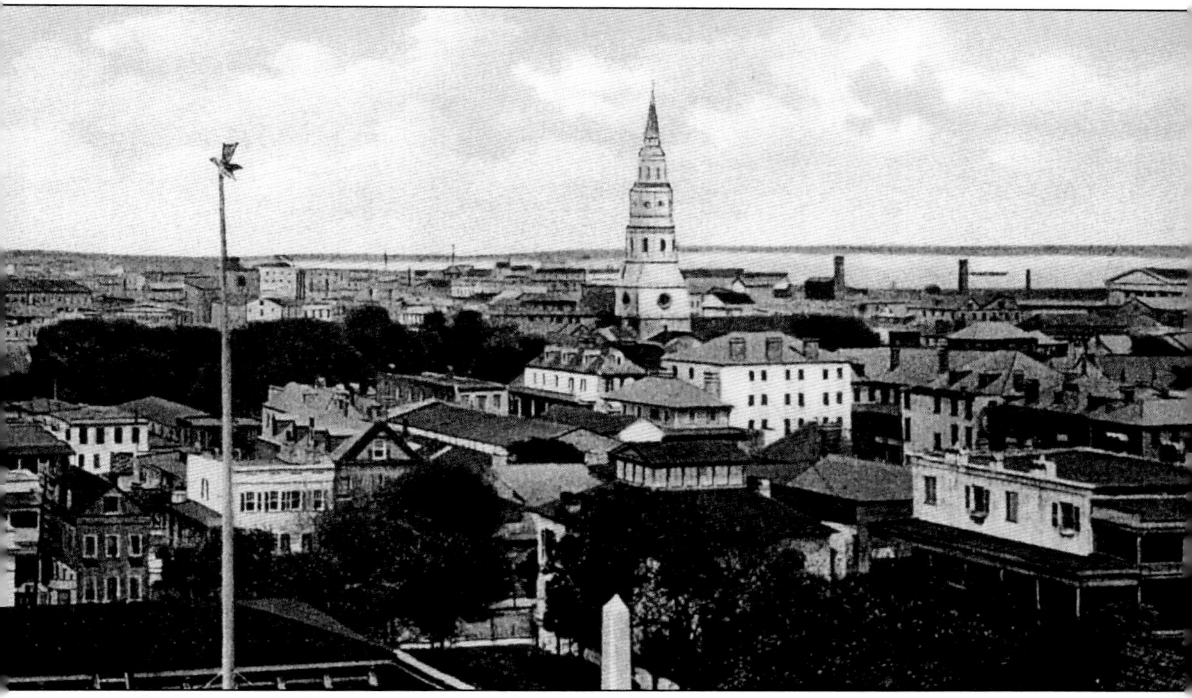

towards the port facilities beyond St. Philip's Church. To the far left are the towers of the Unitarian Church and St. John's Lutheran Church on Archdale Street (see p. 45).

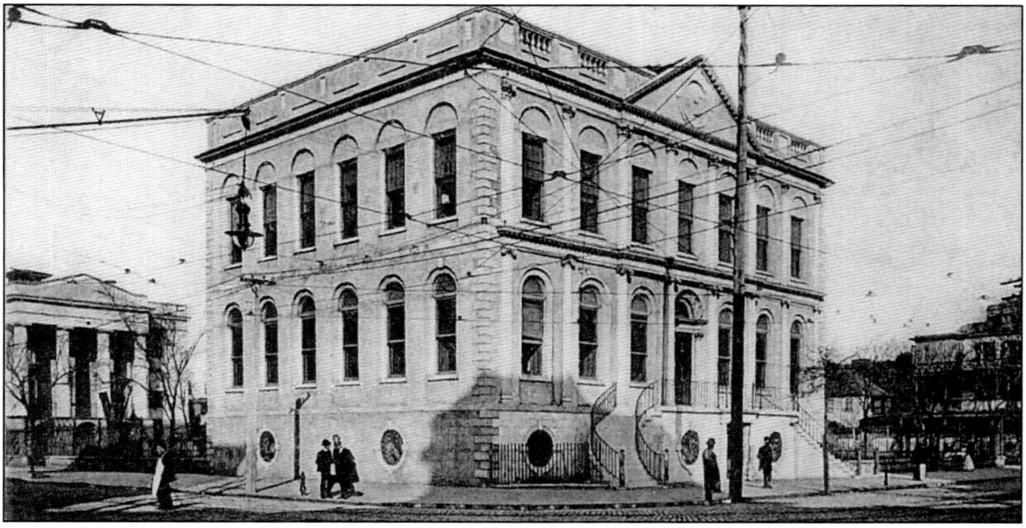

CITY HALL, CHARLESTON, S.C. (Collotype, [Knackstedt and Nather Co., Hamburg, Germany]; Rotograph Co., #A 12585, New York, NY, importer; cp. 1905.) Charleston City Hall, on the northeast corner of Broad and Meeting Streets, was designed by Gabriel Manigault for the United States Bank and built in 1801–1802 on the site of the old beef market. An imposing edifice with delicate details, it has served as city hall since 1818. To the left is Robert Mills's innovative, neoclassic Fireproof Building (1822–1827). Popular subjects like public buildings were made in lots of one to ten thousand each; these cards were stocked by every merchant selling postcards and are easily found in collections and the postcard marketplace today.

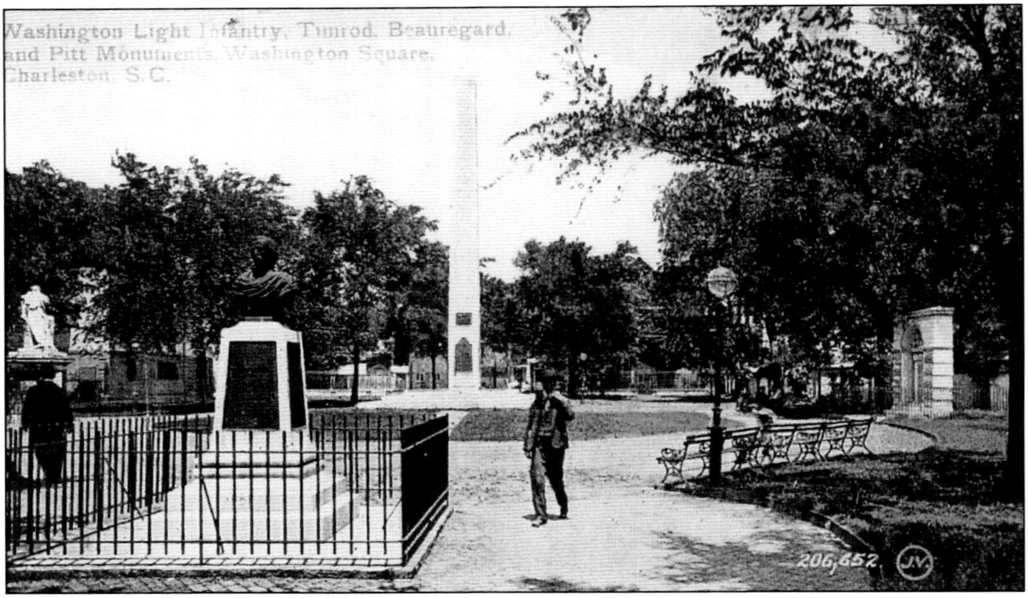


WASHINGTON LIGHT INFANTRY, TIMROD, BEAUREGARD, AND PITT MONUMENTS, WASHINGTON SQUARE, CHARLESTON, S.C. (Color Lithography, Valentine & Sons, #206, 652, Dundee; 1909.) The larger-than-life bronze bust of Henry Timrod (1828–1867), "Carolina's Poet," was unveiled in Washington Park by the Timrod Memorial Association on May Day, 1901. It was sculpted by Edward V. Valentine (1838–1930) of Richmond, Virginia.

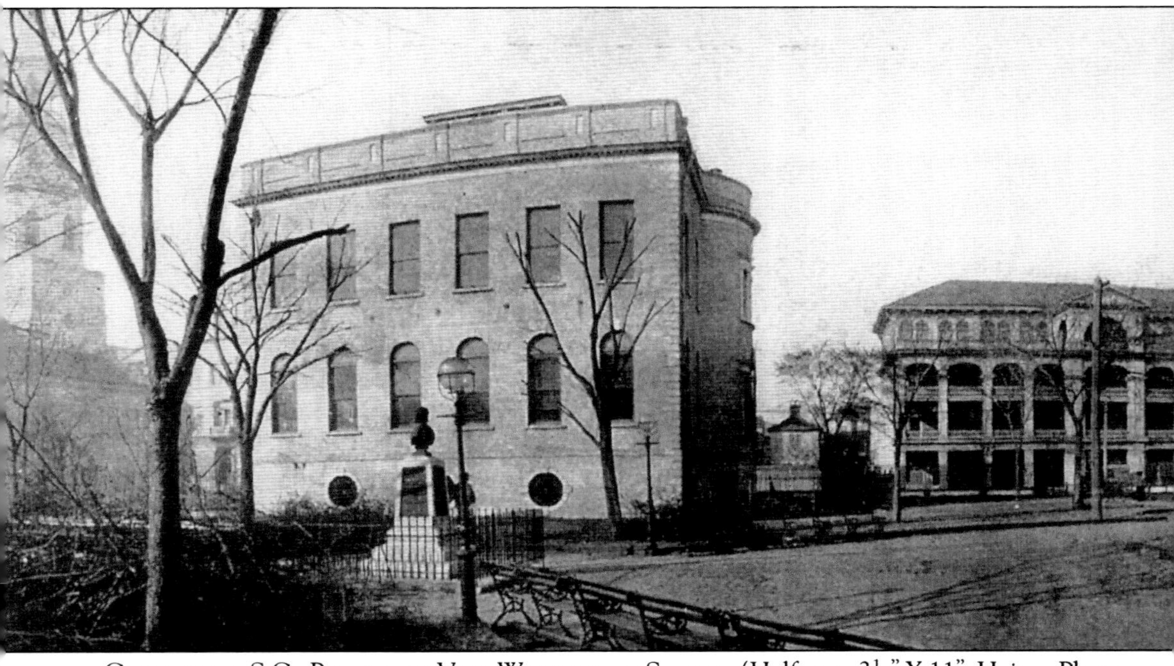

CHARLESTON, S.C., PANORAMIC VIEW WASHINGTON SQUARE, (Halftone, 3½" X 11", Haines Photo Co., #2, Conneaut, OH; *c*. 1915.) This wide-angle view of Washington Park (City Hall Square) shows, from left to right: City Hall, the Commercial Club (later Timrod Inn), the Fireproof Building (South Carolina Historical Society), and in the center of the park the monument

THE HISTORIC PITT MONUMENT, CHARLESTON, S.C. (Color Lithography, $5^{1/2}$" X $3^{1/2}$", [C.G. Röder, #123987, Leipzig, Germany]; American News Co., #C5498, New York, NY, importer; c. 1907.) The statue of William Pitt, Earl of Chatham—created by Wilton, king's sculptor to George III—was erected by order of the Commons House of the Carolina Assembly in commemoration of Pitt's stand for the colonies in the repeal of the Stamp Acts. Considered "a venerable relic of the colonial period," it once stood in the yard of the Charleston Orphan House. The *Year Book* for 1880 contains a statement regarding the removal of the statue "to a prominent position in the newly arranged grounds of Washington Square." Today it can be seen in the lobby of the Charleston Museum.

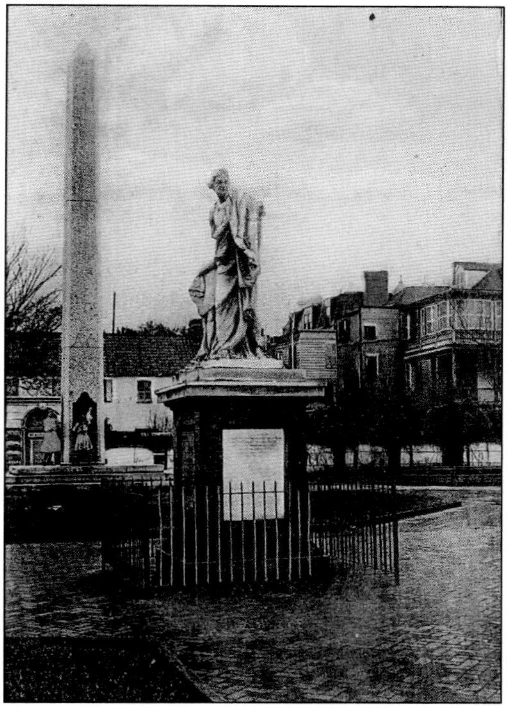

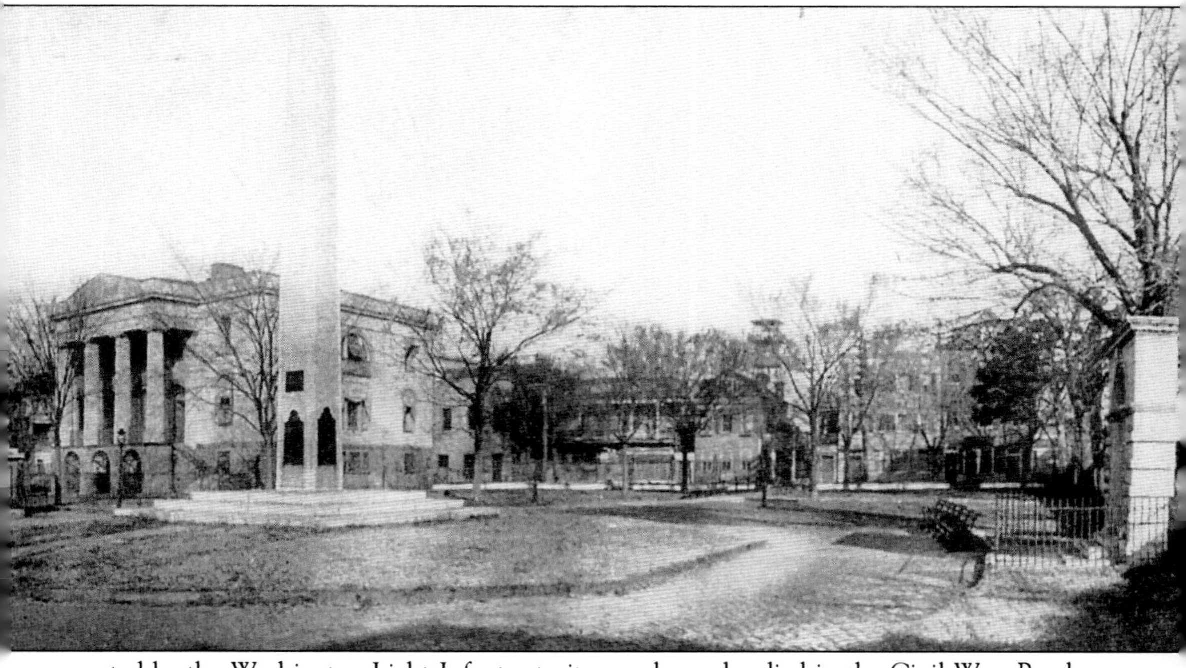

erected by the Washington Light Infantry to its members who died in the Civil War. Barely visible at the far left is St. Michael's Church. The Commercial Club was demolished in 1960 to make room for a county office building.

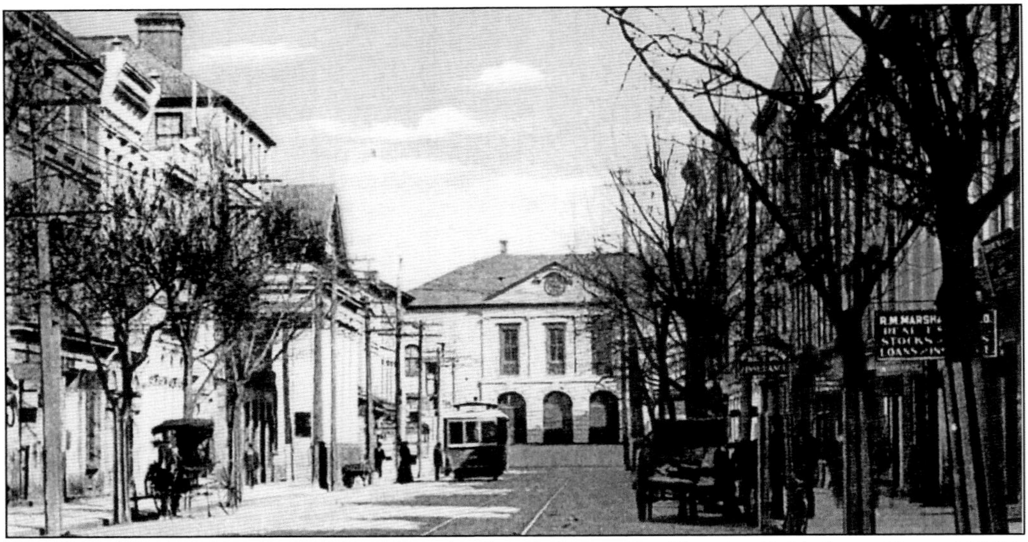

EAST BROAD STREET, CHARLESTON, S.C. (Color Lithography, Detroit Publishing Co., #10554, Detroit, MI; cp. 1906.) The Old Exchange and Provost Dungeon, shown in the distance where Broad intersects with East Bay, has been called one of the three great buildings in Colonial America. Completed in 1771, it was used as a prison by the British after their capture of Charleston in 1780. It was ceded to the federal government in 1818 and served as a custom house and post office, and then as a post office only, until 1896. In March 1975 it was designated a National Historic Landmark.

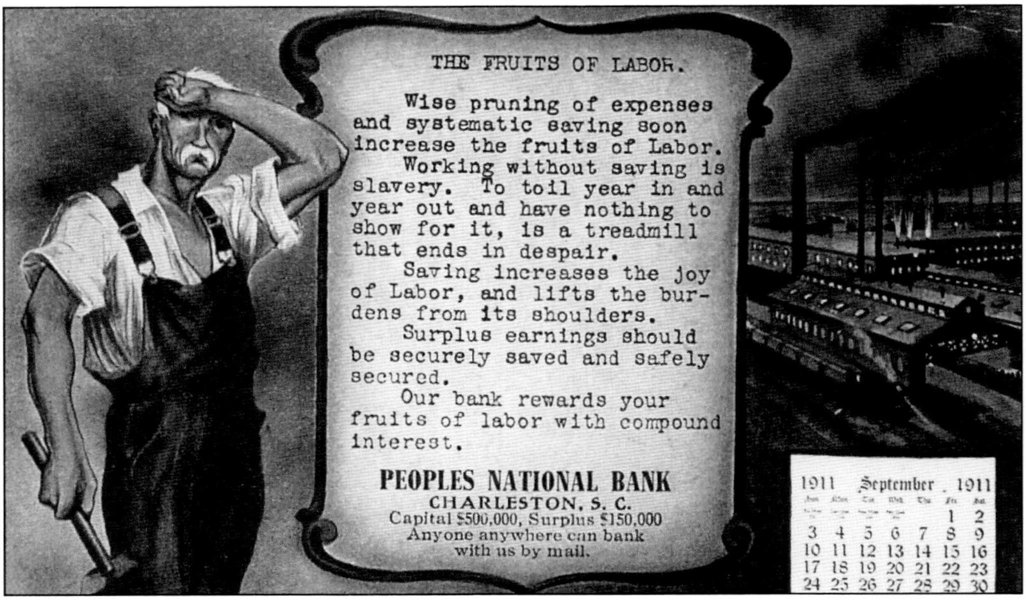


THE FRUITS OF LABOR, PEOPLES [SIC] NATIONAL BANK, CHARLESTON, S.C. (Color Lithography, A.J. Scritsmier, Chicago, IL; 1911.) The People's National Bank promoted the virtues of labor, systematic saving, and banking by mail on this advertising card issued in 1911, the year the bank opened offices in the new "skyscraper" on the northwest corner of Broad and State Streets. This bank card comes from generic sets, with one card for each month, that were printed in bulk without names and addresses—which were added before shipping to the relevant bank.

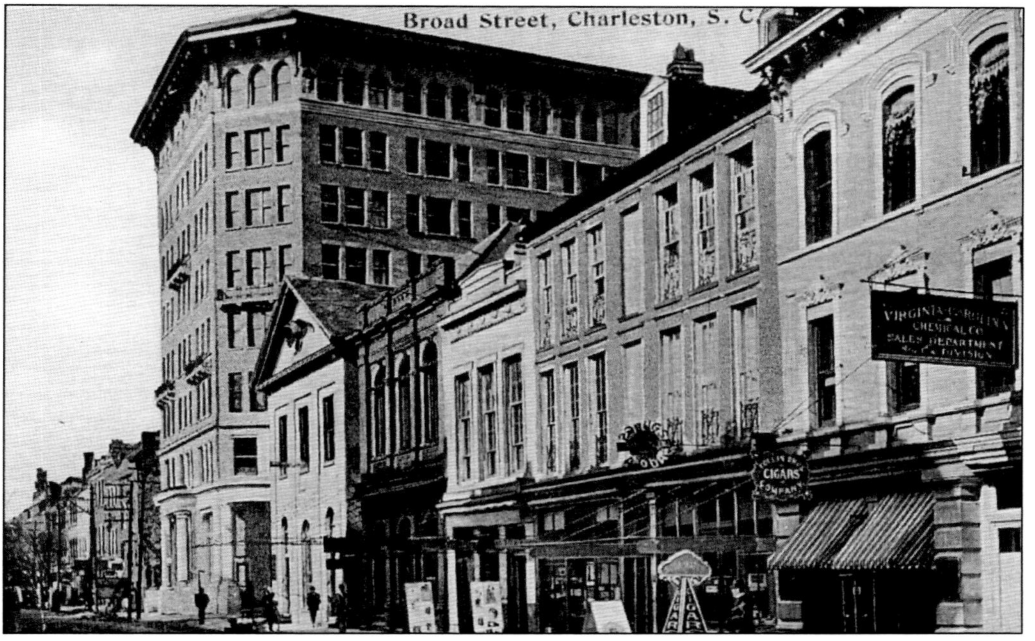


BROAD STREET, CHARLESTON, S.C. (Color Lithography, [Tichnor Bros., Inc., Boston, MA]; c. 1910.) Dominating this view is Charleston's first skyscraper, the People's Office Building, on the northwest corner of Broad and State. A furor accompanied the construction of the $300,000, eight-story "architectural folly" in 1909. The People's National Bank, which moved into the new building on April 18, 1911, acquired it but eventually lost it in the Depression.

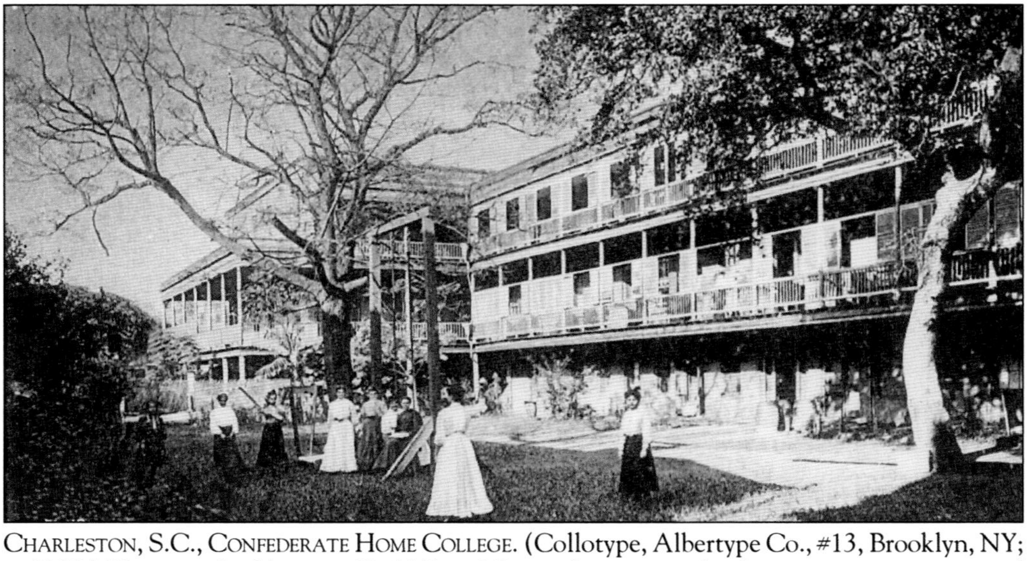

CHARLESTON, S.C., CONFEDERATE HOME COLLEGE. (Collotype, Albertype Co., #13, Brooklyn, NY; c. 1905.) The main building, at 60–64 Broad Street, has seen multiple uses since it was erected c. 1800. In 1867, what had since 1834 been the Carolina Hotel was rented as "a Home for the Mothers, Wives, and Daughters of Confederate Soldiers," founded by Amarinthia Snowden and her sister, Isabella Snowden. In 1870 a "female seminary" was established on the premises and became known as the "college" between 1900 and its closing in 1923. The "Home" is currently used for apartment, studio, and commercial space.

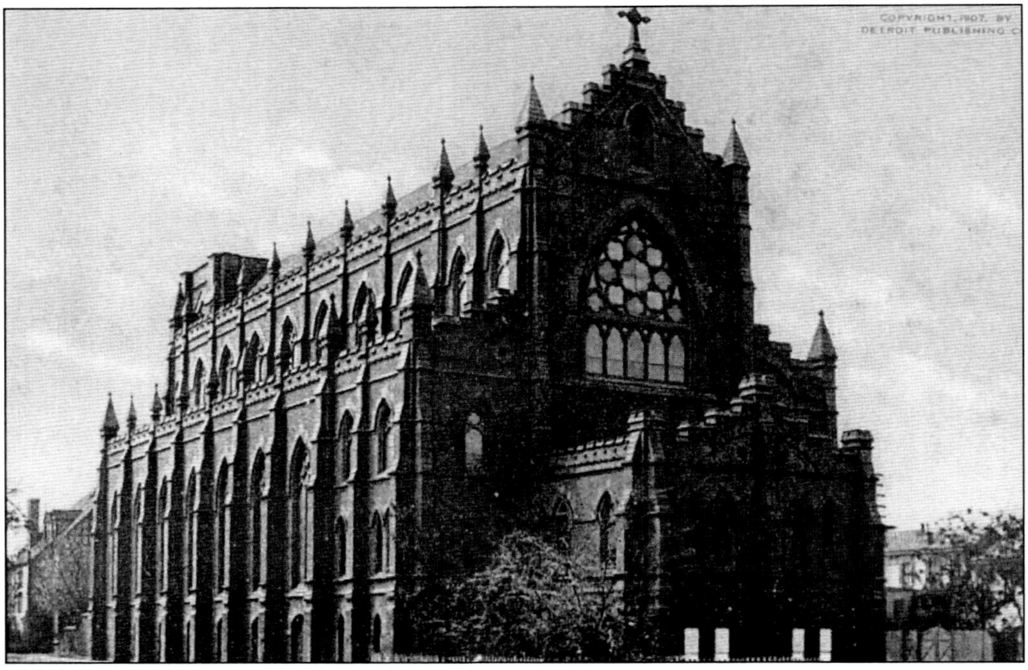


THE CATHEDRAL, CHARLESTON, S.C. (Color Lithography, 3½” X 5½”, Detroit Publishing Co., #11600, Detroit, MI; cp. 1907.) The Cathedral of St. John the Baptist, at Broad and Legare Streets, was completed in 1907, replacing the first cathedral which was destroyed during the fire of 1861. Constructed along plans almost identical to those of the earlier edifice, the cathedral is built of Connecticut brownstone. This rear view reveals the large stained-glass unit made up of a rose window showing the Baptism of Christ and five vertical panels containing a rendering of Da Vinci's *Last Supper*.

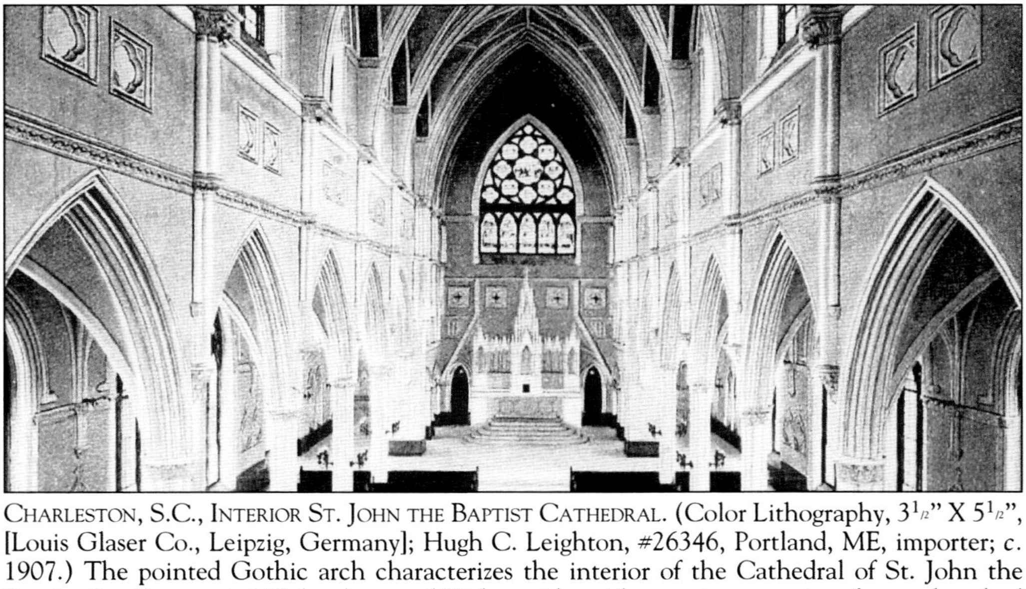

CHARLESTON, S.C., INTERIOR ST. JOHN THE BAPTIST CATHEDRAL. (Color Lithography, 3½” X 5½”, [Louis Glaser Co., Leipzig, Germany]; Hugh C. Leighton, #26346, Portland, ME, importer; *c.* 1907.) The pointed Gothic arch characterizes the interior of the Cathedral of St. John the Baptist. Its tile nave is 150 feet long and 80 feet wide, with a seating capacity of seven hundred persons. The ornately carved main altar was fashioned out of Vermont marble.

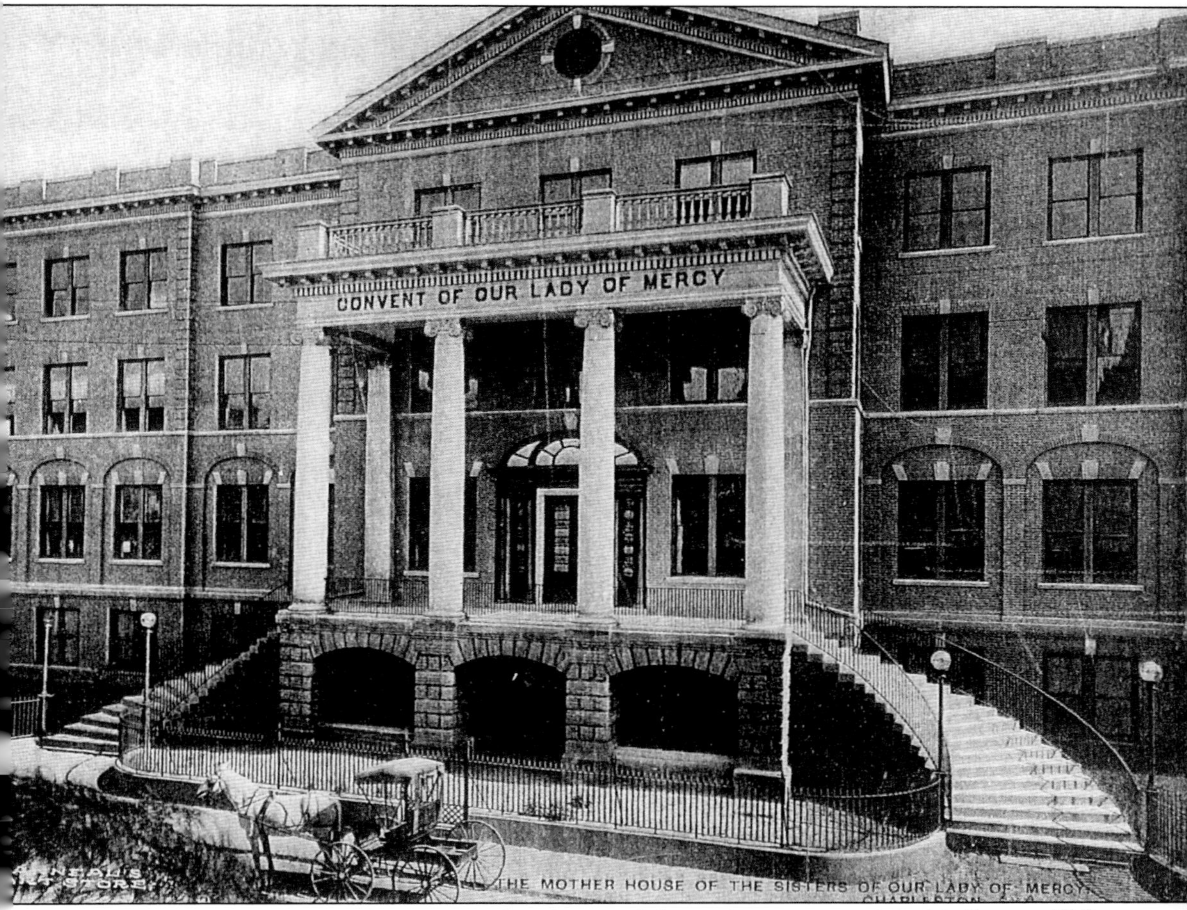


THE MOTHER HOUSE OF THE CONVENT OF OUR LADY OF MERCY, CHARLESTON, S.C. (Collotype, $5\frac{5}{16}$" X $7\frac{5}{16}$", Albertype Co., Brooklyn, NY; *c.* 1910.) This four-story convent, which once stood at 68 Legare Street, was built in 1909. Through the years, the structure also functioned variously as academy, kindergarten, and junior college until the congregation relocated to James Island in 1958. Sold for $125,000 in 1971, it was razed in March of the next year and replaced by twelve two-story townhouses.

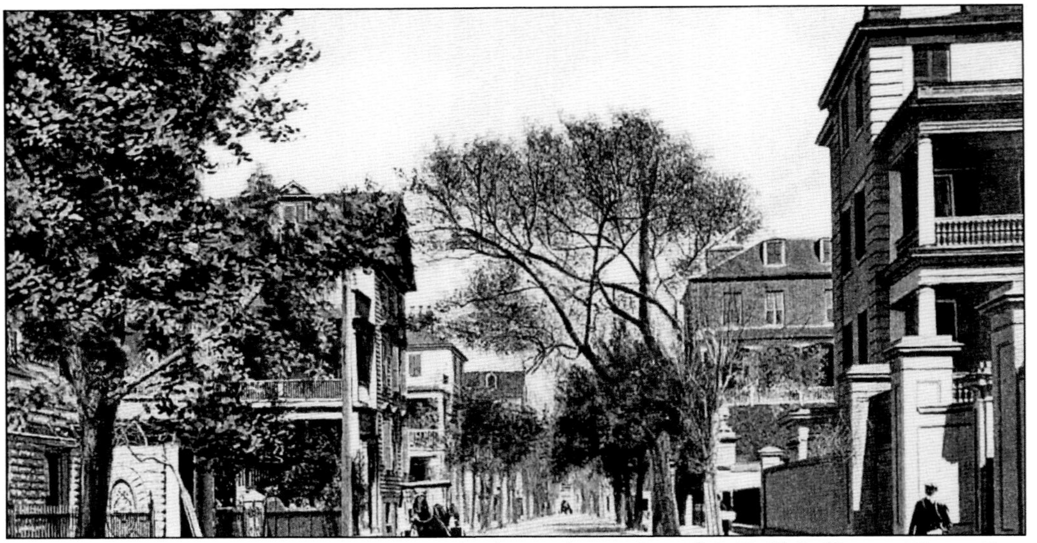

CHARLESTON, S.C., OLD LEGARE STREET. (Color Lithography, 3½" X 5½", [Louis Glaser Co., Leipzig, Germany]; Hugh C. Leighton, #26343, Portland, ME, importer; *c.* 1907.) This view of "Old Legare Street," looking north just above the intersection with Gibbes Street, shows the John Fullerton house in the middle distance at the left and the Simmons-Edwards house farther up on the right.

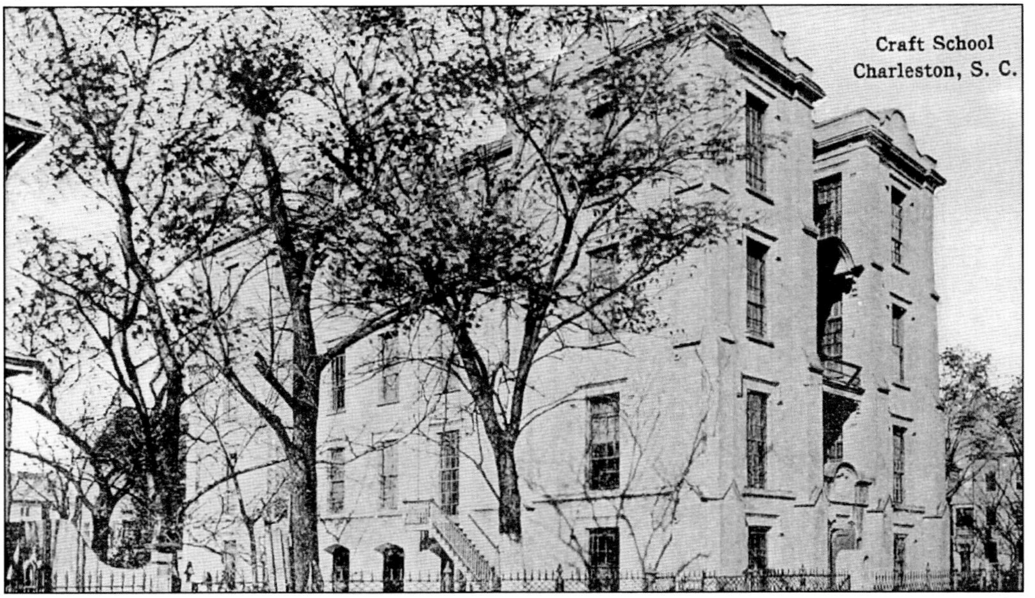


CRAFT [SIC] SCHOOL, CHARLESTON, S.C. (Color Lithography, [Tichnor Bros., Inc., Boston, MA].; *c.* 1913.) The Crafts School, 67–69 Legare Street, which opened in October 1881, was named in honor of William Crafts, who was early identified with the cause of public education in South Carolina. Considered "an ornament to the city," the three-story brick structure built on a high basement contained three large main rooms and fourteen classrooms, and from its upper floors commanded a magnificent view of the city, rivers, and harbor. By 1901 it had 1,244 students. Now known as The Crafts House in Harleston Village, the school was adapted into a stylish condominium complex in the 1990s. This card is postmarked October 15, 1915.

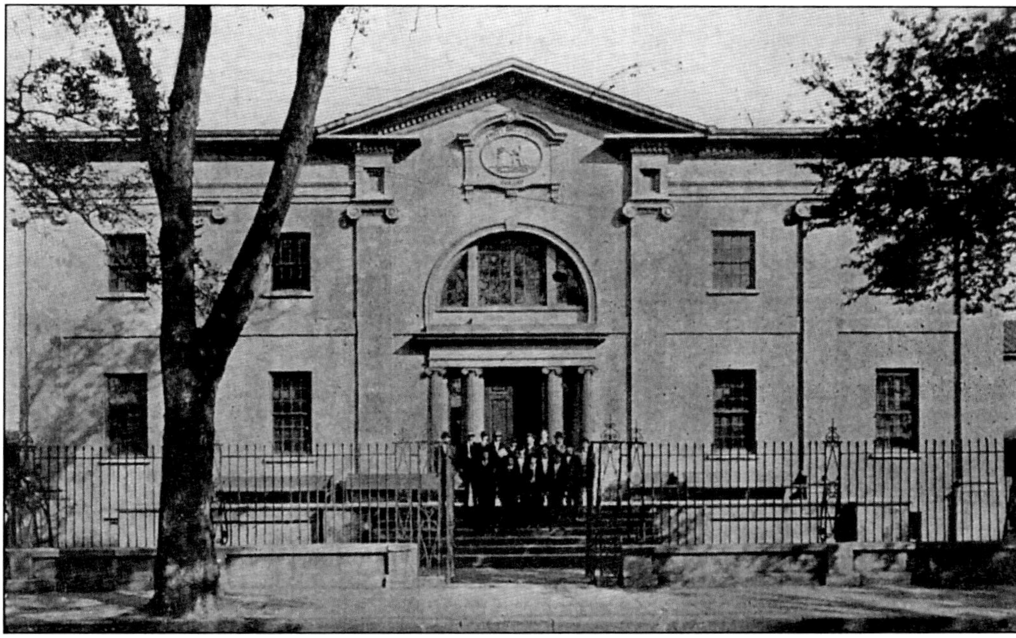

Medical College, Charleston, S.C. (Halftone; G.G. Chapman, publisher; *c.* 1909.) From 1826 to 1913 the Medical College of South Carolina occupied this building, which once stood at the corner of Queen and Franklin Streets. It had been designed by Charleston architect Frederick Wesner (1788–1848). This card is postmarked December 6, 1909.

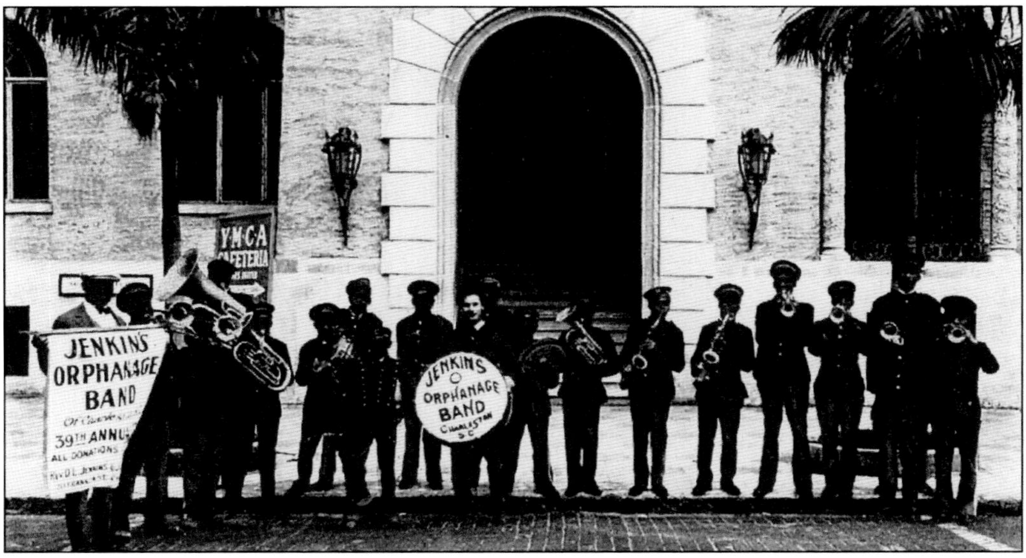


Jenkin's [sic] Orphanage Band Playing at the Y.M.C.A. Building, St. Petersburg, Fla. The Sunshine City. (Color Lithograph, [Curt Teich Co., #128954, Chicago, IL]; The Hartman Card Co., Portland, ME; 1930s.) The Jenkins Orphanage, established by the Reverend Daniel J. Jenkins in 1891, occupied the Robert Mills-designed United States Marine Hospital, 18–20 Franklin Street, from 1895 to 1939. The Orphanage became famous for its children's band which traveled widely and produced some well-known jazz musicians. Here the band is pictured during a stop in St. Petersburg, Florida, on one of its annual fund-raising tours.

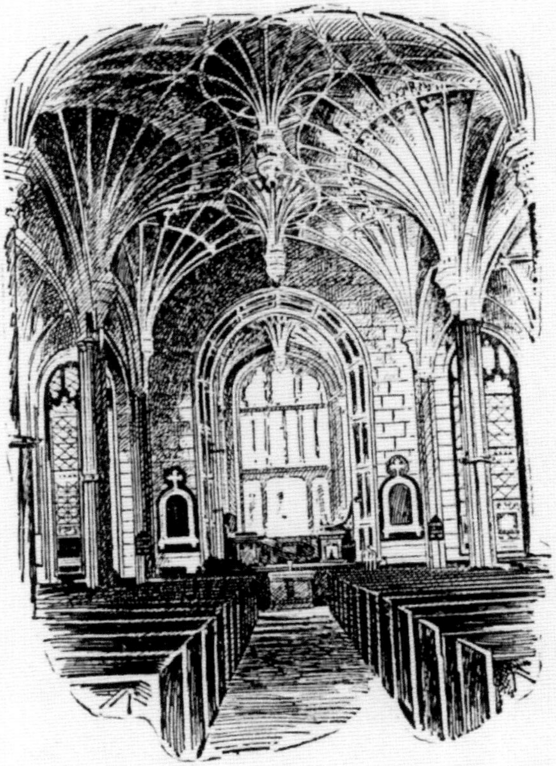

**Unitarian Church, Charleston, S. C.**

—o—

Erected 1774. Remodeled 1854, after King Henry VII Chapel, Westminster Abbey. One of the most beautiful interiors in the South.

In the Tower of this Church the Harvard Men of America have erected a Memorial Room to Samuel Gilman, author of "Fair Harvard." Open to the Public from 2 to 5 P. M.

The Rosa Thompson Memorial Organ, a recent Gift to the Church represents the highest skill in the organ builder's art.

In the love of truth and in the spirit of Jesus, you are invited to join with us here to worship God and serve man.

UNITARIAN CHURCH, CHARLESTON, S.C. (Photoengraving, 5½" X 3½"; *c.* 1915.) This unusual card—one of a two-card, locally published set—was probably used for outreach and promotion by the Unitarian Church about 1915, when the church installed the Austin organ mentioned here. The card features a sketch of the church's interior which highlights its fan tracery Gothic ceiling. Installed during major renovations between 1852 and 1854, this ceiling is considered by many to be the most striking in Charleston. The inexpensive uncoated paper used in this set, which darkens badly with age, dictated that this card to be copied on an extra-light setting to remove the unwanted discoloration. Only two examples of each card have been located.

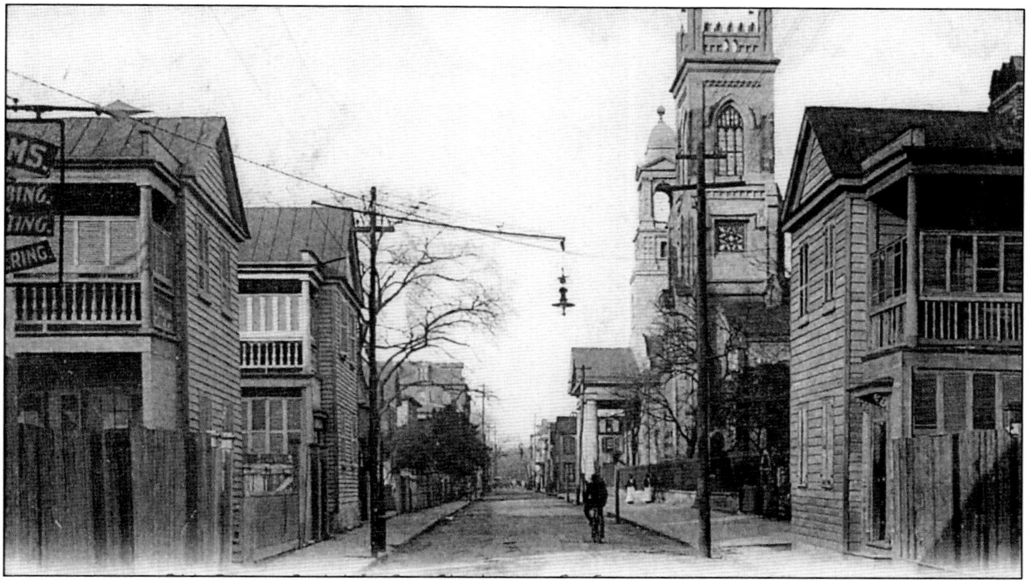

Old Quaint Archdale St., Charleston, S.C. (Collotype, [Knackstedt and Nather Co., Hamburg, Germany]; Rotograph Co., #A 12587, New York, NY, importer; 1905.) In view just beyond the Gothic-towered Unitarian Church at 8 Archdale (right) is St. John's Lutheran at 10 Archdale, the mother church of Lutheranism in Charleston and one of the oldest congregations of the Evangelical Lutheran Church in America. The sanctuary was designed by Frederick Wesner and dedicated in 1817.

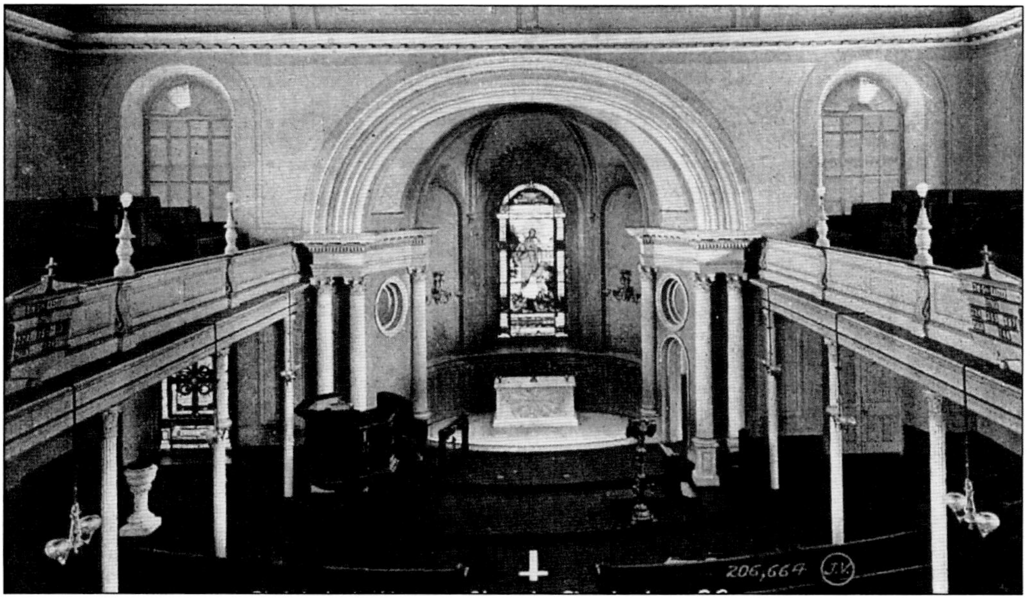


St. John's Lutheran Church, Charleston, S.C. (Color Lithography; Valentine & Sons, #206, 664, Dundee, Scotland; c. 1907.) The recessed chancel and window featured in this interior view of St. John's Lutheran Church were designed by the Reverend E.T. Horn and were added in 1896. The church installed ornamental organ pipes and case by Henry Erben in 1823.

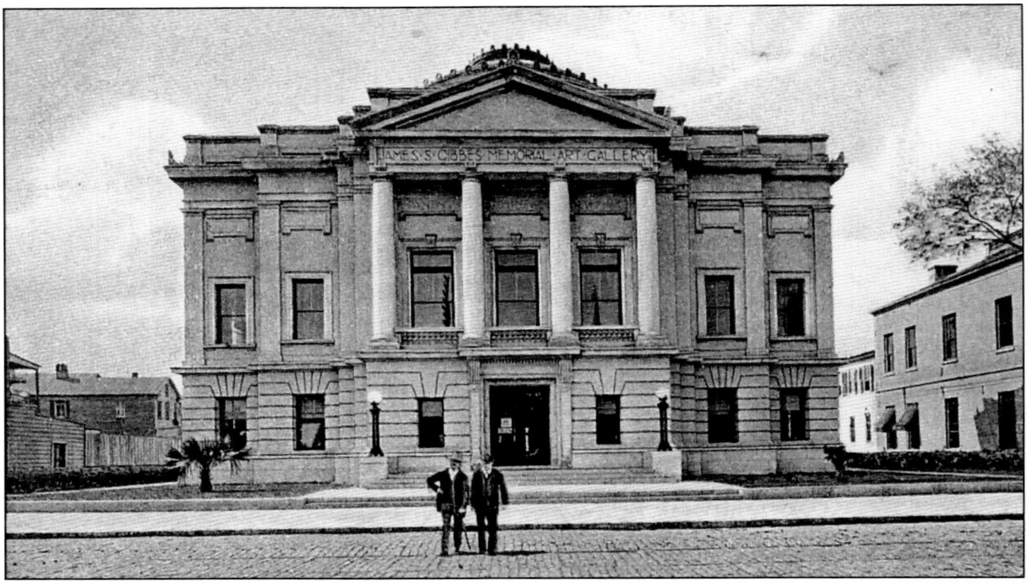


CHARLESTON, S.C., JAMES S. GIBBES MEMORIAL ART GALLERY. (Color Lithography, [Louis Glaser Co., Leipzig, Germany]; Hugh C. Leighton, #26333, Portland, ME, importer; *c.* 1907.) The Gibbes Memorial Art Gallery, 135 Meeting Street, was built in 1905 on the site of the first modest offices of the *Charleston Evening Post*. Started with a bequest from James Shoolbred Gibbes (1819–1888), the museum would come to house valuable permanent collections and has long been at the center of the city's formal artistic life.

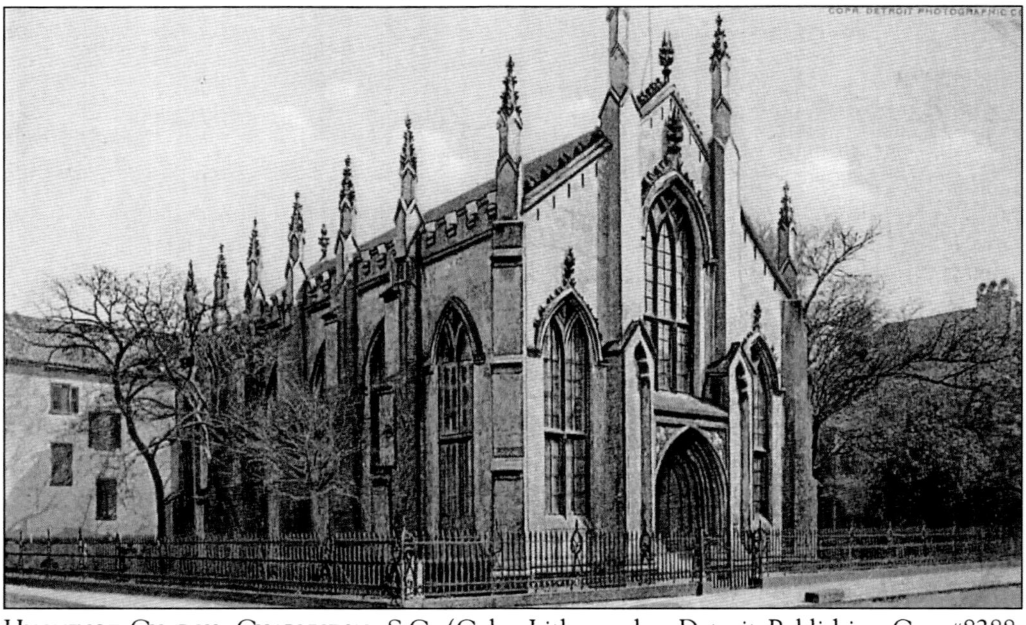

HUGUENOT CHURCH, CHARLESTON, S.C. (Color Lithography, Detroit Publishing Co., #8288, Detroit, MI; cp. 1904.) The sanctuary of the French Huguenot Church, 136 Church Street, is the third to have been erected on this site by the "French Church of Charles Town," which was organized in 1681. It was erected in 1845 and was the city's first church in the Gothic Revival style, which was favored by its designer, Edward Brickell White.

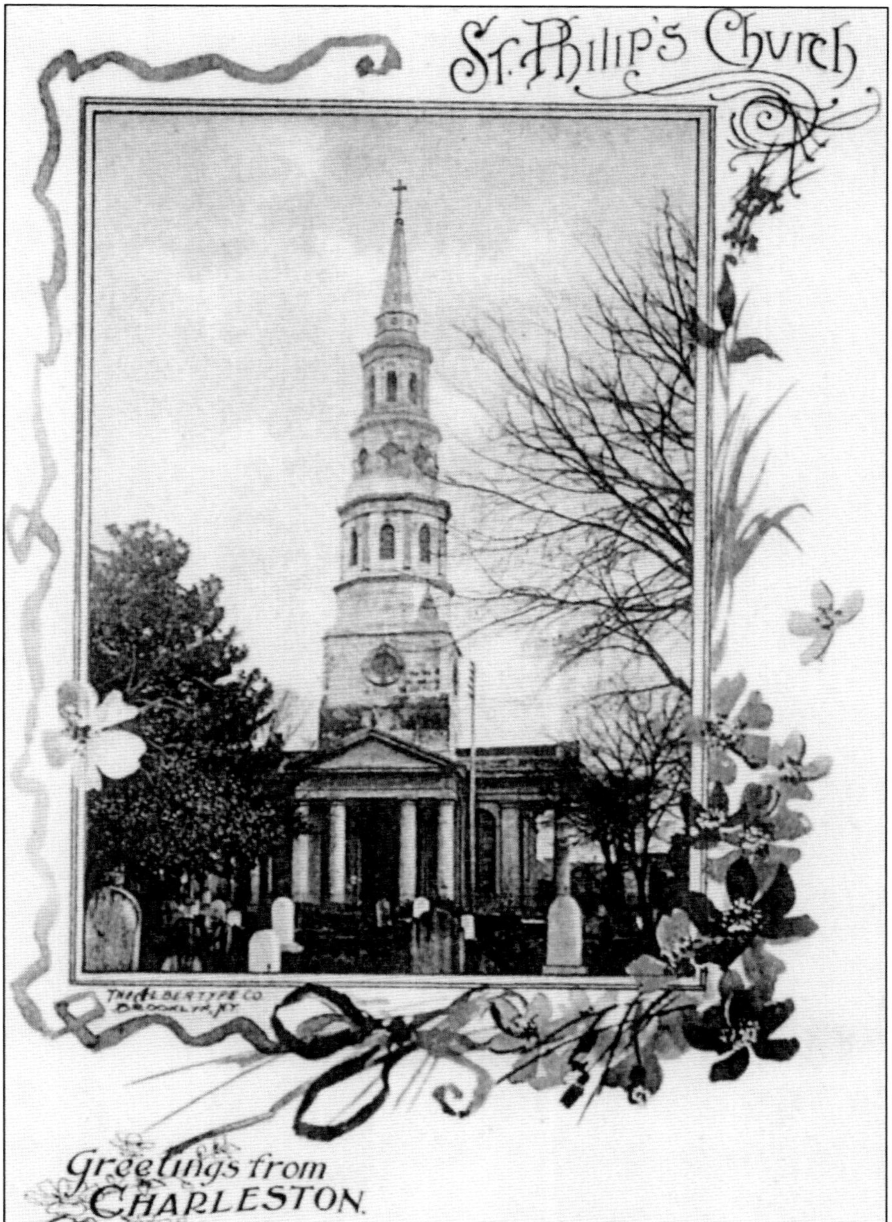


ST. PHILIP'S CHURCH, GREETINGS FROM CHARLESTON. (Collotype, $5^{1/2}$" X $3^{3/10}$", Albertype Co., Brooklyn, NY; *c.* 1899.) This early, beribboned, flower-framed portrait of St. Philip's at 146 Church Street, sometimes referred to during this period as the "Westminster Abbey of the South," was suitably celebratory of what for over three hundred years has been considered the mother church of the Episcopal Diocese of South Carolina. The present sanctuary is the second one to have been built on this "new" site, the first one having been destroyed by fire in 1835. It has been in use since 1838. During the period when this card was published, its steeple functioned as a lighthouse to aid ships entering Charleston Harbor. The decorative composition of this early issue illustrates the stylistic designs of the era.

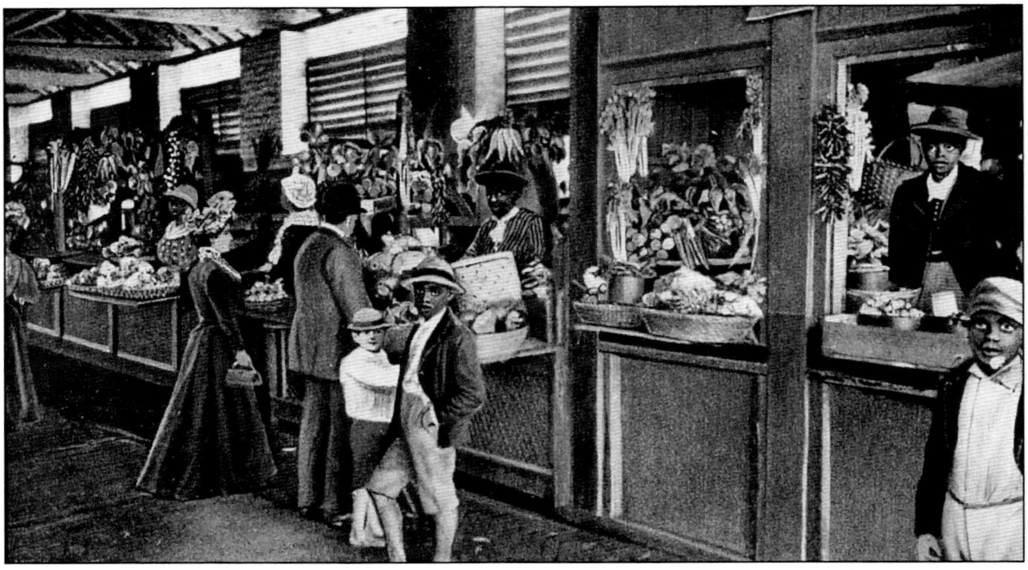

CHARLESTON, S.C., SECTION OLD MARKET. (Color Lithography, 3½" X 5½", [Rosenblatt Lithographic Institute, #202817, Frankfurt, Germany]; 1908.) Erected between 1788 and 1804, the Market extends behind the hall in a series of low arcades which were spaced for large and small meats, vegetables, fruits, and fish. "This is the Vegetable Section," reads the printed note on the back of this card, "where the old 'Maumas' presided in their stalls and dispersed their wares to merchants and professional men who, accompanied by their servants, were accustomed to make their own purchases in the old days." It is postmarked July 28, 1908.

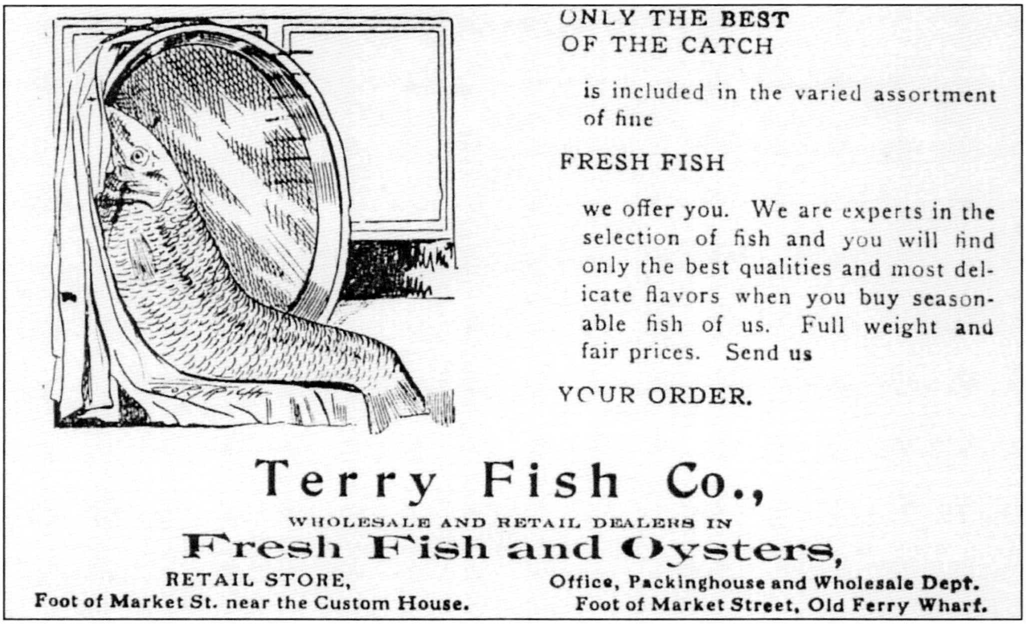


TERRY FISH COMPANY. (Photoengraving; 1912.) The name Terry was prominently identified with a retail and wholesale fish business at the east end of Market from at least 1860 into the early 1930s. This limited-edition card—postmarked May 14, 1912—was drawn, copyrighted, and produced by a Charleston printer.

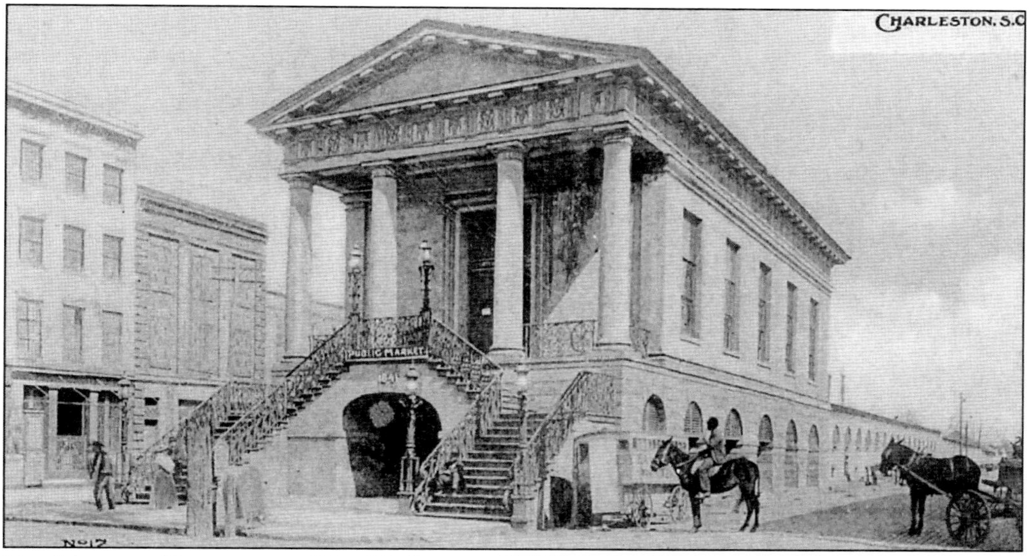


OLD MARKET, CHARLESTON, S.C. (Collotype, 3½" X 5½", Albertype Co., #17, Brooklyn, NY; c. 1905.) Market Hall, which anchors Charleston's Central Market located on Meeting Street through Church and State to East Bay, was designed by Edward Brickell White, erected in 1841, and hailed as an excellent adaptation of the Grecian-Doric "Temple of the Wingless Victory" at Athens. Others have cited it as a fine example of Roman Doric. The City Market was designated a National Historic Landmark in 1975.

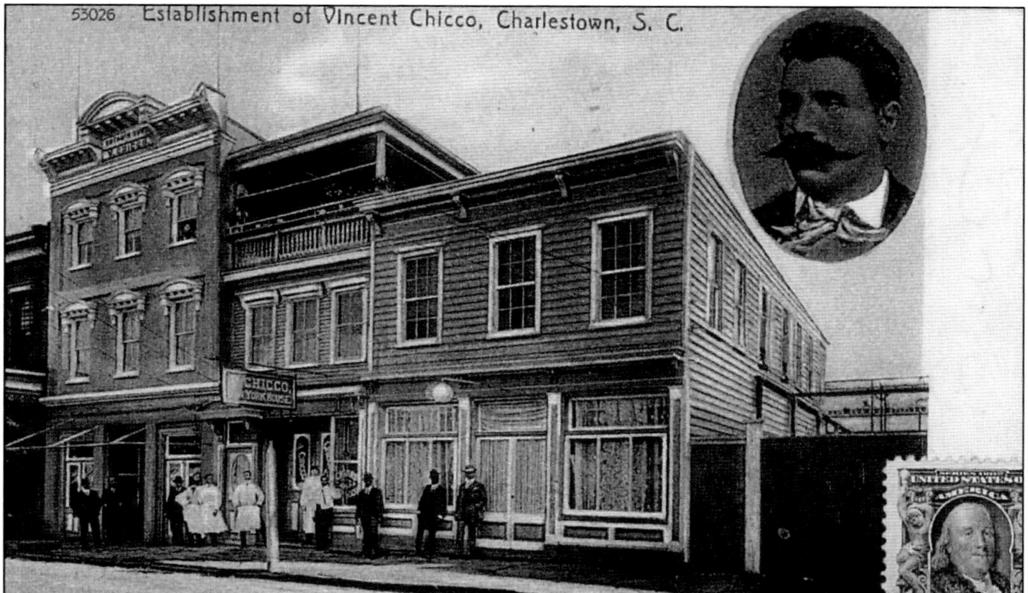


ESTABLISHMENT OF VINCENT CHICCO, CHARLESTON, S.C. (Color Lithography, 3½" X 5½", [Knackstedt and Nather Co., Hamburg, Germany]; Rotograph Co., #53026, New York, NY, importer; 1906.) Vincent Chicco's "establishment," 83–85½ Market Street, was founded in the early 1890s and occupied two three-story buildings divided into three departments: hotel, café, and store. The café was spoken of as one of the most popular and most orderly in the city. Chicco owned extensive property and was a former policeman.

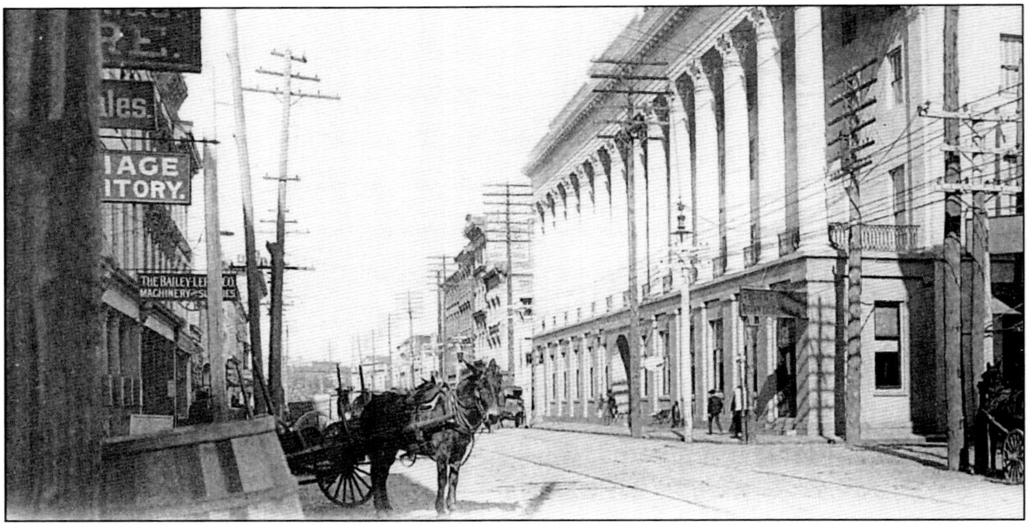

CHARLESTON HOTEL, CHARLESTON, S.C. (Collotype, 3½” X 5½”, [Knackstedt and Nather Co., Hamburg, Germany]; Rotograph Co., #12574, New York, NY, importer; cp. 1905.) The Charleston Hotel, a Greek Revival structure built in 1838–39 to a design by Charles F. Reichardt, once stood at 200 Meeting Street. Its elegant colonnade of fourteen Corinthian columns fronted the block from Pinckney to Hayne. Considered architecturally valuable to the city, it was nevertheless demolished in March 1960. In 1991 NCNB erected an office building on the site, now NationsBank Plaza, with a colonnaded facade which echoes the style of the old hotel.

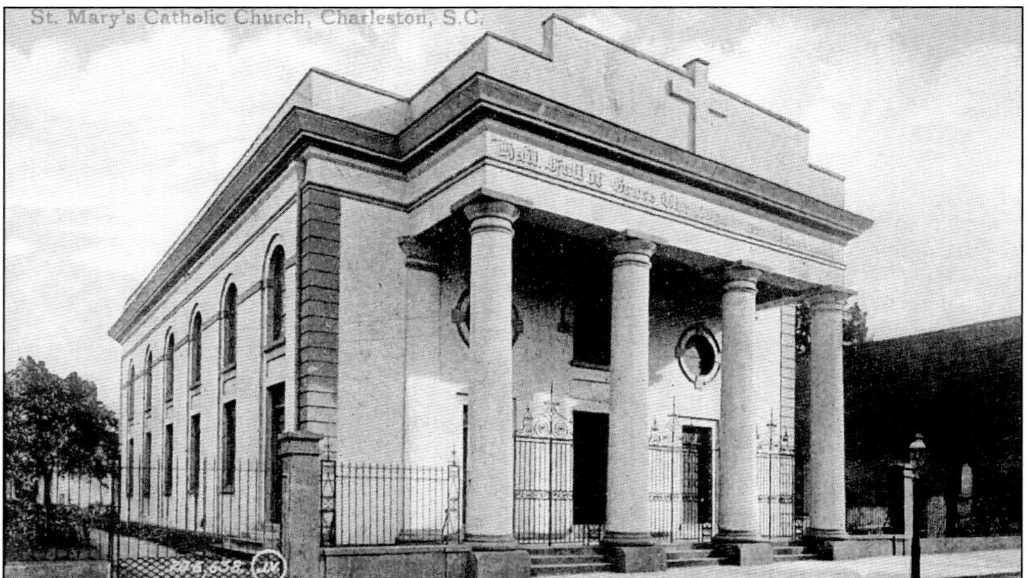


ST. MARY’S CATHOLIC CHURCH, CHARLESTON, S.C. (Color Lithography, 3½” X 5½”, Valentine & Sons, #206, 658, Dundee, Scotland; 1909.) St. Mary’s Catholic Church, at 89 Hasell, was established in 1789 and is the oldest Roman Catholic congregation in the Carolinas and Georgia. The third edifice to have been built on this site, the sanctuary opened for worship in 1839.

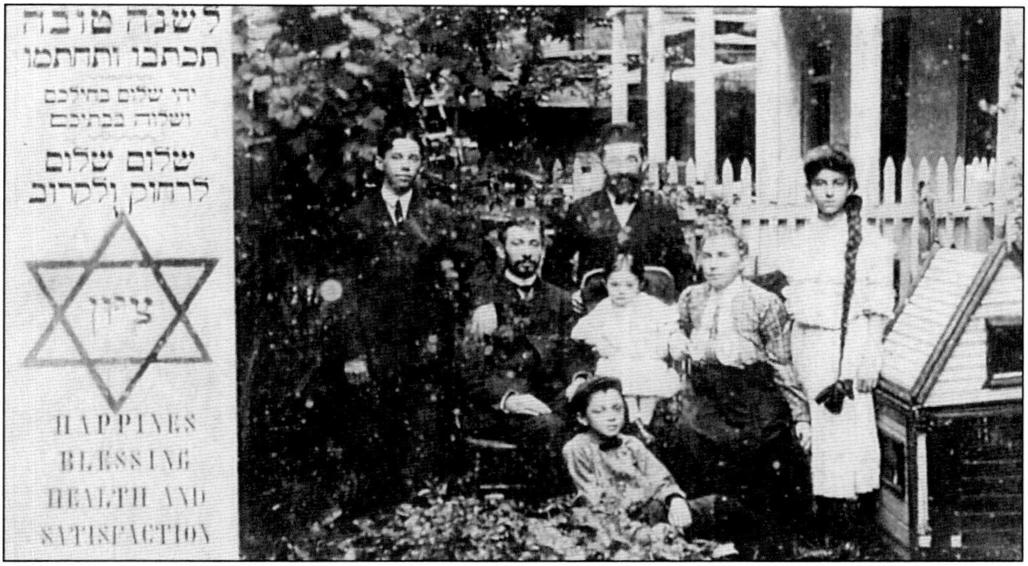


RUBINS' NEW YEAR'S CARD. (Photoprint; *c.* 1913.) This New Year's card, with greetings in both Hebrew and English, was sent out no earlier than 1913, the first year that the Rubins are listed in the *City Directory* as residing at 151 Broad Street. For at least thirty years (1897–1927), Isaac David ("Dave") Rubin was in business as a pawnbroker or merchant of clothing, luggage, and jewelry, with commercial addresses variably at Market and King Streets. The Rubins family would have been members of Charleston's Orthodox Jewish temple, B'rith Sholom, to which he presented a silver menorah. The figure in the center of the picture is probably Isaac David's father.

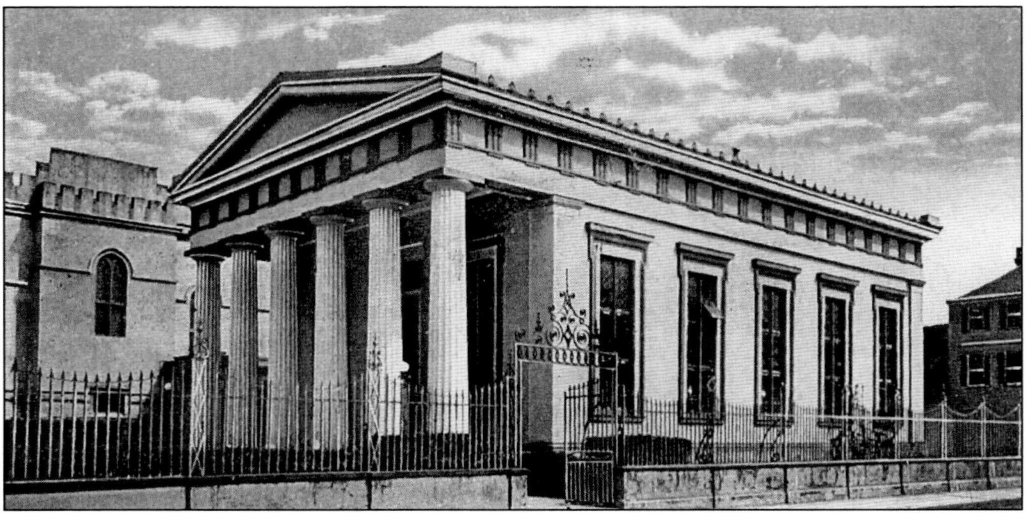

THE SYNAGOGUE, CHARLESTON, S.C. (Color Lithography, 3½" X 5½", Curt Teich Co., #A-65987, Chicago, IL; 1916.) Kahal Kadosh Beth Elohim (Holy Congregation, House of God), 90 Hasell Street, is the latest temple (erected between 1839 and 1841) for a congregation which occupied sanctuaries on this site since the 1790s. The claim is made that it is the oldest one in continuous use in the United States and the oldest surviving Reform synagogue in the world. A significant example of the Greek Revival style in America with a front of the Doric order, it is on the National Register of Historic Places.

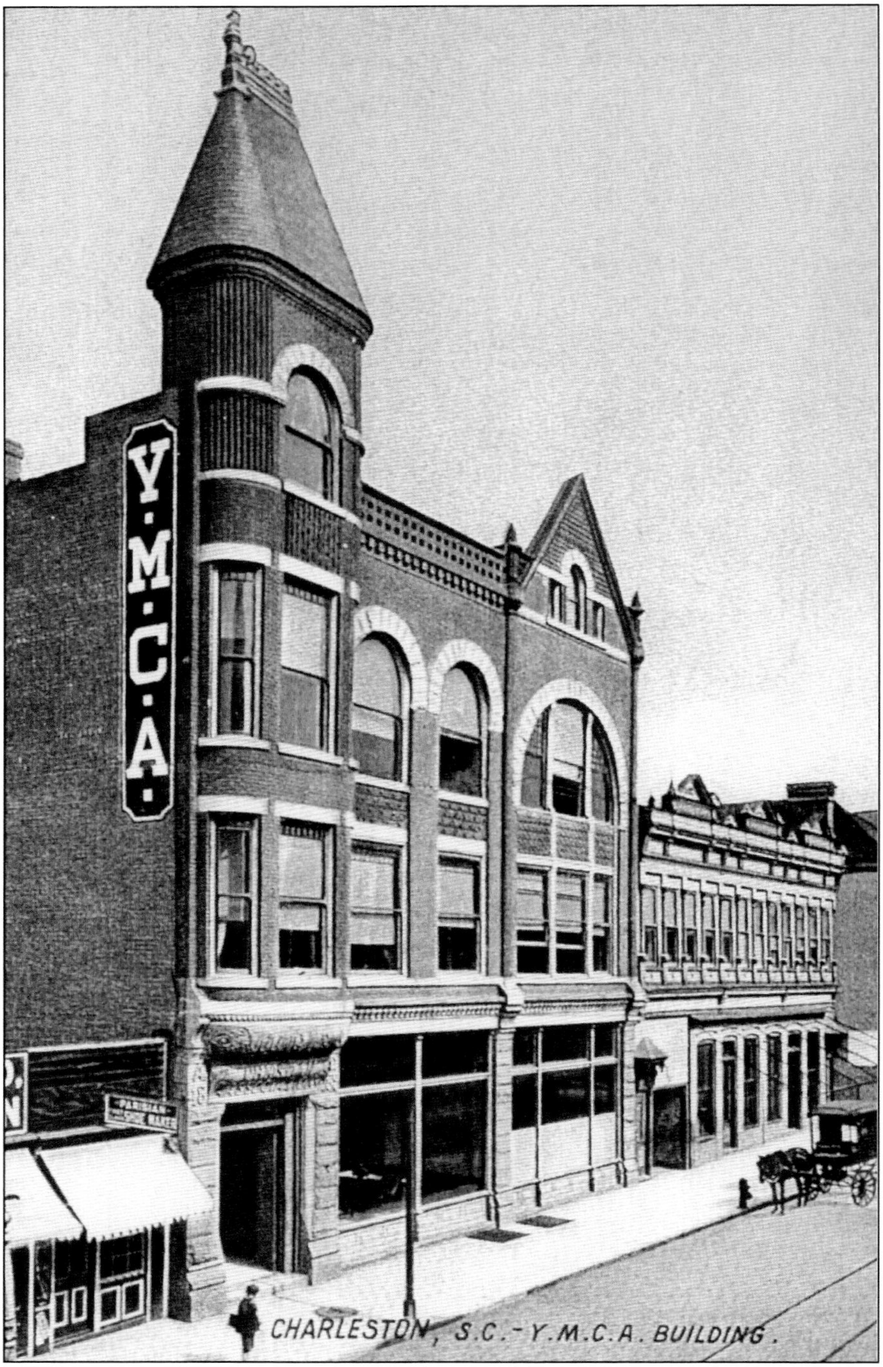


Y.M.C.A. BUILDING, CHARLESTON, S.C. (Color Lithography, 3 1/2" X 5 1/2", [Rosenblatt Lithograph Institute, #202803, Frankfurt, Germany]; *c.* 1908.) Considered one of the "show" places of Charleston in the 1890s, this turreted structure at 298 King Street was home to the local YMCA from 1889 to 1912, when it moved into new quarters at 26 George. Demolished in the early 1960s, it was replaced by a gymnasium for the College of Charleston.

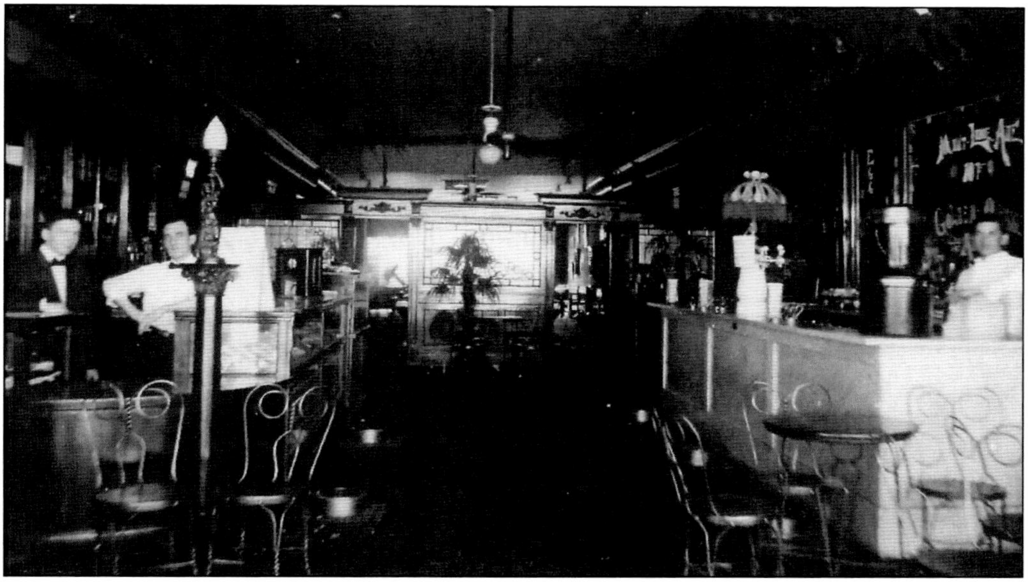

INTERIOR VIEW OF DRUG STORE. (Photoprint, 3½" X 5½"; c. 1910.) This card was in circulation about 1910, the year that Walsh's Charleston *City Directory* listed forty-four retail druggists in the city. The unidentified commercial interior here may have been one of the eighteen that were located on King Street. Store managers often commissioned a local photographer to produce special pictorial cards in bulk to use for announcements, advertisements, and notifications. Only one copy of this card has been located.

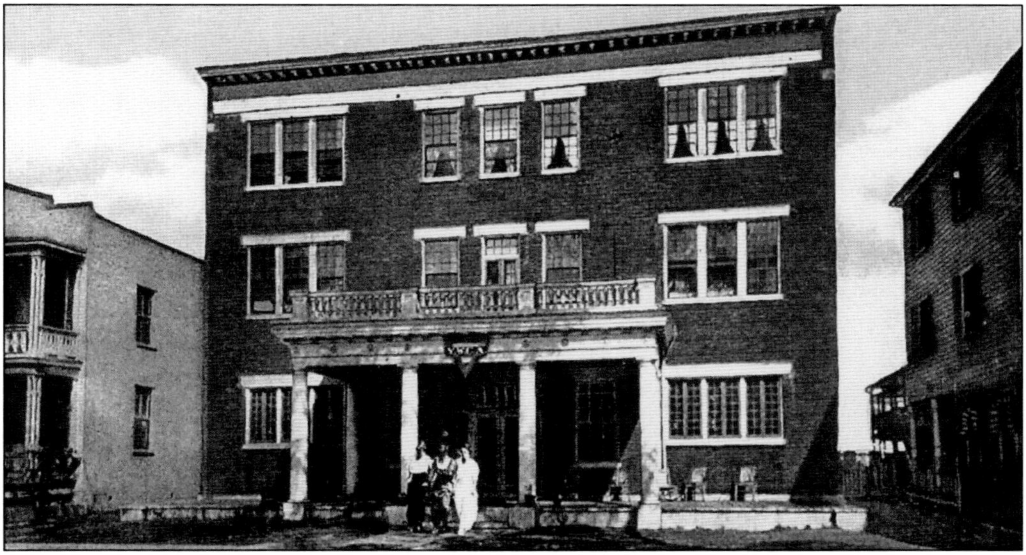

Y.W.C.A., Charleston, S.C. (Color Lithography, [Tichnor Bros., Inc., #116131, Boston, MA]; c. 1921.) A printed note on the back of this card indicates that the YWCA in Charleston was first established in two rooms on King Street in 1903. It goes on to say that they moved several times "before settling in the present building, number 21 George Street, which was completed on March 4, 1920." But the building pictured here is not the 1840s Greek Revival Ripley home which once stood at 21 George. Rather, it must be the structure at 76 Society, which is the organization's address starting in 1918. Today this site is used for parking.

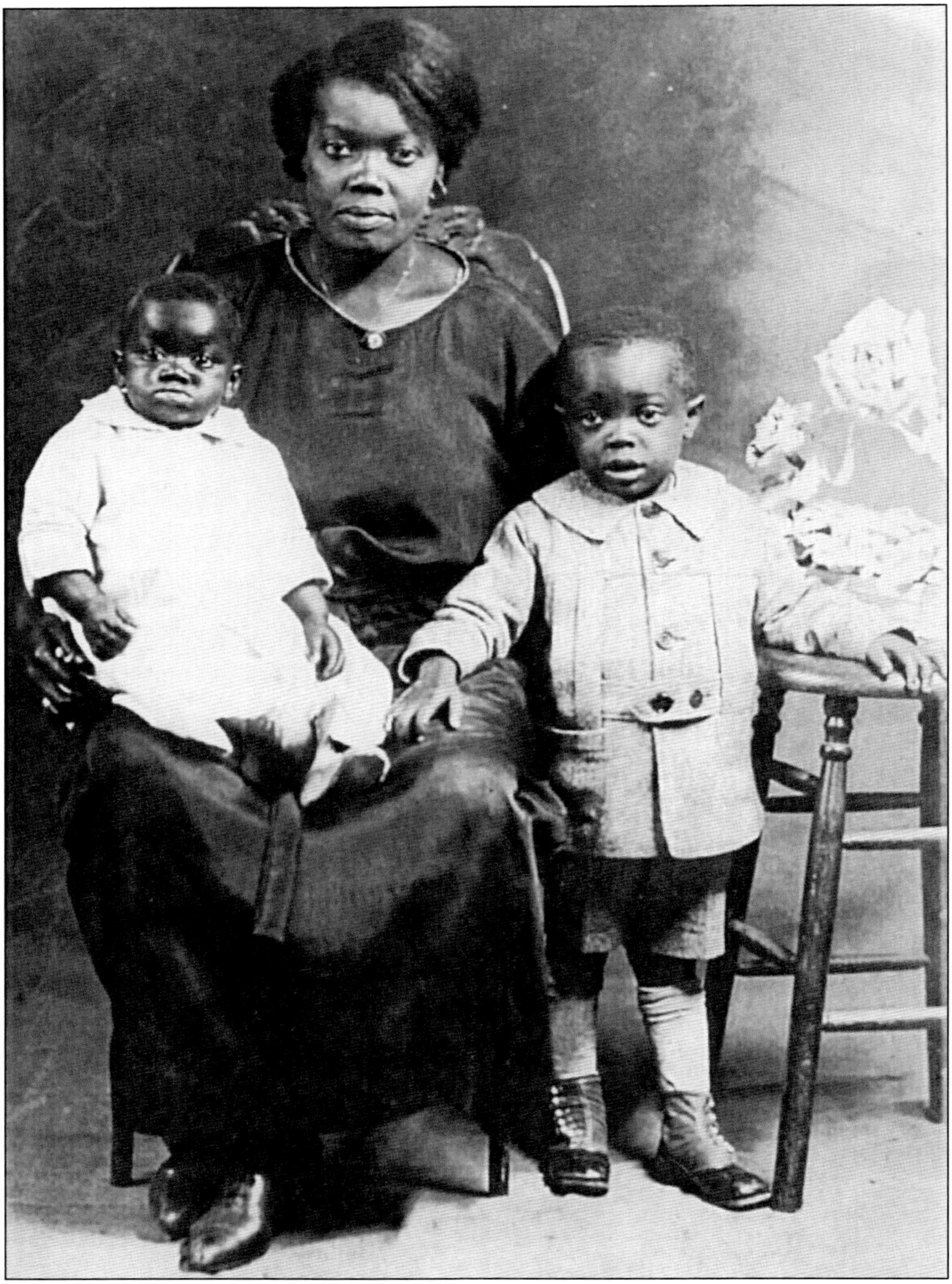

MRS. ISAIAH AIKEN AND SONS. (Photoprint, 3 1/2" X 5 1/2", M.F. Blake, Charleston, S.C.; c. 1925.) This portrait of Anna Beatrice Green (Mrs. Isaiah N.) Aiken, with her sons Isaiah Jr. and Arthur, was made by black photographer Michael Francis Blake, probably in the late 1920s. A Race Street family, the Aikens lived first at 406 and then at 429. Mrs. Aiken, a graduate of Avery Institute, was principally a homemaker; in 1985 she died at the age of 92. Mr. Aiken was a sheet metal worker, roofer, and musician. The sons seen here were the first two of the Aikens' seven children.

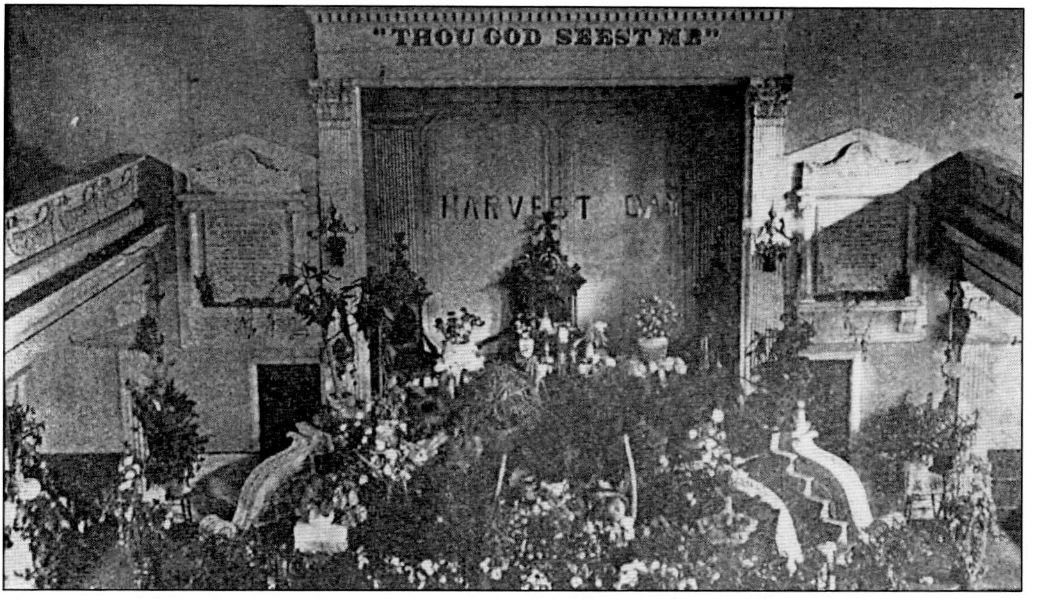


CENTENARY M.E. CHURCH, CHARLESTON, S.C. (Halftone, 3½" X 5½", Thomas D. Small, Summerville, S.C., publisher; 1909.) Centenary Methodist Episcopal Church was established in 1865 when black members of Trinity Methodist Episcopal Church withdrew to form their own congregation and subsequently purchased the Second Baptist Church on Wentworth Street for $20,000 in gold. This unusual card, postmarked October 7, 1915, bears on its reverse the handwritten words: "Getting ready for Harvest Day on the 17th."

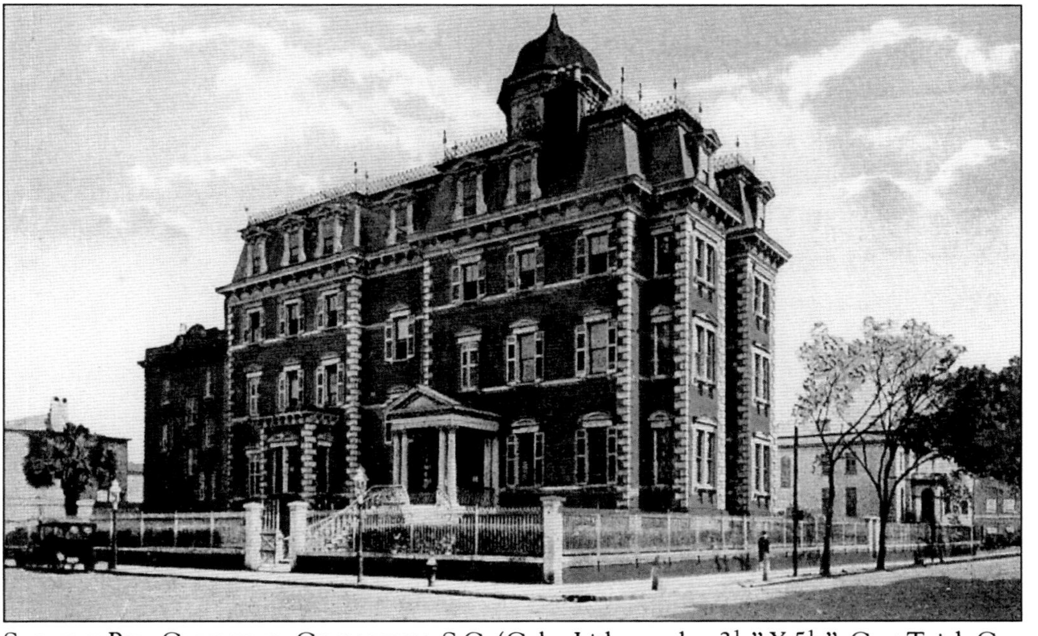

SCOTTISH RITE CATHEDRAL, CHARLESTON, S.C. (Color Lithography, 3½" X 5½", Curt Teich Co., #A88701, Chicago, IL; *c.* 1920.) The Scottish Rite Cathedral, formerly known as the "Rodgers Mansion," still stands on the southeast corner of Wentworth and Smith Streets. Until recently it has served as the headquarters of the Atlantic Coast Life Insurance Company.

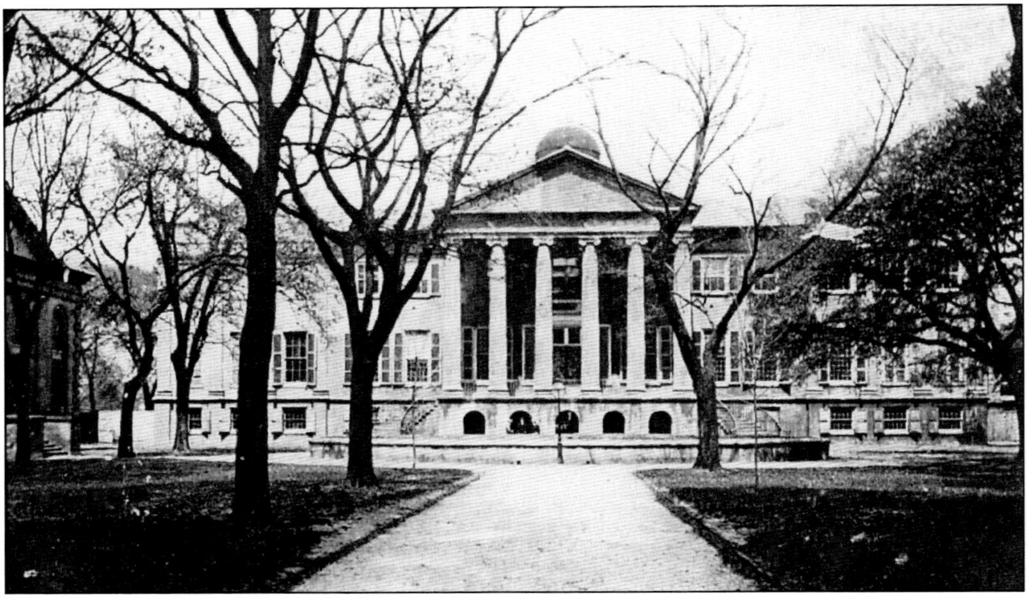

COLLEGE OF CHARLESTON, MAIN BUILDING, CHARLESTON, S.C. (Halftone; 1907.) Designed by William Strickland (approx. 1787–1854), the central portion of the main building of the College of Charleston, 66 George Street, dates from 1828. The portico and wings by Edward Brickell White were added by 1850. It is of national importance architecturally, along with its Library and Lodge on the same block. The school claims to be the oldest municipal college in America.

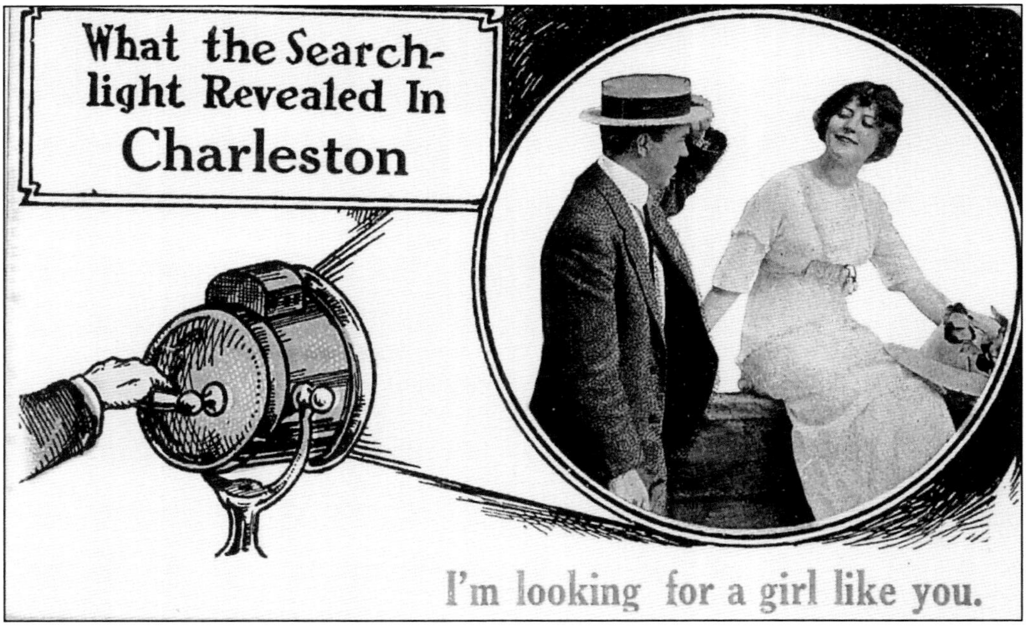


WHAT THE SEARCH LIGHT REVEALED IN CHARLESTON, CHARLESTON, S.C. (Color Lithography, McGown-Silsby Lithographic Co., New York, NY; *c.* 1914.) This novelty card, dating from about 1914, might have been a generic stock item which any jobber, local or otherwise, could imprint with the appropriate name in the available space.

ST. PAUL'S CHURCH RADCLIFFEBOROUGH, NEAR CHARLESTON, S.C.; (Color Lithography, 3½" X 5½", Detroit Publishing Co., #11544, Detroit, MI; *c.* 1907.) St. Paul's Radcliffeborough—now the Cathedral of St. Luke and St. Paul, 126 Coming Street—was nicknamed the "Planters' Church" because it was built with subscriptions from the planters who summered in the area. Erected in 1815, it was consecrated in 1816 and was the first Episcopal church in the area to be formally consecrated by an American bishop. Architecturally, it is a curious but strangely harmonious blend, with its Gothic Revival-style parapet superimposed upon a Classical Revival structure below. In 1949 St. Paul's merged with St. Luke's, Charlotte Street, and the new parish later became designated the Cathedral Church for the Diocese of South Carolina.

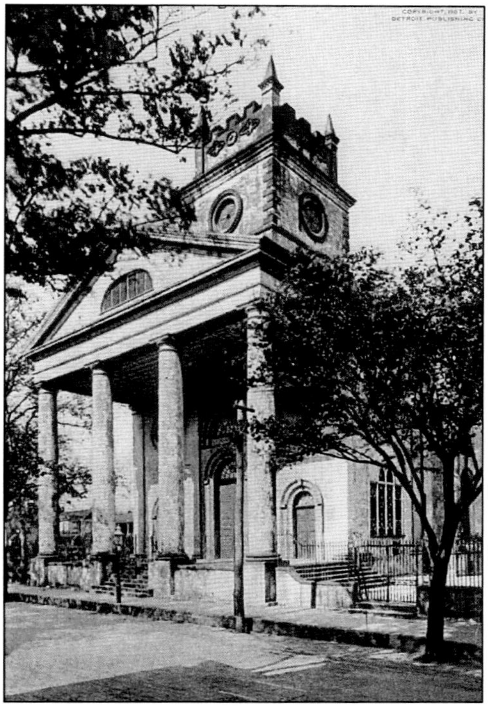

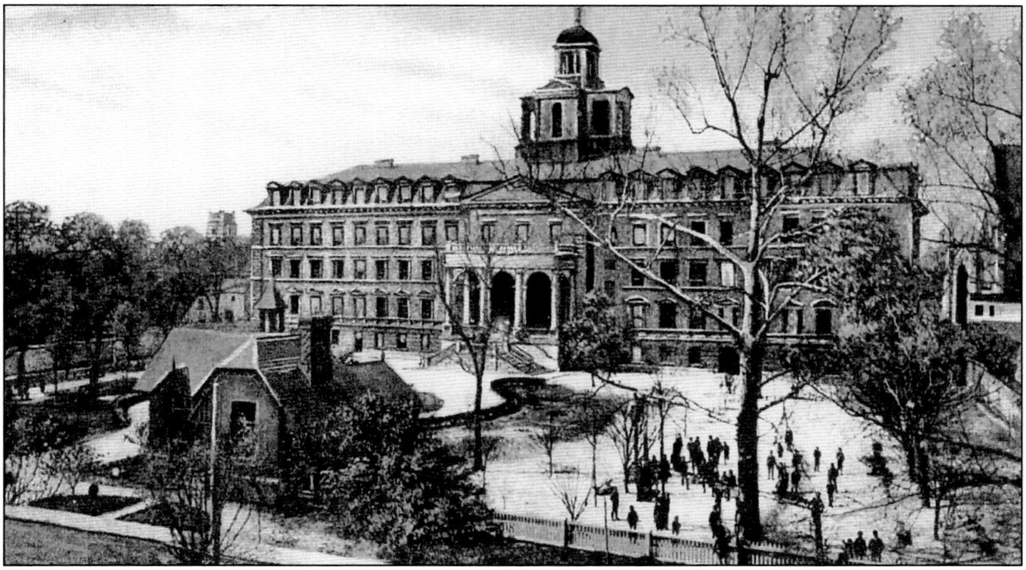

ORPHAN-HOUSE, CHARLESTON, S.C. (Color Lithography, 3½" X 5½", [Trenkler, Leipzig, Germany]; *c.* 1908.) The Charleston Orphan House, which once stood at 160 Calhoun Street between St. Philip and King, was built on the site of old Revolutionary War barracks by soldiers of that war, opened in 1794, and came to be hailed as "the finest edifice of its kind in the New World." The four-story, 170-foot-long brick structure was remodeled in 1855 to provide a modern steam heating system and space for a library. In 1950 the City sold the property for $350,200 to the Sears, Roebuck Company, which in 1952 demolished the Orphan House to make way for a new store. Today the block is part of the campus of the College of Charleston.

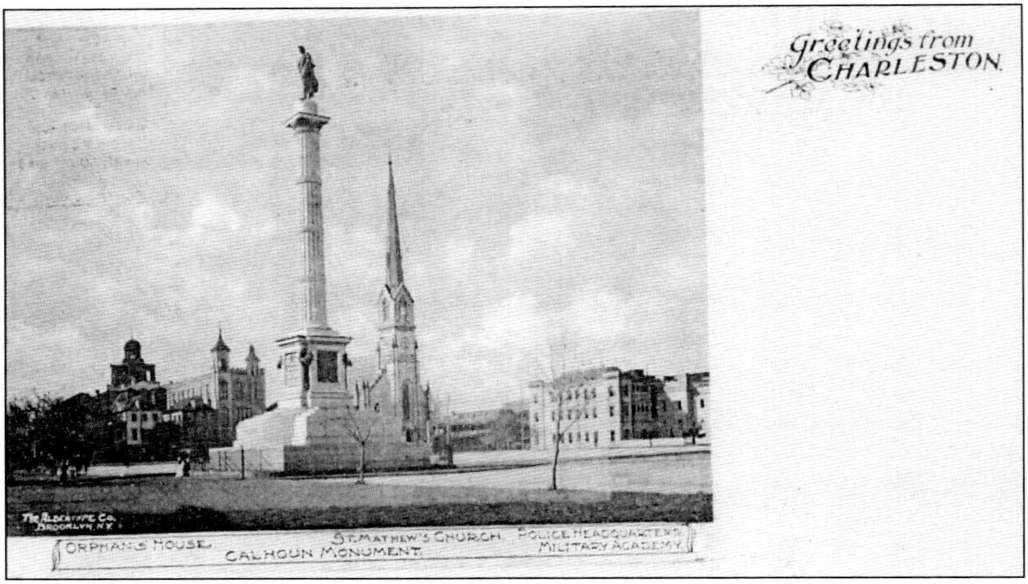


GREETINGS FROM CHARLESTON. (Collotype, Albertype Co., Brooklyn, NY; *c.* 1900.) The Calhoun Monument dominates this very early Private Mailing Card, which looks west across Marion Square and King Street towards the Orphan House, St. Matthew's Lutheran Church, the old police headquarters, and the military academy.

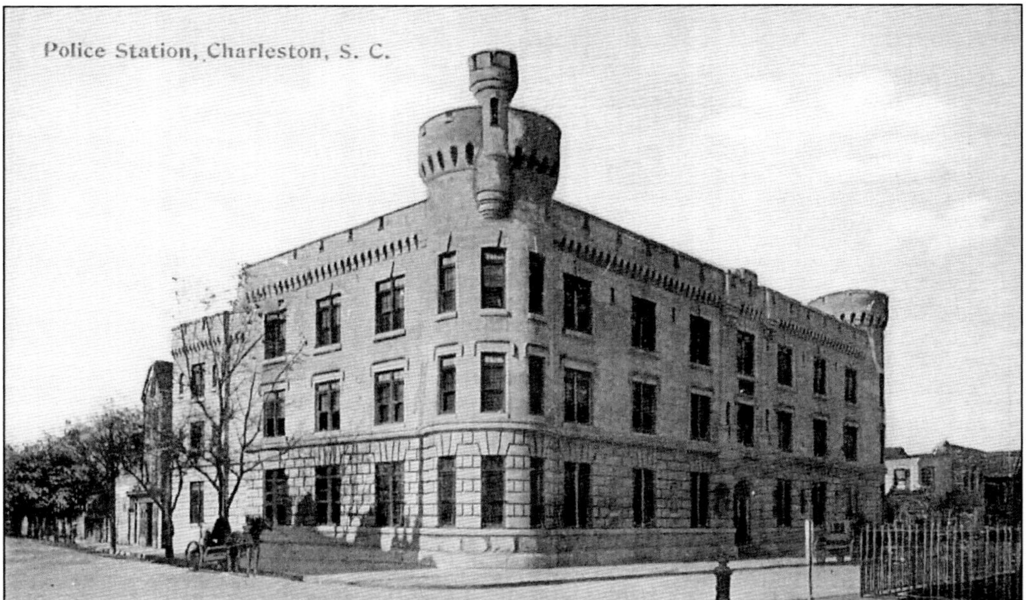


POLICE STATION, CHARLESTON, S.C. (Color Lithography, [Tichnor Bros., Inc., Boston, MA]; *c.* 1910.) The "new" Police Station, at the northwest corner of St. Philip and Vanderhorst (within a block of the old one), was completed in the spring of 1908. Valued at $90,000, it was considered one of the finest in the South. Its demolition in the 1970s allowed for the eventual erection on this site of a city public works administrative office building, which was dedicated on June 5, 1985.

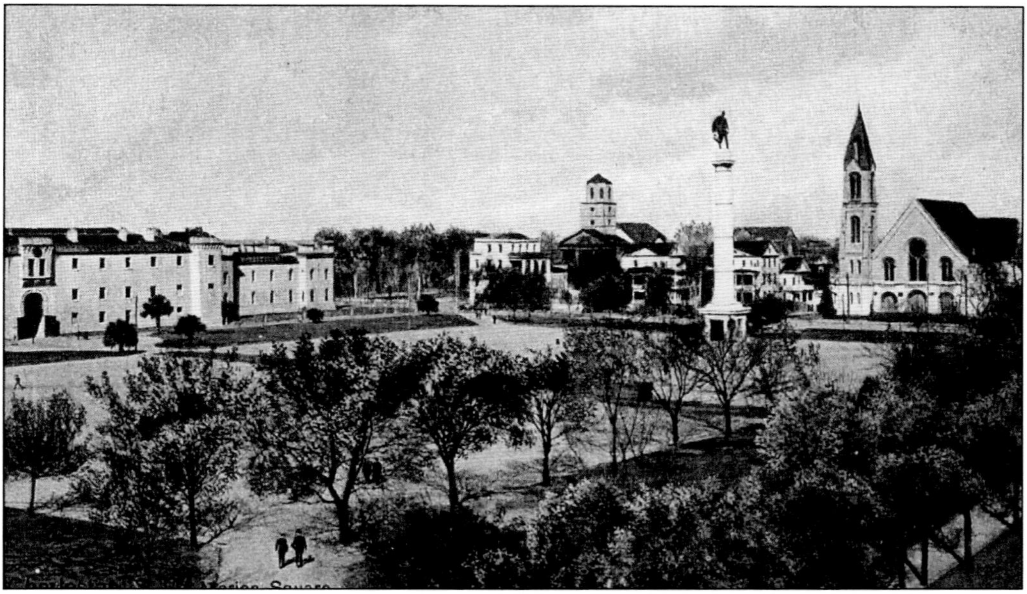

CHARLESTON, S.C., MARION SQUARE. (Color Lithography, [Louis Glaser Co., Leipzig, Germany]; Hugh C. Leighton, #26322, Portland, ME, importer; c. 1907.) This panoramic view of Marion Square, or "Citadel Green," looks east across Meeting Street to the Second Presbyterian Church (center) and Citadel Square Baptist Church (right). At left is the Military College of South Carolina, The Citadel.

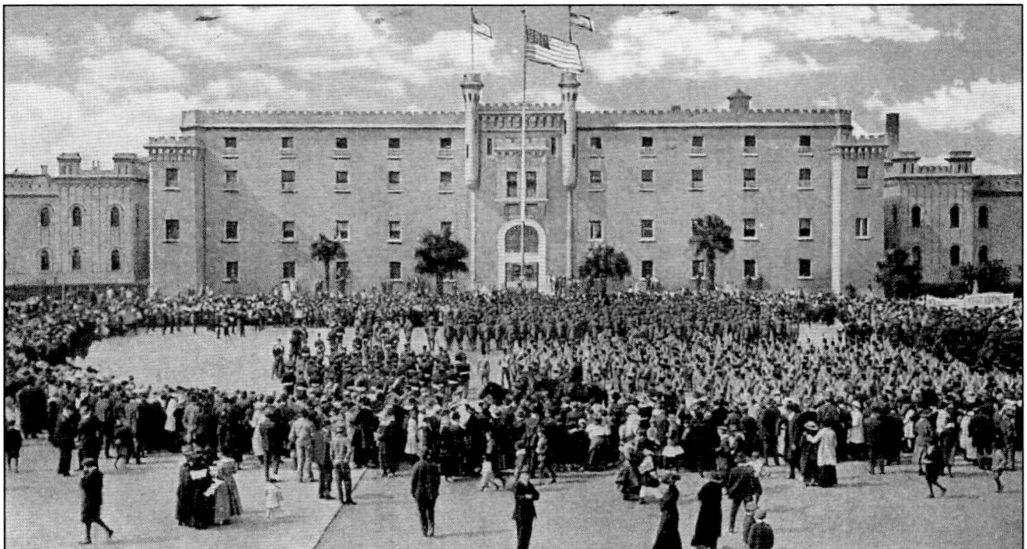

CITADEL AND SOLDIERS RETURNING FROM THE FRONT, CHARLESTON, S.C. (Color Lithography, 3½" X 5½", Curt Teich Co., #A74787, Chicago, IL; 1917.) Citadel Square has always been the drill and parade ground for local militia, as well as a major place of rendezvous for various other military and civic groups in Charleston. On the back of this card, postmarked November 1917, a printed note describes The Citadel as "the foremost military school of the South" and identifies the gathering here as "National Guards" returning from their duties on the Mexican border.

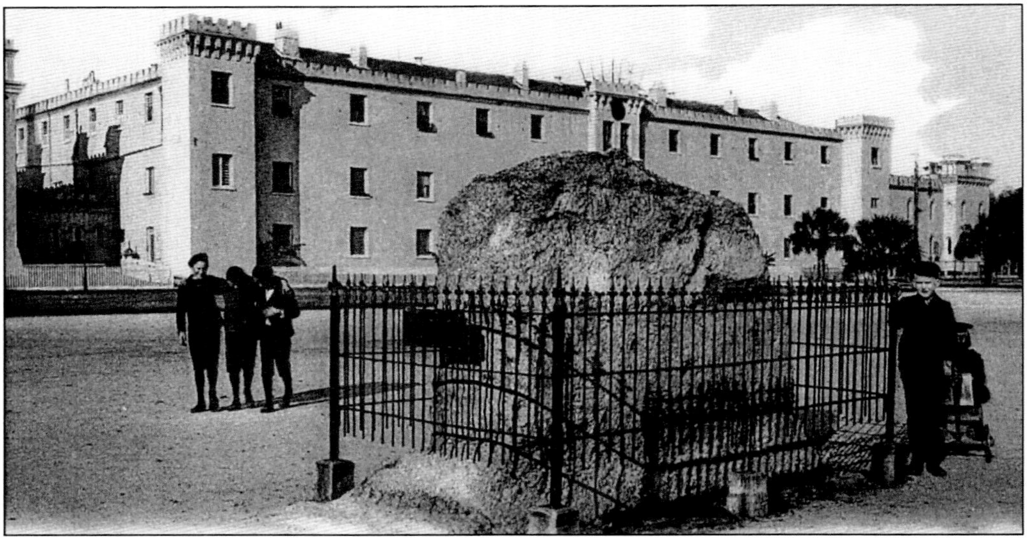

REMNANT OF HORN WORK, SIEGE OF CHARLESTON 1780, CHARLESTON, S.C. (Color Lithography, 3½" X 5½", [Knackstedt and Nather Co., Hamburg, Germany]; Rotograph Co., #G 12577, New York, NY, importer; cp. 1905.) Depicted here, on Marion Square, is the surviving segment of the ancient city wall and tabby hornwork (c. 1757), a fortification which protected the city gates and was part of the town's defenses when the British captured Charleston in May 1780. Because it was printed on coated stock, this issue still looks almost new.

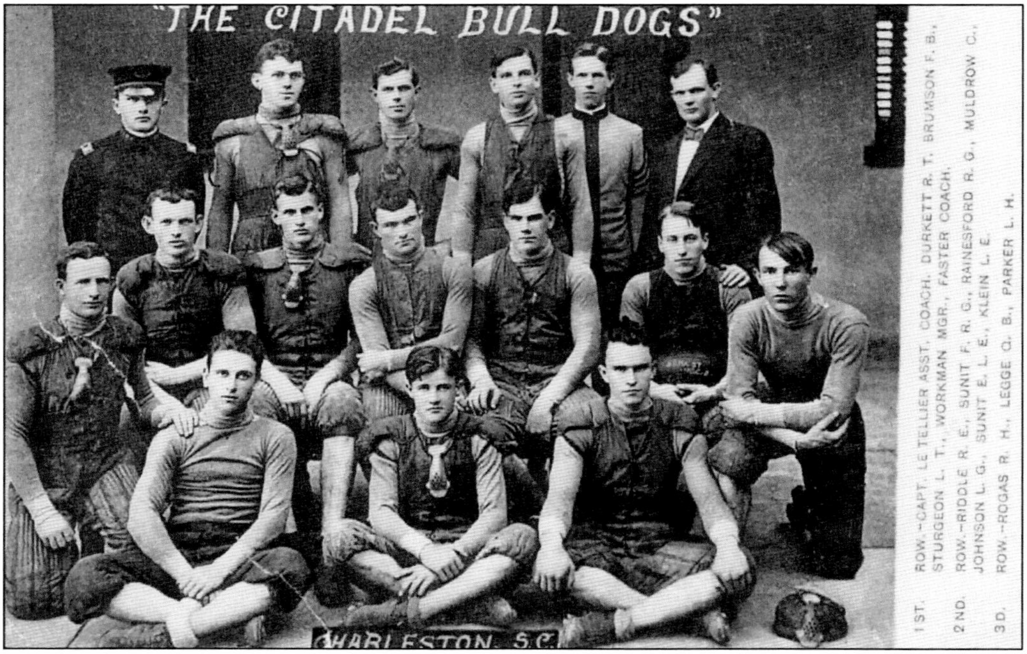


THE CITADEL BULL DOGS, CHARLESTON, S.C. (Hand-Colored Collotype, Germany; 1909.) This rare postal portrait of the Citadel Bull Dogs, complete with a listing of the football coaches and players, along with initialed indications of their positions on the team, was sent to Miss Claudia Fraser in Sumter on May 27, 1909. Only one example of this limited-issue card has been found.

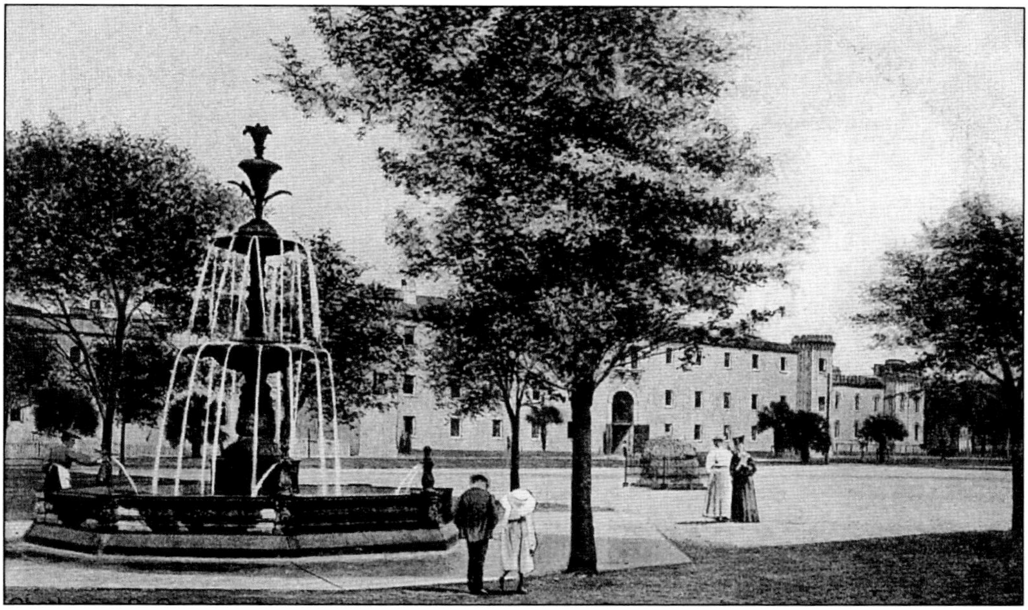

CHARLESTON, S.C., SOUTH CAROLINA MILITARY ACADEMY SHOWING FOUNTAIN AND OLD STONE RELIC. (Color Lithography, [Louis Glaser Co., Leipzig, Germany]; Hugh C. Leighton, #26323, Portland, ME, importer; *c.* 1907.) The old Citadel, seen here beyond the fountain and the fragment of historic tabby hornwork, was erected about 1825. The Military College of South Carolina relocated from this site north to the Hampton Park area in 1922.

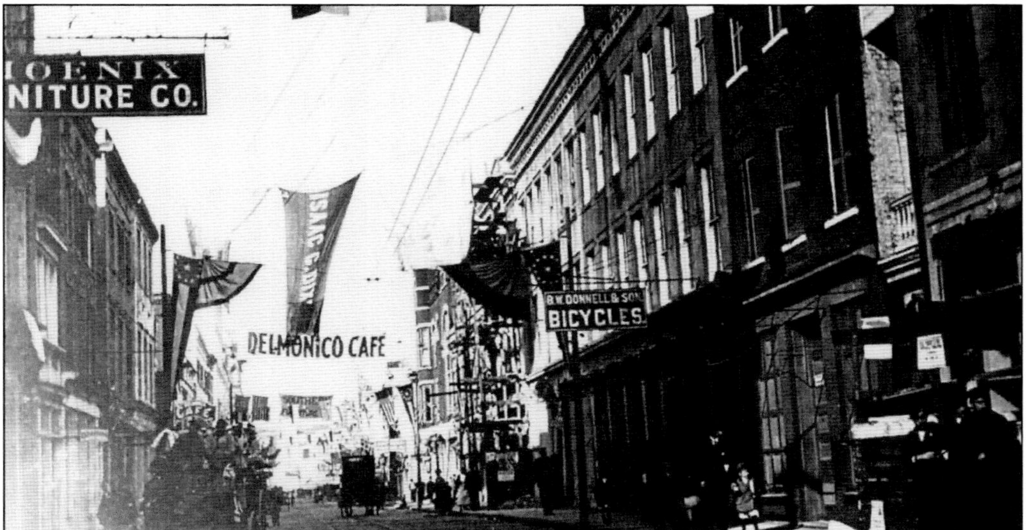


KING STREET, CHARLESTON, S.C. (Photoprint, 3½" X 5½", F.R. Sargent, photographer; *c.* 1911.) A.W. Litschgi's Phoenix Furniture Company, whose sign is visible here (upper left), was a commercial fixture at 187–191 King Street for more than a quarter century (from at least 1892 to 1919). But Delmonico's, a Greek restaurant whose banner can be seen up the street at number 199, was in business no earlier than 1915 and was gone by 1926. This view, with its patriotic decorations, probably dates from some special celebration or occasion during World War I.

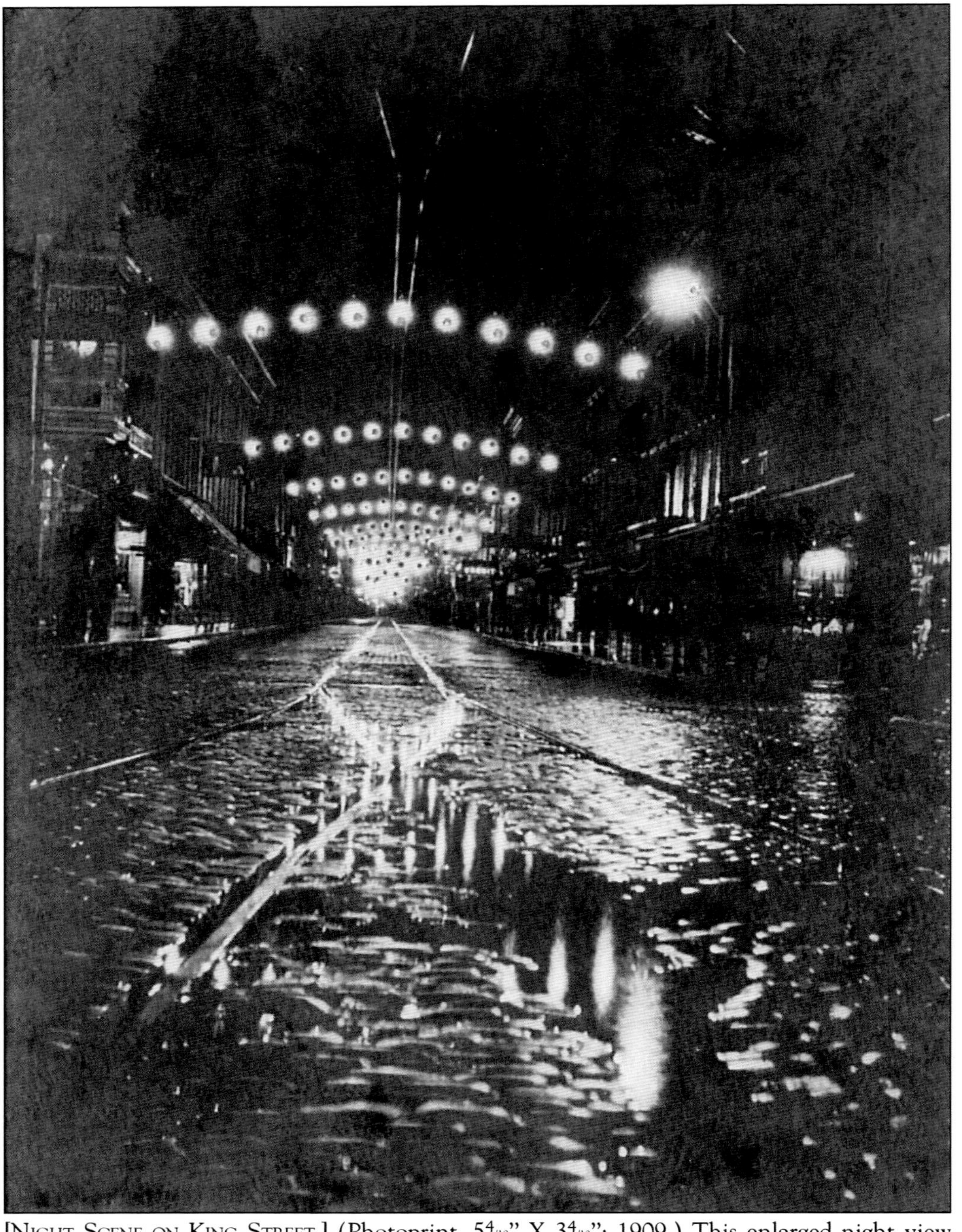

[NIGHT SCENE ON KING STREET.] (Photoprint, 5 4/10" X 3 4/10"; 1909.) This enlarged night view of King Street looking north features the arches of lights which the Charleston Consolidated Railway and Lighting Company put up each year for the holiday season. The idea behind this experimental photographic postcard was to record a night scene that captured the bright quality of the lights above the street and their reflections on the wet brick pavement below. The visual possibilities were increased by the placing of pin-size holes in the center of each light, which actually permitted light to come through the openings.

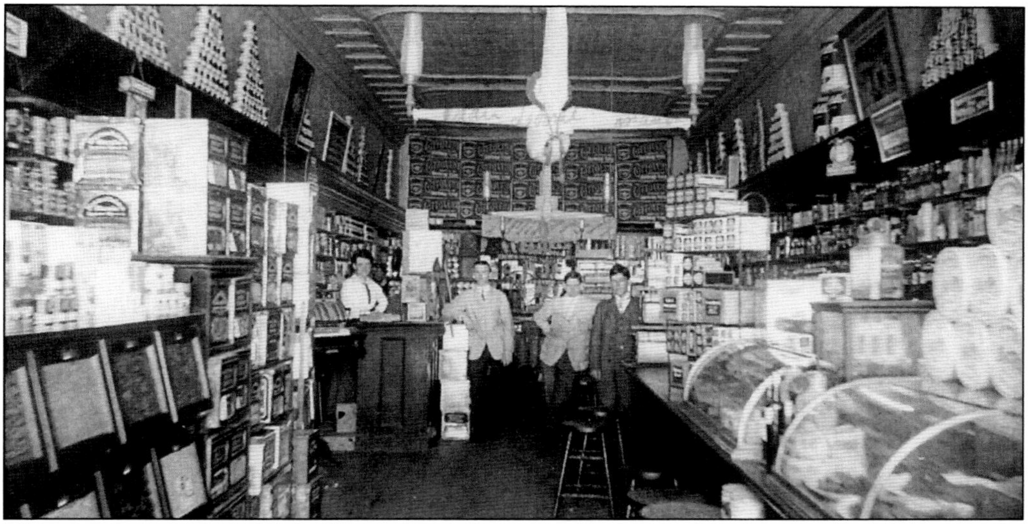

INTERIOR, J.M. PEECKSEN STORE, KING STREET. (Photoprint; 1911.) For more than forty years, John N. Peecksen was one of Charleston's leading grocers, conducting a wholesale and retail business in staple and fancy goods and specializing in the production of "the best and purest" self-rising flour on the market. By 1912 he owned six outlets, three of them on King Street. This rare interior view of the store at 289 King Street pictures manager Rudolph V. Torck, clerks Dorrill Muckenfuss and Edwin J. Cart, and cashier Gertrude Kugley.

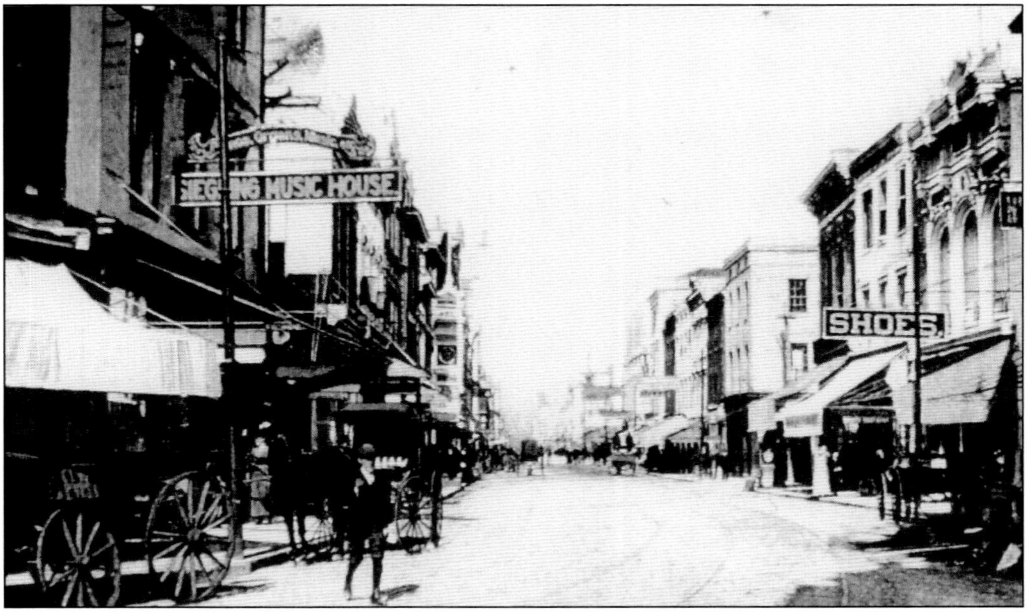


KING STREET LOOKING NORTH, CHARLESTON, S.C. (Color Lithography, 3½" X 5½", [C.G. Röder, #12398, Leipzig, Germany]; American News Co., #C5492, New York, NY, importer; c. 1908.) This view of King Street looking north from the bend shows the Siegling Music House on the left, built in 1839. The oldest of its kind in the United States, it was founded in 1819 by John Zachariah Siegling, a native of the Germanic Kingdom of Saxony. The business closed its doors in 1970 after more than one hundred and fifty years of service to the music lovers of Charleston.

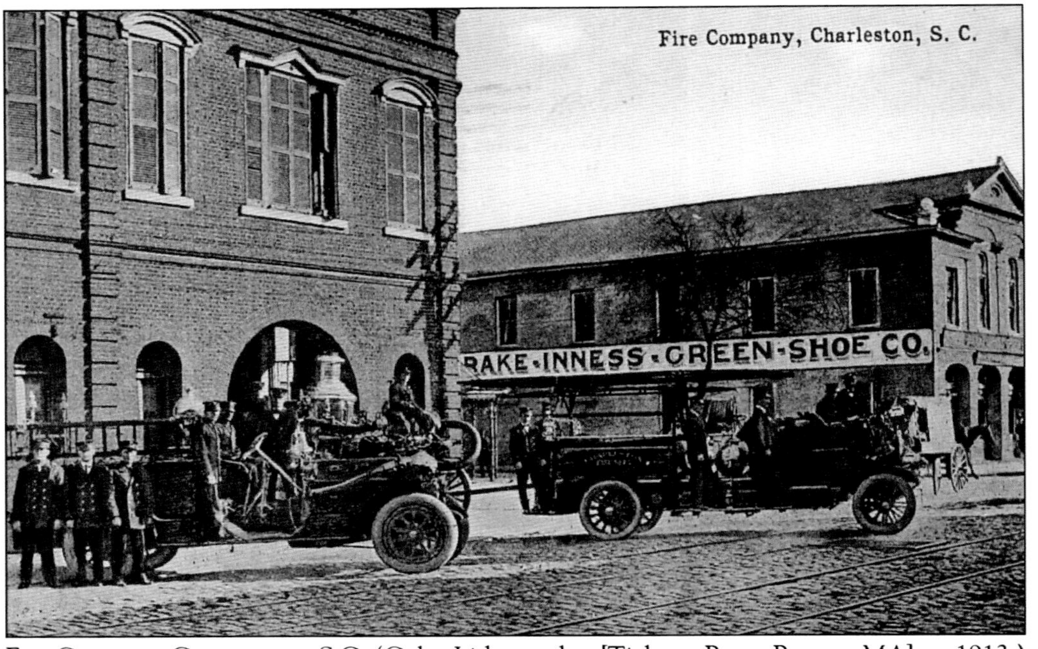


FIRE COMPANY, CHARLESTON, S.C. (Color Lithography, [Tichnor Bros., Boston, MA]; *c.* 1913.) The building to the left here, at 262 Meeting Street, was erected in 1887 as Charleston's Central Fire Station and more than a century later still functions in this capacity. The building across Wentworth Street occupied by the Drake-Inness-Green Shoe Company from 1902 to 1919 now houses offices of the Bank of South Carolina. Some fire companies had postcard portraits made to raise funds for special projects.

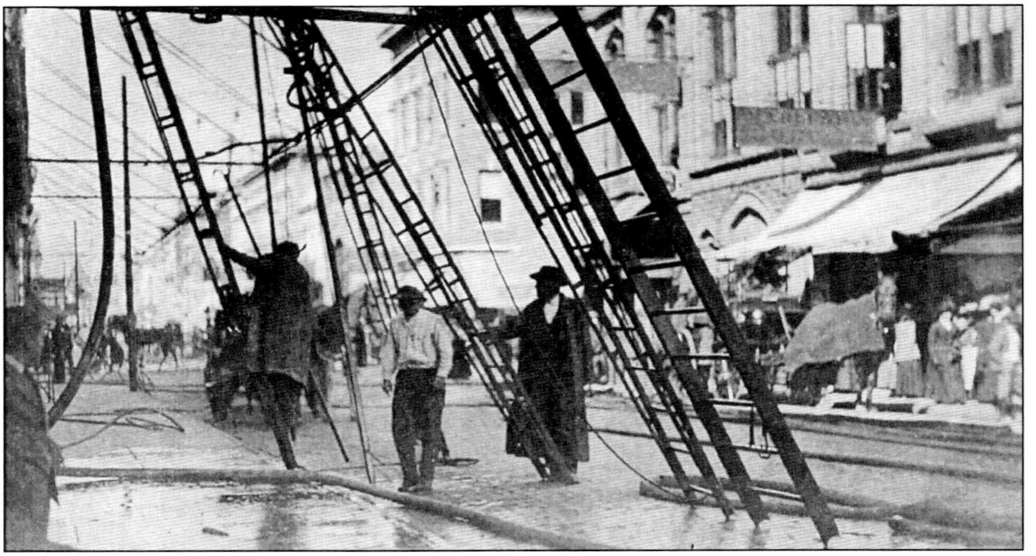

[FIRE ON KING STREET.] (Photoprint, 3½" X 5½"; *c.* 1909.) Author E. Milby Burton claimed that the city's "greatest devastator" through the years had been fire (*Charleston*, 1946). The one documented by the cards on these two pages may have been that of February 18, 1909, when three stores in the 200 block of King Street suffered $18,575 worth of damage. The blanketed horse in the background was one of thirty in service with the fire department at that time.

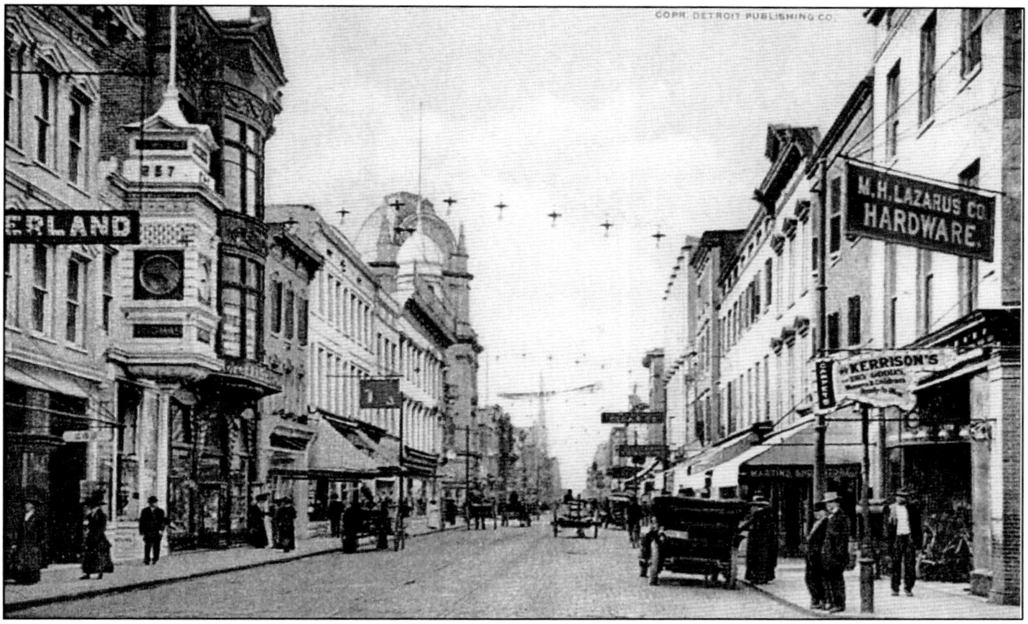


KING STREET LOOKING NORTH, CHARLESTON, S.C. (Color Lithography, Detroit Publishing Co., #70248, Detroit, MI; *c.* 1910.) Conditions of normalcy and of emergency are contrasted in these two views taken from the same place at different times. This picture of King Street looking north was made sometime after 1909. The M.H. Lazarus Hardware store on the corner of Hasell Street (right) is not listed at this 254 King Street site until 1910.

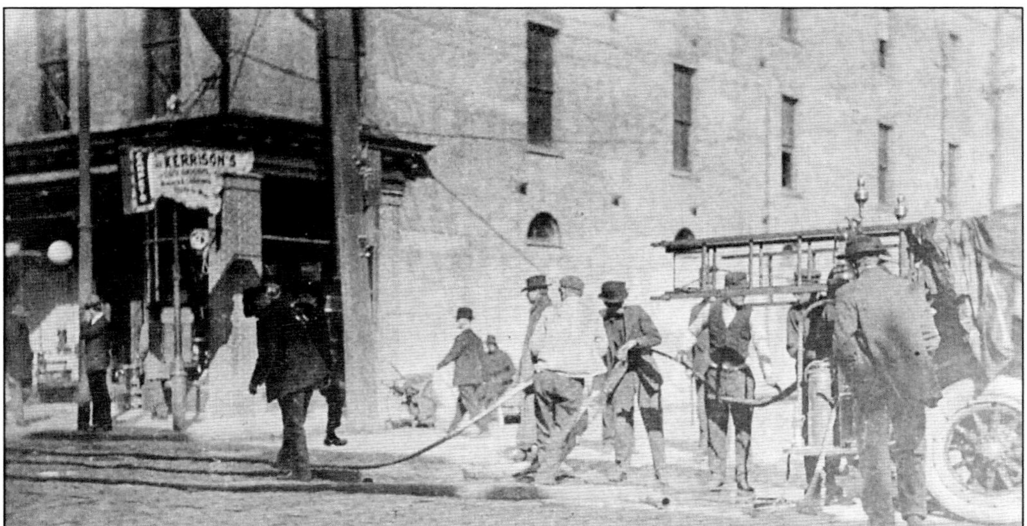


[FIRE ON KING STREET.] (Photoprint; *c.* 1909.) Firefighters work with the hose running up King Street from the fire truck at the same Hasell Street corner location as is shown in the card above. The large Kerrison's hand sign is in both of them. These amateur photoprints—probably taken under the worst of conditions—provide a relatively good dark and light definition of this fire scene.

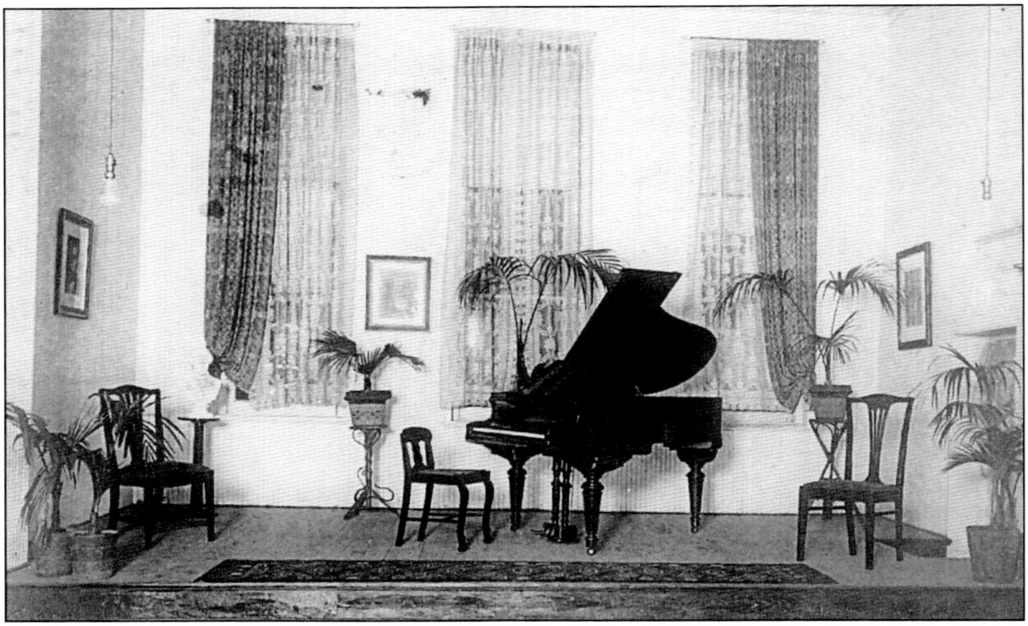

[MUSICAL ART CLUB.] (Photoprint; $3^{1/2}$" X $5^{1/2}$", 1913.) An item in the *Charleston News and Courier* on November 17, 1912, reveals that the Musical Art Club opened its "attractive rooms" at 289 King Street with an entertainment "last evening." This card, postmarked November 3, 1913, invites Miss Mary Stein to purchase a $2 season ticket, thus helping the club to attain its goal of enrolling a thousand members. A local commercial photographer took this promotional, stage-set-type image and produced them by the hundreds. This is the only known copy.

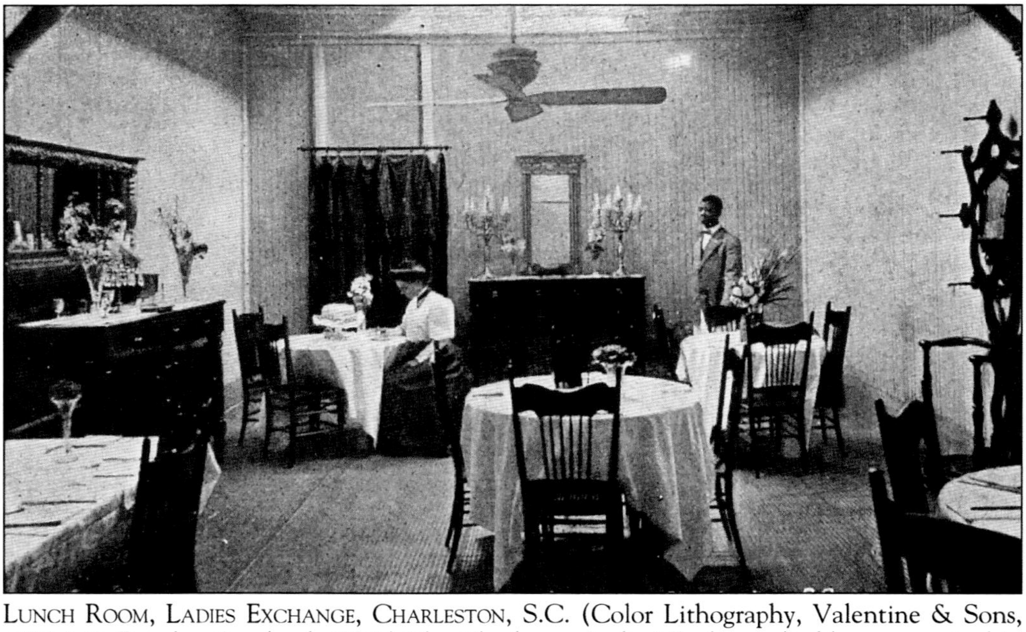

LUNCH ROOM, LADIES EXCHANGE, CHARLESTON, S.C. (Color Lithography, Valentine & Sons, #403,169, Dundee, Scotland; 1909.) The Charleston Ladies' Exchange had been organized in December 1884. It was located at 215 King Street in 1910, the year after this card was mailed.

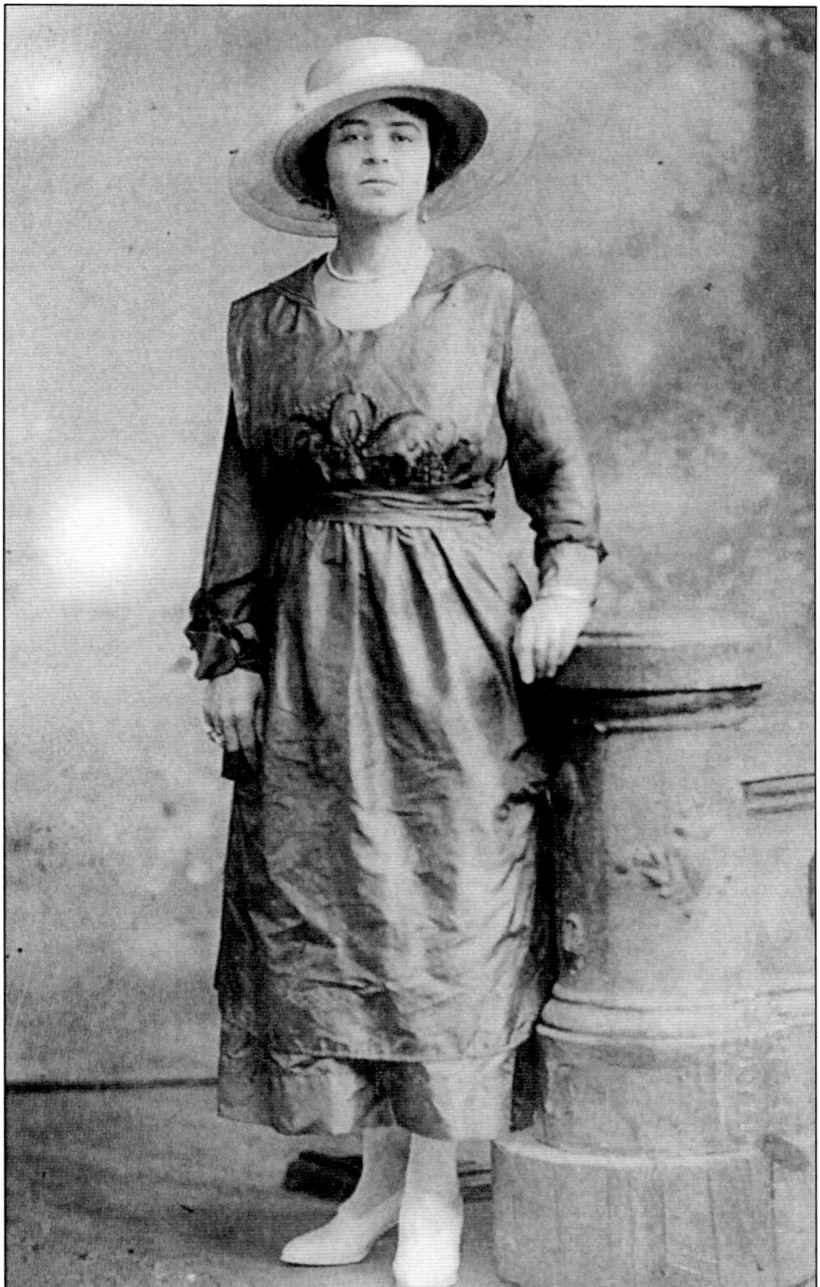

[PORTRAIT OF A LADY.] (Photoprint, $3^{1/2}$" X $5^{1/2}$", W.B. Austin, Charleston, S.C.; *c.* 1918.) The logo in the lower right-hand corner here indicates that the portrait of this unidentified woman was made by William B. Austin, who for more than twenty-five years operated a photographic studio in Charleston. This picture belongs to his mature years, 1915–1919, when he was located at 251 King Street. When Austin opened his studio in the early 1890s, he was one of five commercial photographers in the city. By the time he had disappeared from the scene, *c.* 1921, there were nine—all of them located on King.

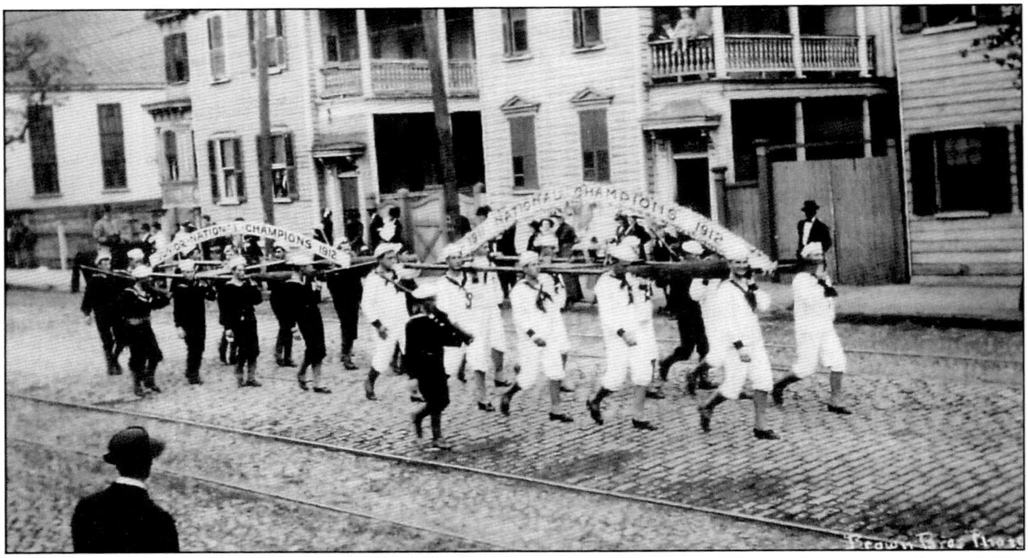

[FLEET WEEK PARADE.] (Photoprint, 3½" X 5½", Brown Brothers, Photo, Newport News, VA; 1912.) The crowning achievement of 1912, Mayor Grace would write in his annual report for the year, was the management of Fleet Week, November 17–24—the "greatest event in the history of Charleston." The big day of "fleet, fair and fashion week" was Thursday, November 21, when a huge parade of seven thousand sailors and soldiers—Artillery men, Bluejackets, Marines, Cadets, National Guardsmen, and Reserves—wound its way from the Battery up through Meeting, Broad, King, Columbus Streets, and then back down Meeting to Broad.

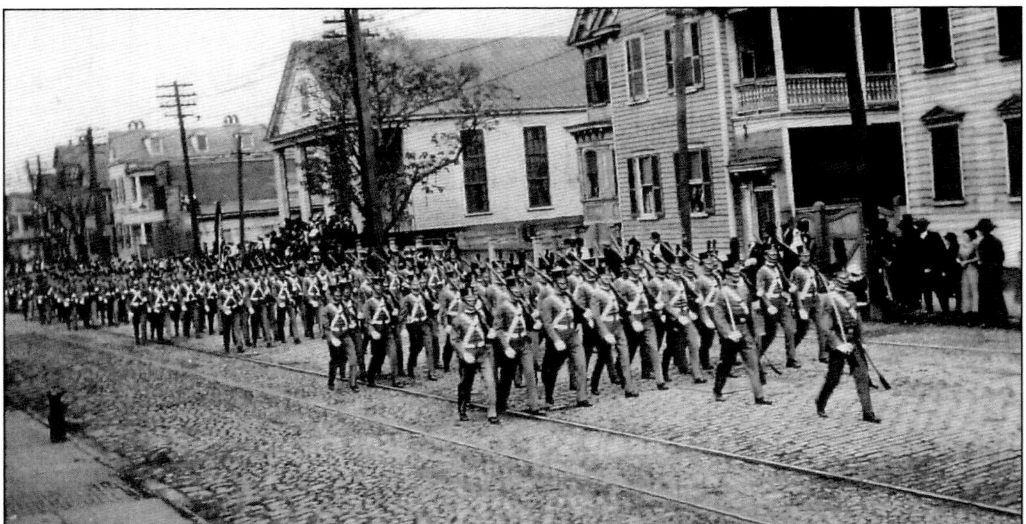

[FLEET WEEK PARADE.] (Photoprint, 3½" X 5½", Brown Brothers, photo, Newport News, VA; 1912.) Cadet battalions from both The Citadel and the Porter Military Academy were represented in the Fleet Week parade of November 21, 1912. Mayor Grace, reflecting upon this Fleet Week "as one of the most beneficial and successful events in our history," would remark finally: "The visit of the fleet served to bring out two things in particular. The affection between Charleston and the Navy and the great value and possibilities of Charleston Harbor." The three Fleet Week views shown here are the first such items to be uncovered in decades.

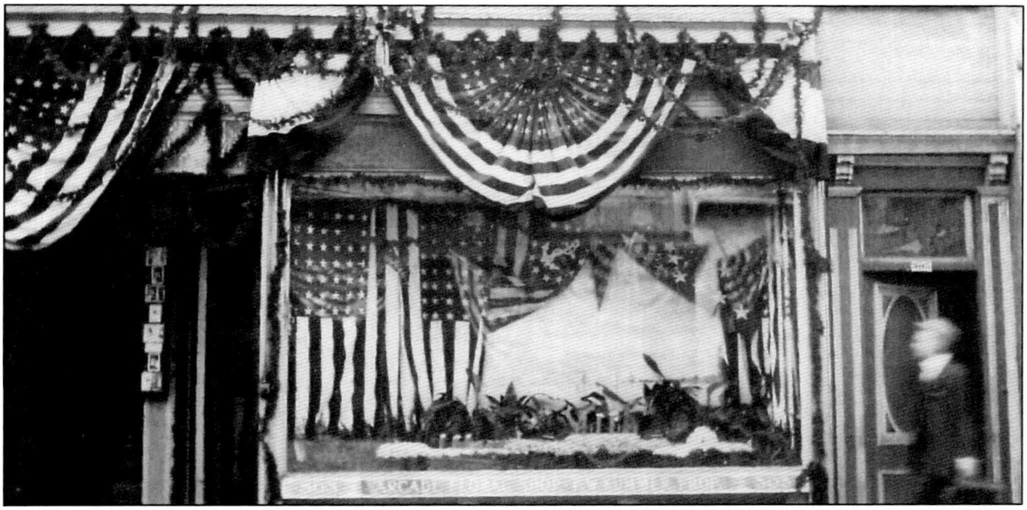

A PATRIOTIC WINDOW DISPLAY, CHARLESTON, S.C. (Photoprint, 3½" X 5½", Brown Brothers, Photo, Newport News, VA; 1912.) One much-anticipated feature of "fleet, fair and fashion week," 1912, was the competition in window dressing and illumination which engaged fifty-five of Charleston's leading merchants along King Street. This patriotically draped and dressed window was that of the Arcade Floral Shop, 303 King, operated by Frank W. Kummer.

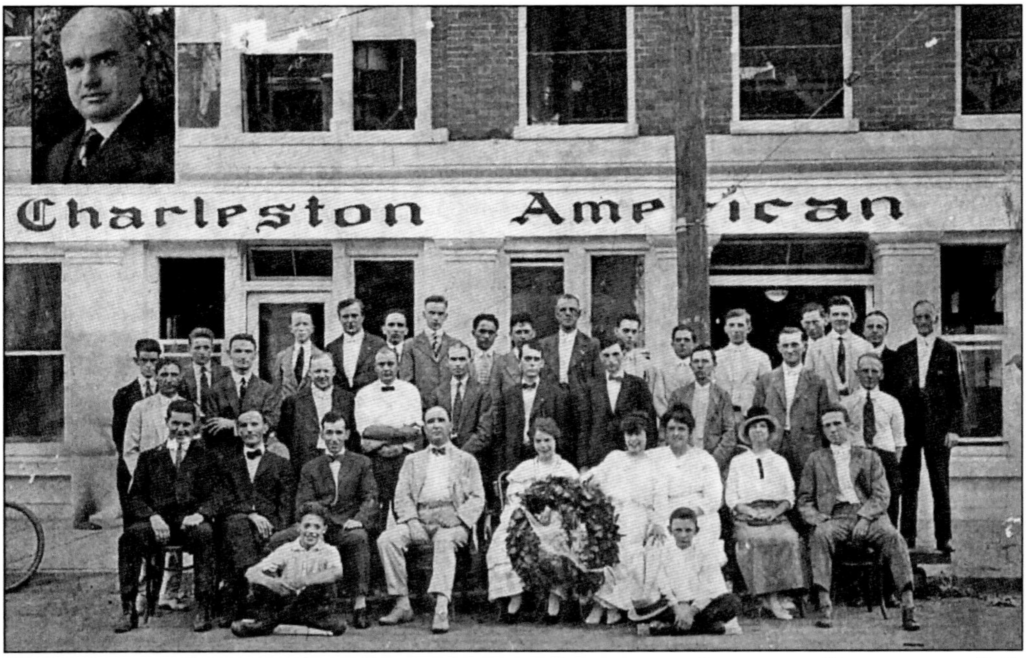


EDITORIAL AND BUSINESS OFFICE FORCE OF THE *CHARLESTON AMERICAN*, CHARLESTON, S.C. (Halftone; c. 1915.) *The Charleston American*, initially edited by John P. Grace (portrait insert, top left), was a daily newspaper published from 1916 to 1923, with offices at 267–269 Meeting Street. John Hammond Moore, in his 1988 book *South Carolina Newspapers*, characterized it as Hearst-like, Progressive Democrat, and "Grace's answer to the *News and Courier*." Grace served as mayor of Charleston from 1911 to 1915 and also from 1919 to 1923. Within a month after his defeat for a third term, the *Charleston American* ceased publication.

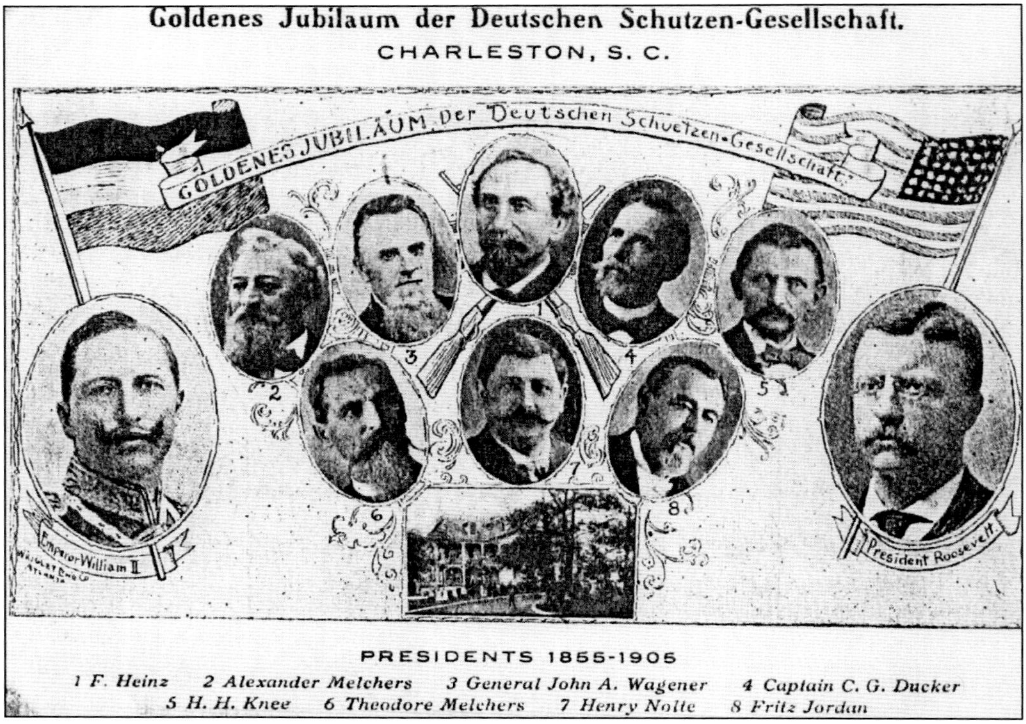


GOLDENES JUBILÄUM DER DEUTSCHEN SCHÜTZEN-GESELLSCHAFT, CHARLESTON, S.C. (Halftone, 3$^{8/10}$" X 5$^{6/10}$" Wrigley Engraving Co., Atlanta, GA; 1905.) German and American flags and presidential portraits—of national leaders, as well as of those of Charleston's German Rifle Club from 1855 to 1905—adorn this card, which also features a small picture of the Schützen-Platz, issued in celebration of the club's Golden Jubilee. Walter Fraser estimates that about thirty percent of the city's white population was German. Also shown on the card below, the Schützen-Platz, where the German Rifle Club held its exercises, was above the city limits on the west side of the King Street road.

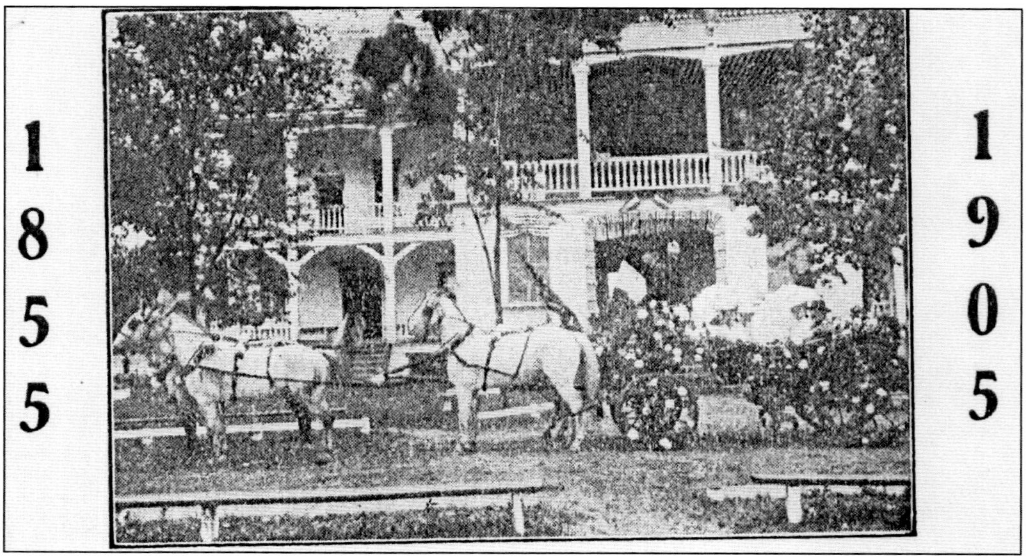

5TH GREAT NATIONAL SHOOTING FESTIVAL OF THE NATIONAL SCHUETZEN BUND OF AMERICA. (Charleston, S.C.; Color Lithography, 5 1/2" X 3 1/2", 1907.) A dramatically illustrated advertising and announcement card, perhaps a nationally generic one, from 1907 reveals that Charleston's German Rifle Club hosted the 5th National Shooting Festival of the National Schuetzen Bund (Rifle Club) of America, held from May 6 to 14 of that year. During this era many state fairs, horse shows, and other special events and occasions used these stock cards for promotional purposes; however, only one example of this issue has been found. This event, which had gone undiscovered in a review of over 100,000 South Carolina postcards, is documented on these two cards (see p. 70) that introduce viewers to an almost forgotten activity.

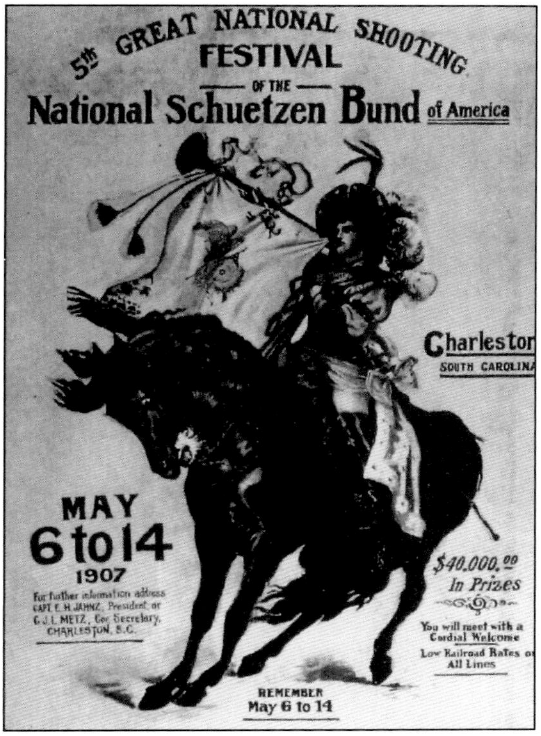


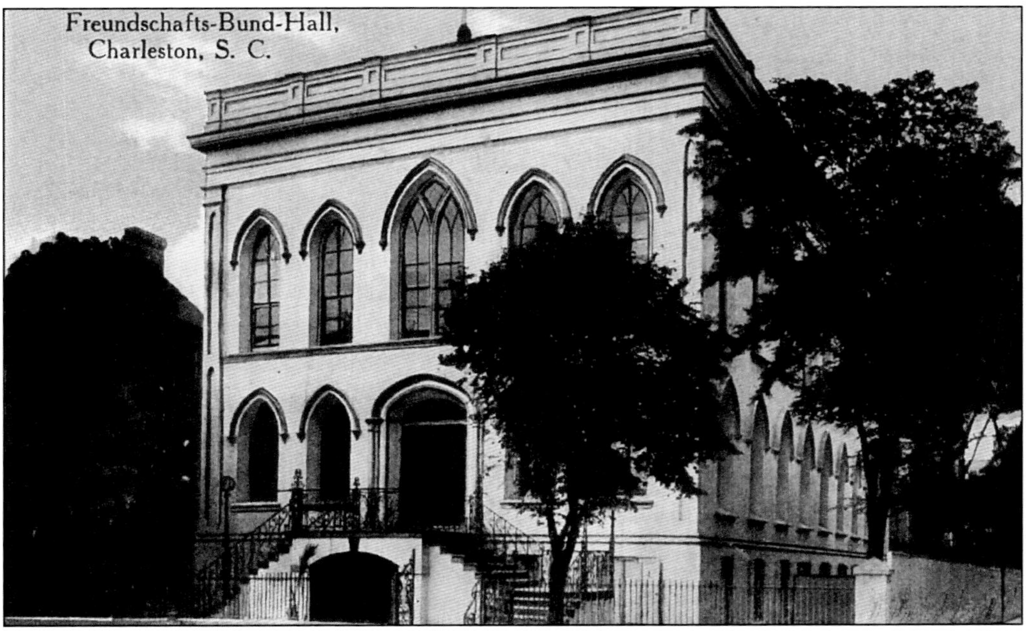


FREUNDSCHAFTS-BUND-HALL, CHARLESTON, S.C. (Color Lithography, E. C. Kropp, #1771, Milwaukee, WI; c. 1911). The Freundschafts Bund Hall, 207 Meeting Street, was built in 1870 and became the meeting place for such organizations as the German Friendly Society and the German Rifleman's Charitable Association. In the early 1920s it was Charleston's Labor Temple. In the 1980s it became the home of the Washington Light Infantry.

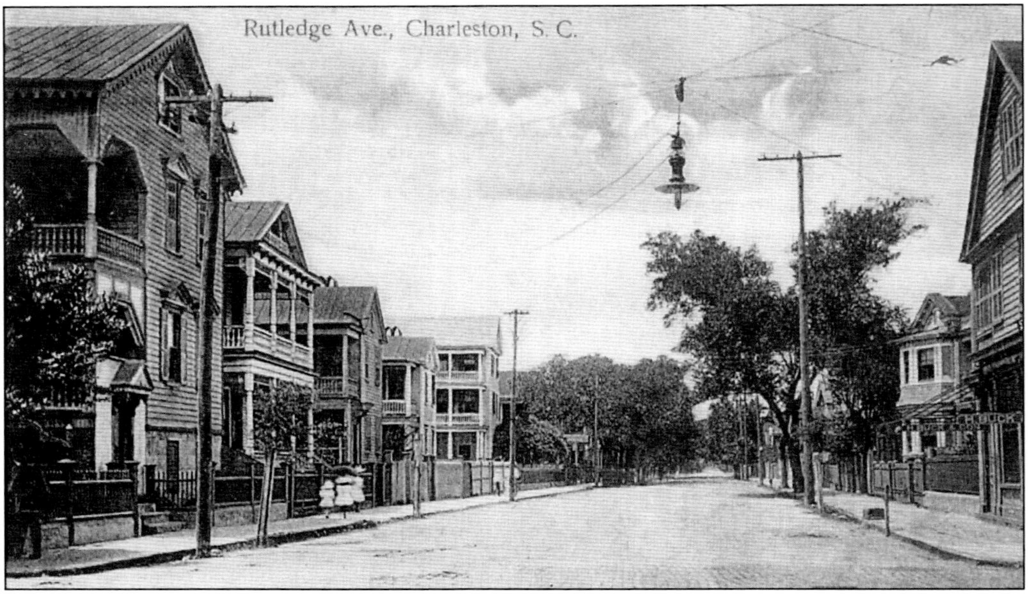


RUTLEDGE AVE., CHARLESTON, S.C. (Collotype, [Trenkler Co., Leipzig, Germany]; A.M. Simon, #12 204, New York, NY, importer; *c.* 1908.) Identified as Rutledge Avenue, this picture postcard actually appears to be a view looking west on Cannon Street at its intersection with Ashley Avenue. Lettering on the structure to the right reads "H. Buck & Son," designating it as the grocery store which existed on this corner, with an address of 114 Cannon Street, from at least 1886 until 1923, under the proprietorship of Henry Buck and his son, Henry William H. Buck. This structure still exists as a commercial establishment.

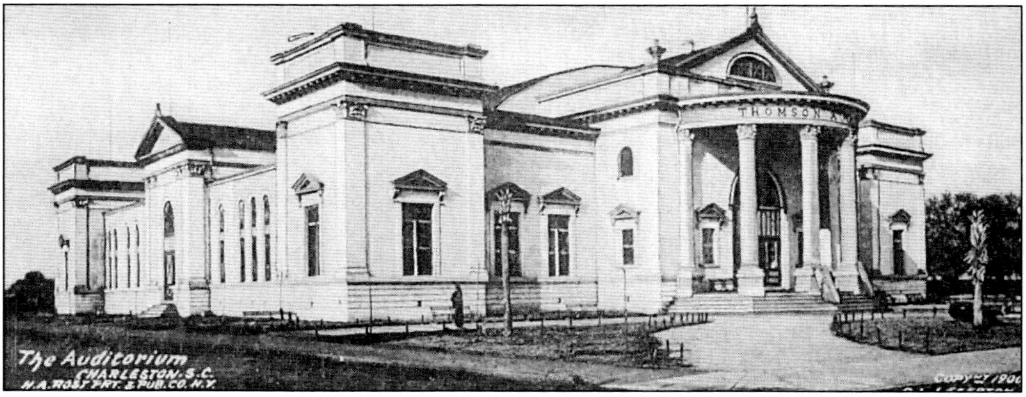


THE AUDITORIUM, CHARLESTON, S.C. (Collotype, 3¼" X 5½"; cp. C.L. Legerton, 1900; H.A. Rost Printing and Publishing Co., #708, New York, NY; *c.* 1900.) Thomson Auditorium, once located at 121 Rutledge Avenue, had been constructed of brick and iron in sixty days in 1899, in time for the United Confederate Reunion that May. Built with funds left to the City by John Thomson and designed in the exposition style by the well-known regional architect Frank P. Milburn, it was the largest building of its kind in the South to that time, but proved to be an acoustic failure and a "maintenance white elephant." After temporary service as a theater and then as a hospital, it was acquired for use by the Charleston Museum, and served as its quarters from 1907 to 1979. It was destroyed by fire on October 18, 1981. Clifford L. Legerton, whose 1900 copyright notice is in the lower right-hand corner here, was a bookseller and stationer whose enterprise at 263 King Street lasted for more than half a century.

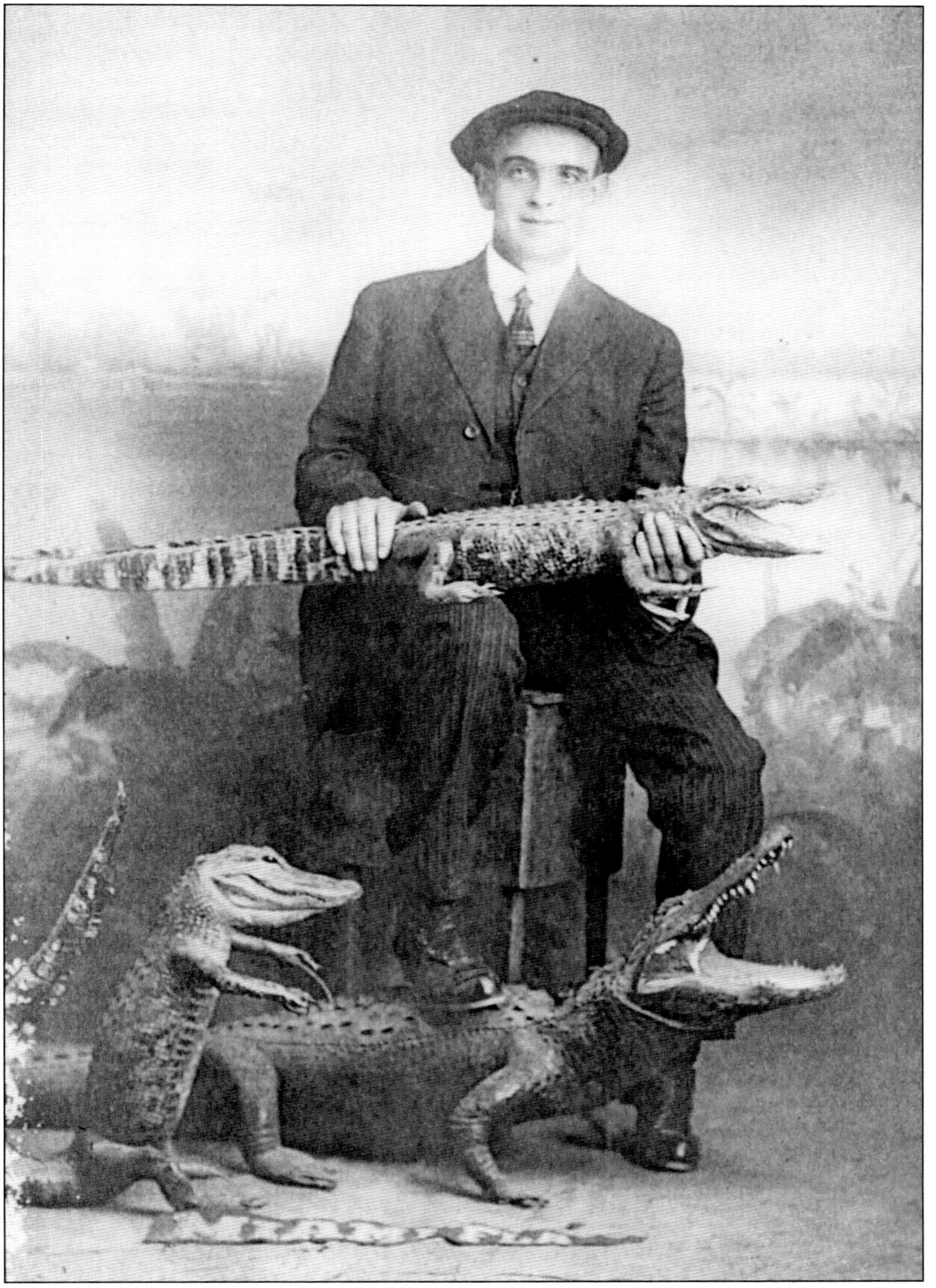

[PORTRAIT OF A MAN.] (Photoprint, 5½" X 3½"; *c.* 1910.) This card is in the collections of the Charleston Museum. The props used in this studio portrait may either indicate the humor of the photographer or the profession or hobby of the subject.

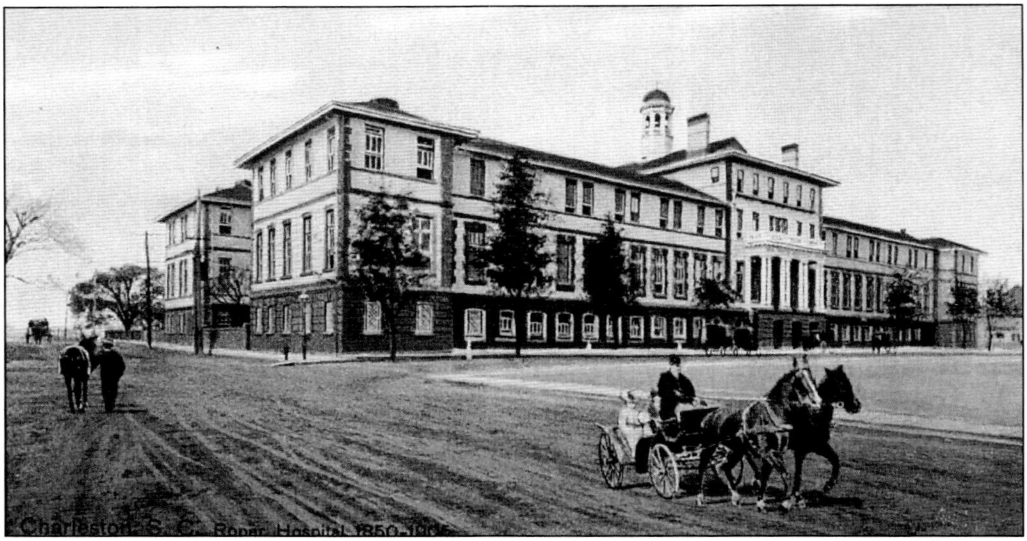

CHARLESTON, S.C., ROPER HOSPITAL, 1850–1905. (Color Lithography, 3½" X 5½", [Louis Glaser Co., Leipzig, Germany]; Hugh C. Leighton, #26326, Portland, ME, importer; c. 1908.) Construction of the new Roper Hospital, at the corner of Calhoun and Lucas, began in 1905 and was completed early the next year at a cost of $140,000. This card illustrates the practice of superimposing images of horse and buggies, automobiles, and strolling people to enliven or modernize the picture.

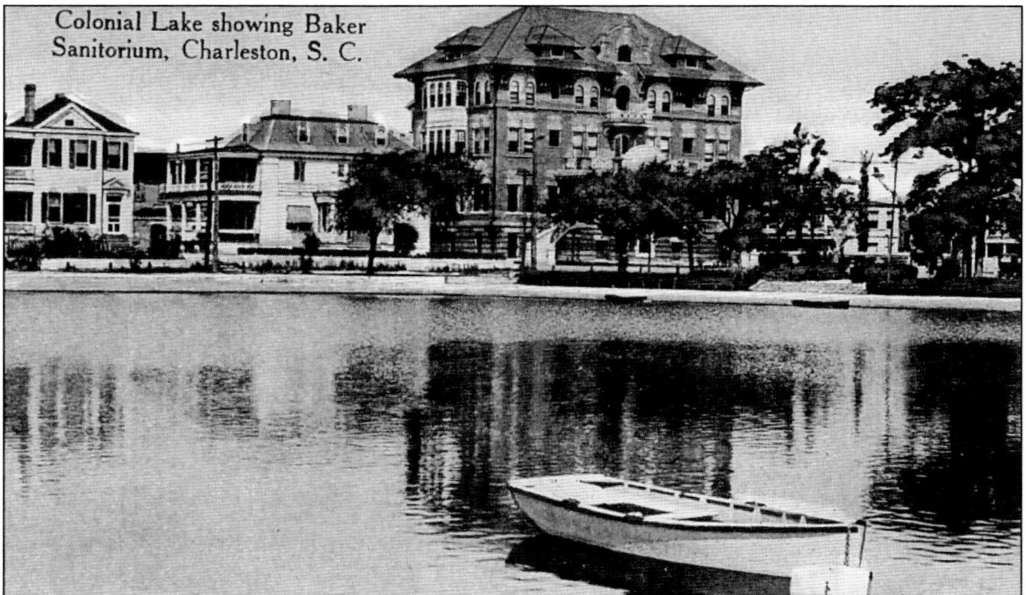


COLONIAL LAKE SHOWING BAKER SANITORIUM, CHARLESTON, S.C. (Color Lithograph, E.C. Kropp, #1783, Milwaukee, WI; 1916.) The Baker-Craig Sanatorium, 55 Ashley Avenue, at the northwest corner of Colonial Lake, was built for $100,000 in 1912 as a sixty-bed private hospital and nursing school by Dr. Archibald E. Baker Sr. and Dr. Lawrence Craig. A rare example of early twentieth-century eclectic architecture in Charleston, it was adapted for residential use in 1983.

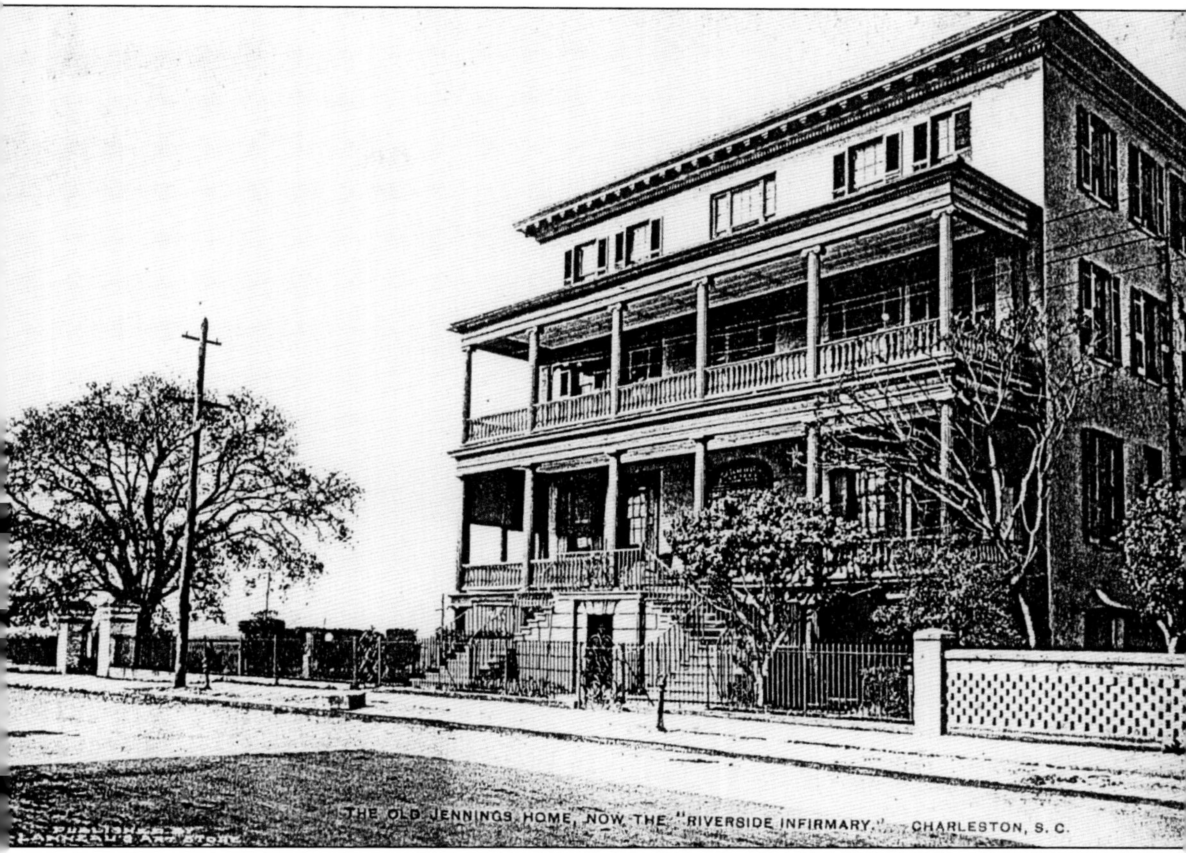


THE OLD JENNINGS HOME, NOW THE "RIVERSIDE INFIRMARY," CHARLESTON, S.C. (Sepia Collotype, $5^{5/16}$" X $7^{5/16}$", Albertype Co., Brooklyn, NY; *c.* 1910. ) The Jonathan Lucas House, 316 Calhoun Street, identified on this oversize card as the "Old Jennings Home," has had intrinsic value through the years not only as "an excellent example of Adamesque architecture" (completed *c.* 1809), but also as one of the few surviving edifices directly associated with Charleston's eighteenth- and nineteenth-century rice empire. The house had been built by the Lucas family, whose name would also be associated with the West Point Mill, the largest rice-pounding mill in the state, built on the Ashley River not far from the house (see p. 21). In 1887 the City of Charleston purchased the house for $20,000, and by 1896 it had become part of the hospital complex as the Riverside Infirmary, furnished and equipped to serve private patients. After 1948 it became known as the Riverside Nurses Home and subsequently the Kinloch Home for Nurses. Currently it is part of Roper CareAlliance's downtown campus, housing offices for various health services.

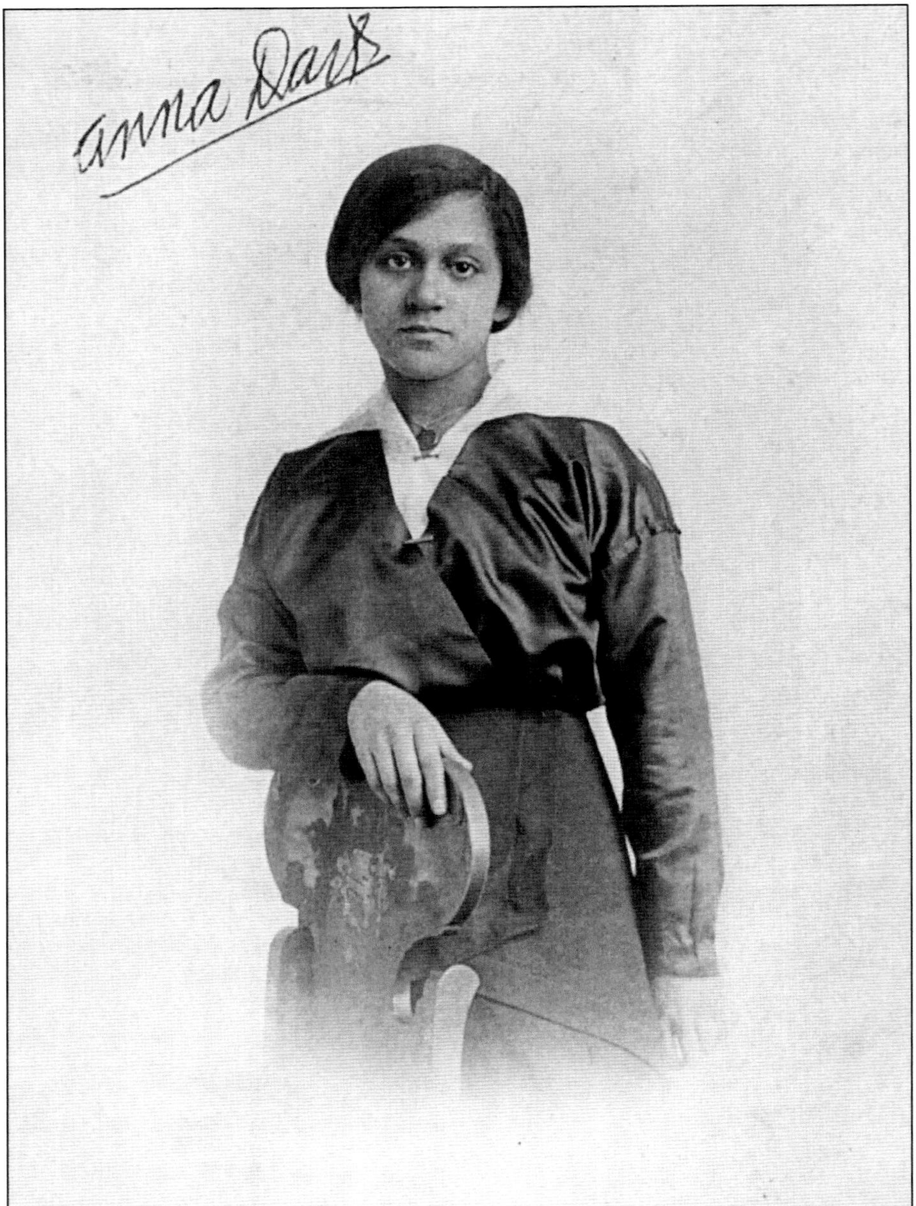


[PORTRAIT OF ANNA DART.] (Photoprint, 3½" X 5½"; c. 1915.) Anna P. Dart, the subject of this postcard portrait by an unknown photographer, was one of three children of the Reverend John L. Dart and his wife, Julia P. Dart, both of whom were associated with the Charleston Industrial Institute as administrators or teachers. A graduate of Avery Institute, John L. Dart attended both the University of South Carolina and Atlanta University, where he graduated in 1879. He was minister of the Morris Street Baptist Church in the 1880s, and later became pastor of the Shiloh Baptist Church. Anna, whose sister Susan Dart Butler became a well-known librarian in Charleston, is shown in the 1919 Charleston *City Directory* as living at home (108 Bogard Street) that year. The 1959 obituary of Susan Dart Butler lists Anna Dart Bronzeaux of New York City as a survivor.

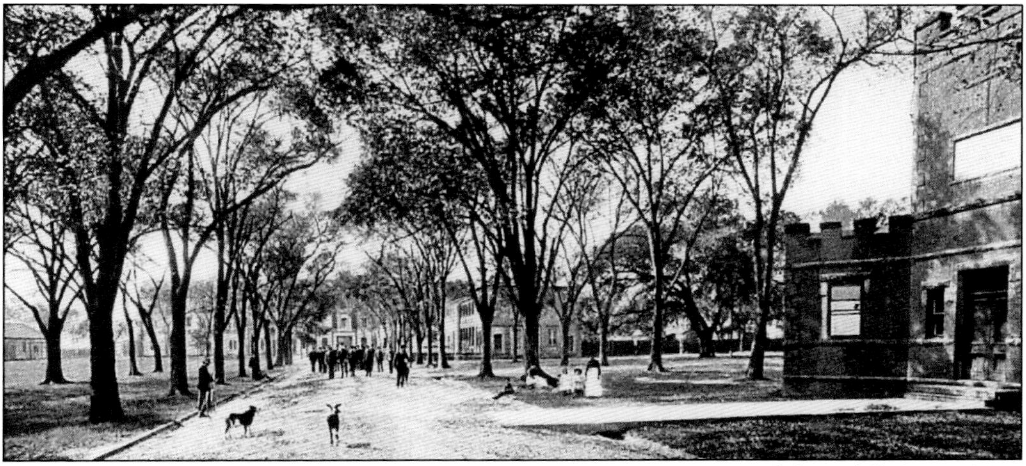

CHARLESTON, S.C., PORTER MILITARY ACADEMY. (Color Lithography, 3½" X 5½", [Rosenblatt Lithograph Institute, #202809, Frankfurt, Germany]; *c*. 1908.) Porter Military Academy once encompassed the block bounded by Ashley Avenue and Bee, and President and Doughty Streets, occupying the grounds of the old Federal Arsenal. Established in 1867 through the efforts of an Episcopal minister, the Reverend Anthony Toomer Porter, it was originally called the Holy Communion Church Institute and began as "a classical school for the children of parents in straitened circumstances" due to the Civil War. The Hoffman Library, seen here at the right, was formally opened on June 26, 1894. It now houses the Medical University's Waring Historical Library.

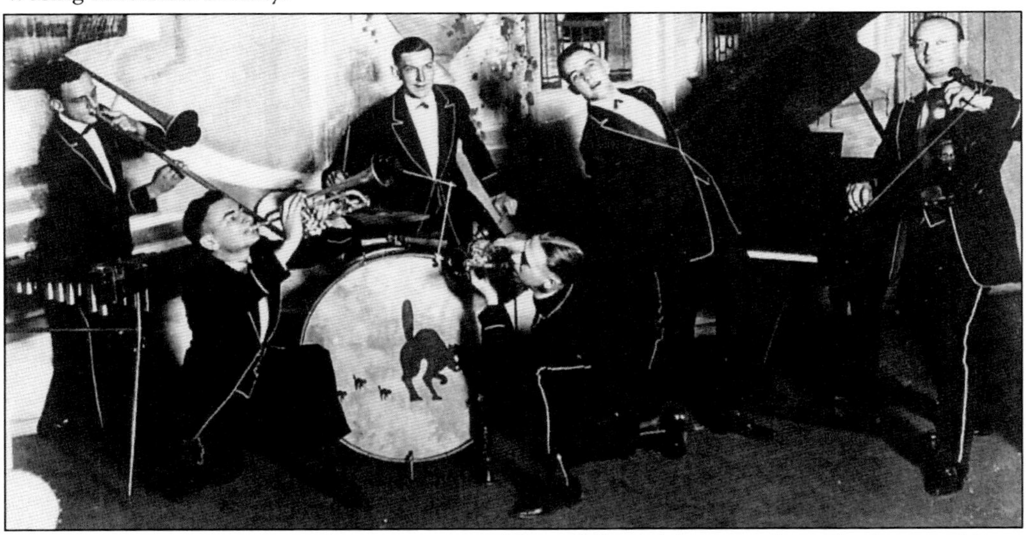

[PORTRAIT OF A DANCE BAND.] (Photoprint, 3½" X 5½", Melchers Studio, Charleston, SC; *c*. 1922.) Charleston has long prided itself on being "a rare old city, stable and decorous, even rigidly punctilious; and yet given to merry-making and entertainment" (*Charleston and Vicinity—Illustrated*, 1901). The area produced its own share of Jazz Age groups whose new music determined much of what the college and society sets sang and danced to in the 1920s. The portrait of this unidentified six-piece band, used for promotional purposes, was made by the Melchers Studio, which about 1921 began operating at the 238 King Street address indicated in the company logo on the back of this card. Only one example of this card has turned up in an archival collection.

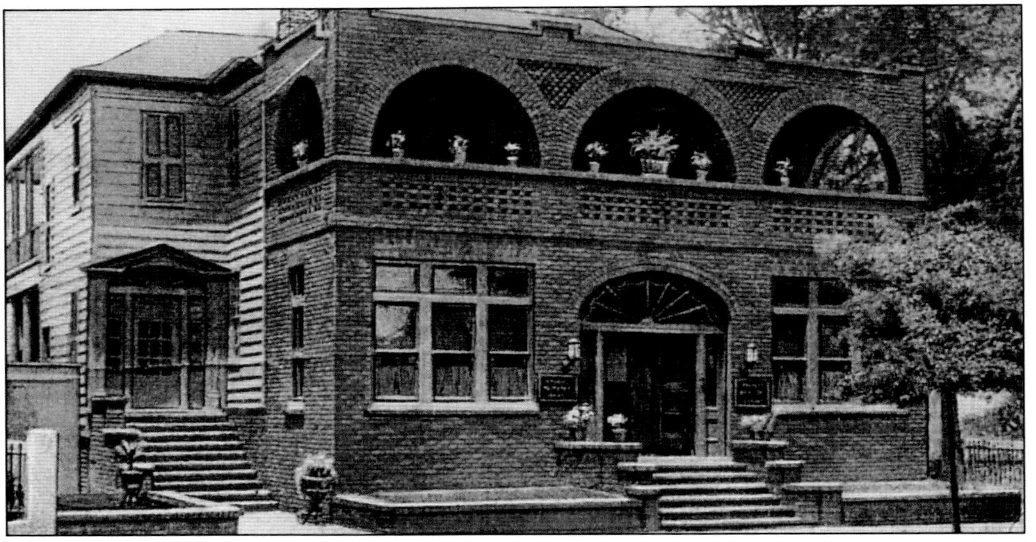

THE MICKEY FUNERAL HOME, CHARLESTON, S.C. (Color Lithography, Detroit Publishing Co., #41397, Detroit, MI; c. 1915.) "This Model Funeral Establishment," reads the printed note on the back of this card, "is an old Colonial residence, rebuilt to meet the needs of the modern funeral by the sons of E.H. Mickey, who established his funeral business in 1884." At the time this picture was made, the Mickey Funeral Home was located at 50 Cannon Street. In the late 1930s Edward Mickey moved his business to New York. The Mickey Home once stood on the north side of Cannon Street, on what is now the vacant lot next to the New Cannon Street Baptist Church. Only two copies of this African-American promotional item have been found in local collections.

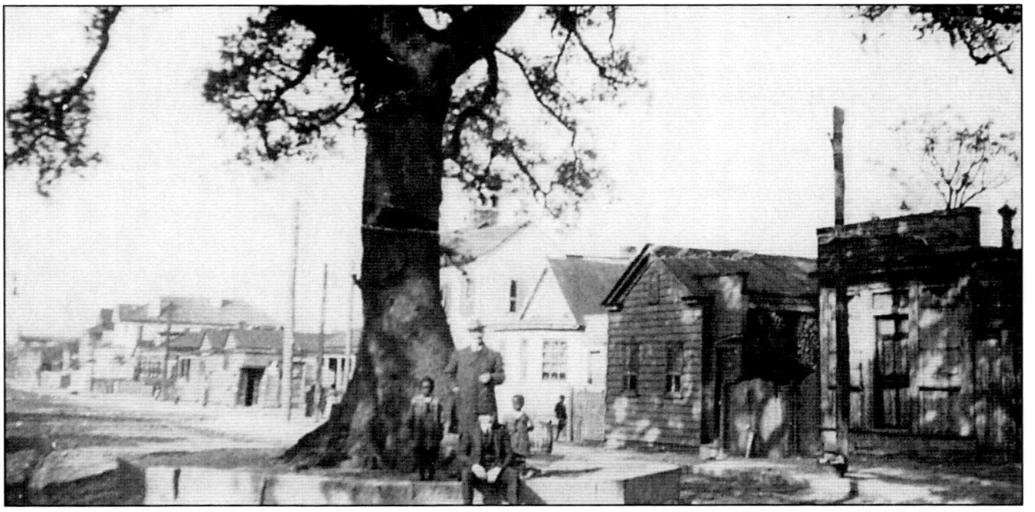

[ASHLEY OAK IN THE MIDDLE OF ASHLEY AVENUE.] (Photoprint, 3 1/2" X 5 1/2"; c. 1918.) The curiosity known as the Ashley Oak was a grand old tree which was so enjoyed by the nearby residents that they refused to cut it down and even protected it, though it was in the middle of the avenue. The huge tree remained there until it died a decade or so ago, only to be replaced by a young sapling to continue that tradition. While the Ashley Oak is the intended focus of this amateur photoprint, it also provides an unadorned contemporary view of the block between Nunan and Fishburne Streets.

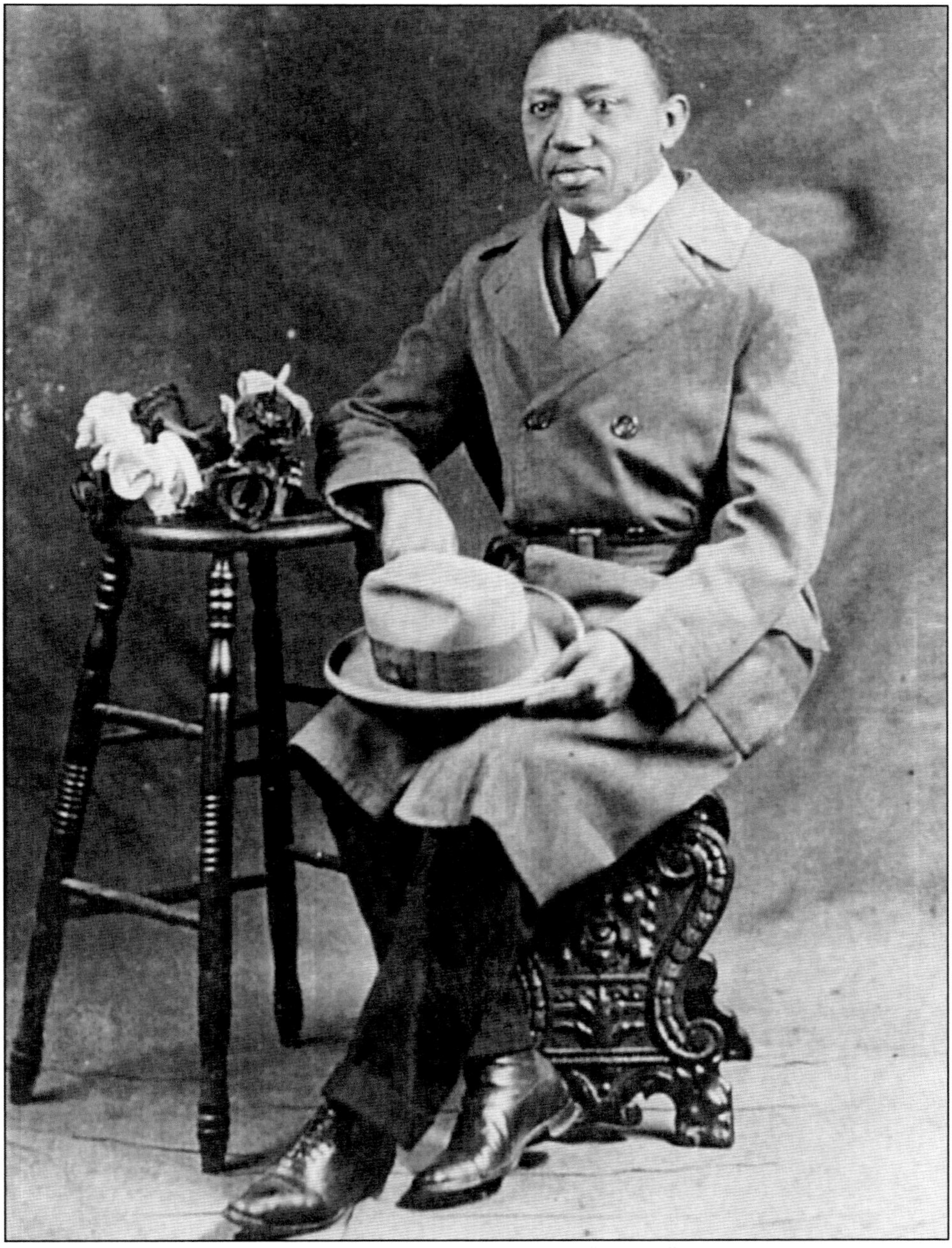

[PORTRAIT OF A MAN IN AN OVERCOAT.] (Photoprint, 5½" X 3½", M.F. Blake, Photographer, Charleston, S.C.; *c.* 1925.) This portrait of an unidentified man was made by black photographer Michael Francis Blake (d. 1934). He operated a studio—which was also his home—on West Sumter Street for at least twenty-two years. Blake was educated at Charleston's Avery Normal Institute. While he was not the city's first black photographer (Arthur L. Macbeth, for one, preceded him), he may have been the only one operating a commercial studio in Charleston for certain periods during the first two decades of the twentieth century. Some 116 samples of his work, ninety-one of which are photographic postcards, have been preserved at Duke University.

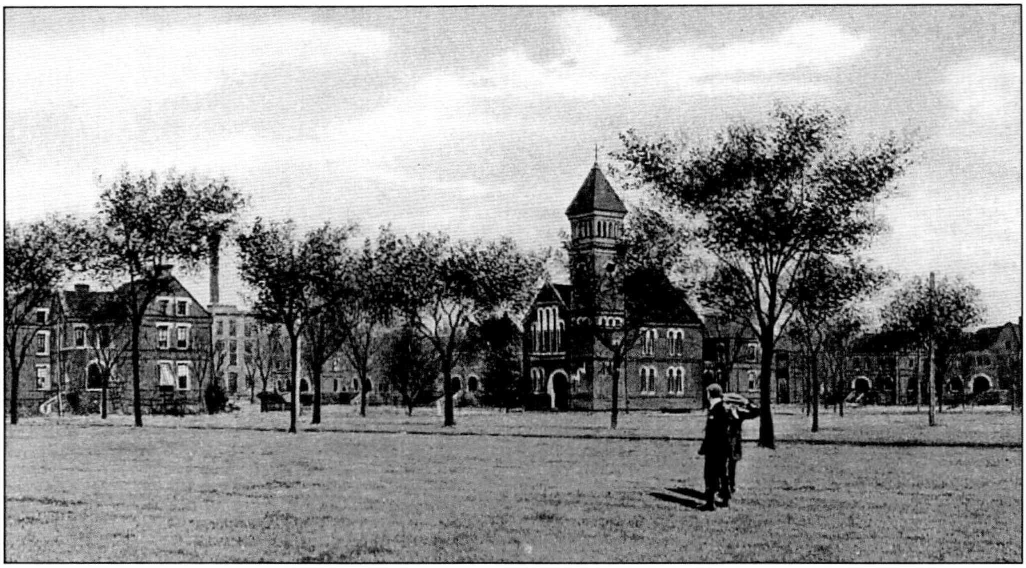

CHARLESTON, S.C., THE WILLIAM ENSTON HOME. (Color Lithography, [Louis Glaser Co., Leipzig, Germany]; Hugh C. Leighton, #26342, Portland, ME, importer; *c.* 1907.) The William Enston Home, 900 King Street, is actually an 11-acre retirement compound consisting mainly of nineteen red brick double cottages of eight rooms each. Founded through a bequest from furniture businessman William Enston (1806–1860), who desired "To Make Old Age Comfortable," the "model village" 2 miles north of the courthouse has long been considered one of the marvels of Charleston.

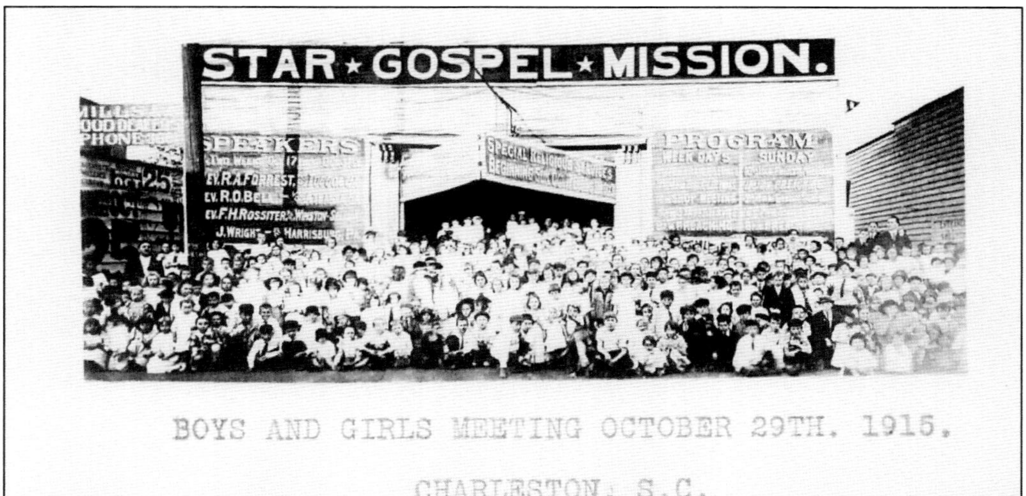


BOYS AND GIRLS MEETING, OCTOBER 29TH, 1915, CHARLESTON, S.C. (Photoprint, 3½" X 5½"; 1915.) From at least 1906 to 1919 the Star Gospel Mission operated out of the old Star Theater at 600 King Street. In addition to the regular Sunday activities of church school and morning and evening preaching hours, the mission featured weekday prayer services, Bible lectures, shop meetings, and street services. During a two-week period of programming from October 17–31, 1915, the mission advertised special religious services featuring speakers from Georgia, North Carolina, and Pennsylvania. Only one known copy exists of this card, which is postmarked November 10, 1915.

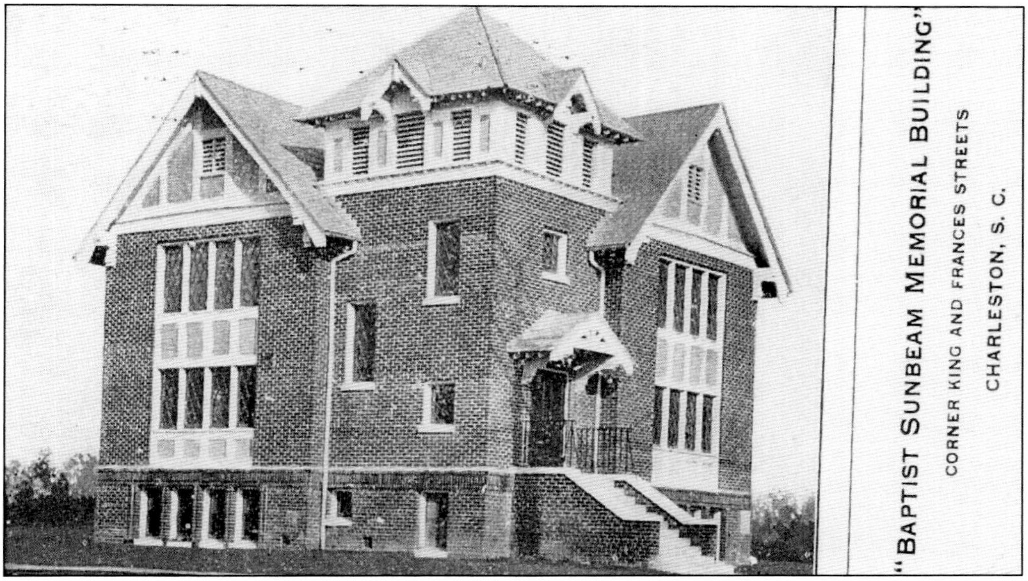


"BAPTIST SUNBEAM MEMORIAL BUILDING". . . CHARLESTON, S.C. (Halftone, 3½" X 5½"; *c.* 1915.) The picture of this building at 981 King Street was probably taken soon after it was erected in 1915 with funds contributed by the Sunbeams, a Baptist children's organization, in memory of Eliza Yoer Hyde, Baptist city missionary in Charleston and pioneer Sunbeam leader in the state. The building served as sanctuary or fellowship hall for a congregation that subsequently became the King Street and then the Hampton Park Baptist Church. Sold as commercial property after the demise of the church, it has been the site of Theatrics Unlimited, a costume shop, since 1992.

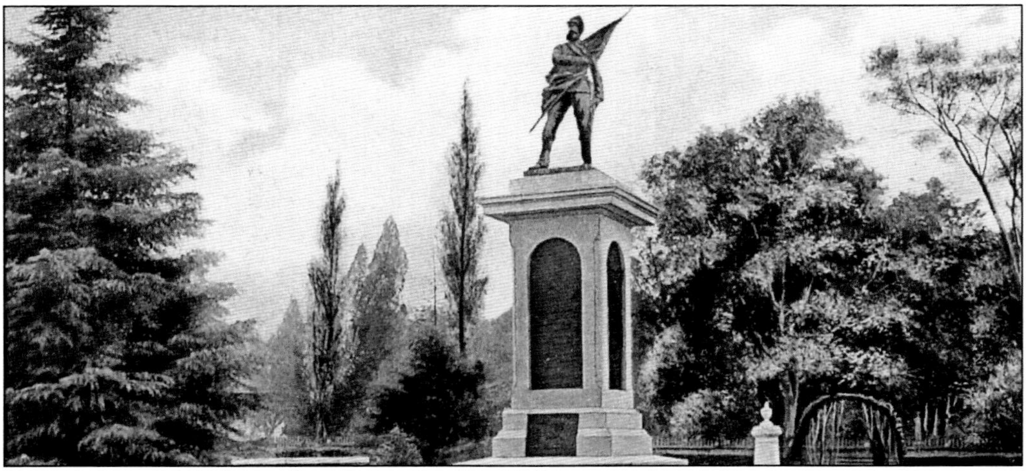

CONFEDERATE MONUMENT, CHARLESTON, S.C. (Blue Collotype, 3½" X 5½", [Trenkler & Co., #80863, Leipzig, Germany]; G.G. Lange, K.L.V. Schwalbach & Co., Germany, exporters; American Historical Art Publishers, NY, importers; *c.* 1908.) *Progressive Charleston*, a promotional booklet published in 1903, claimed that the city was "rich in beautiful cemeteries" and that Magnolia Cemetery was "noted as one of the most artistic homes for the dead." The Confederate Monument, shown here, was erected by the women of Charleston to the memory of the eight hundred Confederate soldiers who died defending the city. The bronze figure is by the Philadelphia sculptor Albert E. Harnisch.

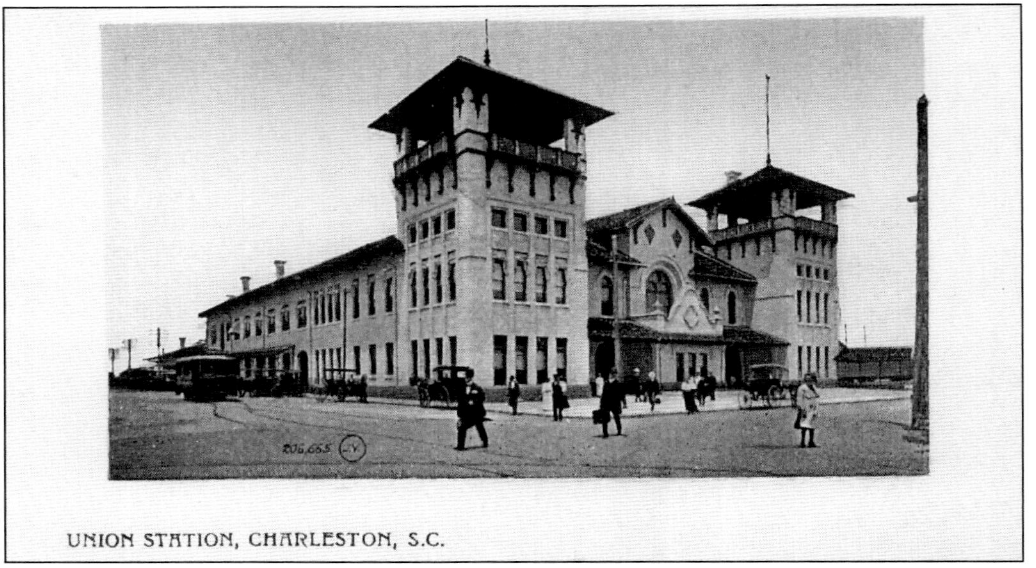


UNION STATION, CHARLESTON, S.C. (Color Lithography, Valentine & Sons, #206, 665, Dundee, Scotland; *c.* 1907.) Union Station, once located at the northeast corner of Columbus and East Bay Streets, opened for service on November 10, 1907. Built in the Spanish Mission style at a cost of $250,000, it was hailed as one of the most magnificent, modern, and convenient terminals in the Southeast. Fire destroyed it on January 10, 1947. It was never rebuilt.

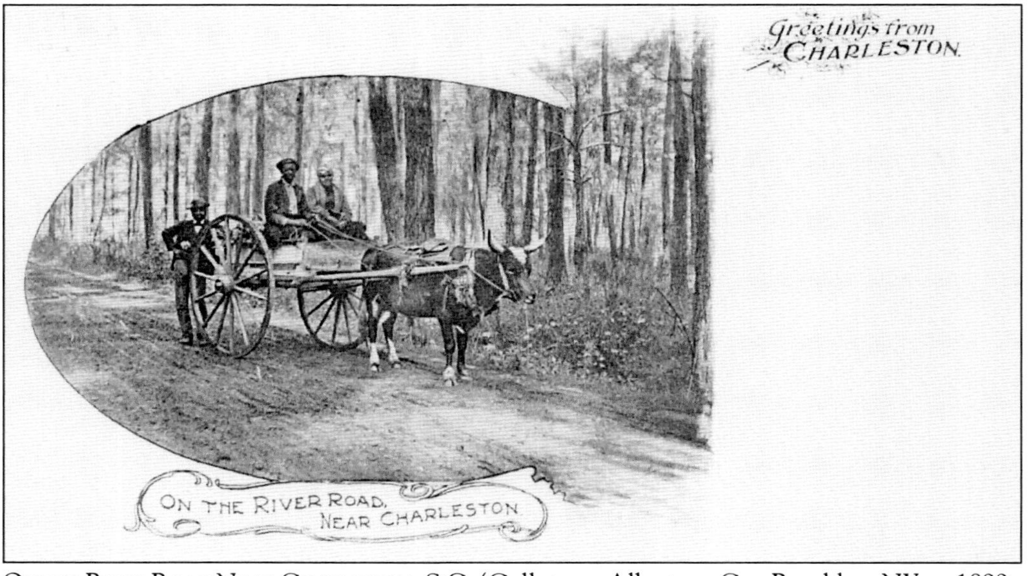


ON THE RIVER ROAD NEAR CHARLESTON, S.C. (Collotype, Albertype Co., Brooklyn, NY; *c.* 1899–1901.) The animal-drawn conveyance would continue to be a routine mode of transportation in the rural areas beyond Charleston for decades to come. The picture on the Pioneer card here depicting this elementary mode of travel also shows the Ashley River Road, the tree-canopied route which has been a busy thoroughfare since the mid-seventeenth century. This popular image was used either as a single vignette or grouped in multi-view compositions in the initial Charleston issues.

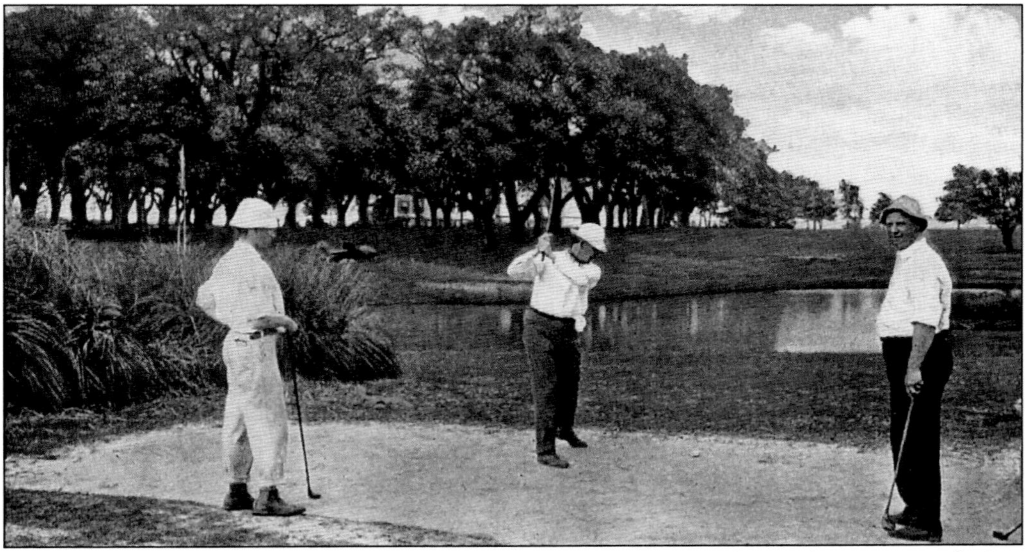

GOLFING AT THE COUNTRY CLUB LINKS, CHARLESTON, S.C. (Color Lithography, Curt Teich Co., #65984, Chicago, IL; c. 1909.) The history of golf in Charleston goes back to 1786, when the South Carolina Golf Club was organized, the first golf club in America. In 1901 the three-hundred-member country club opened the city's first modern golf course on 62 acres of the old Belvedere Plantation, located just north of Magnolia Cemetery. The printed note on the back of this card claims these links as among "the most beautiful in this part of the country." The 1805 Shubrick homestead situated at the end of an avenue of oaks was used as the clubhouse.

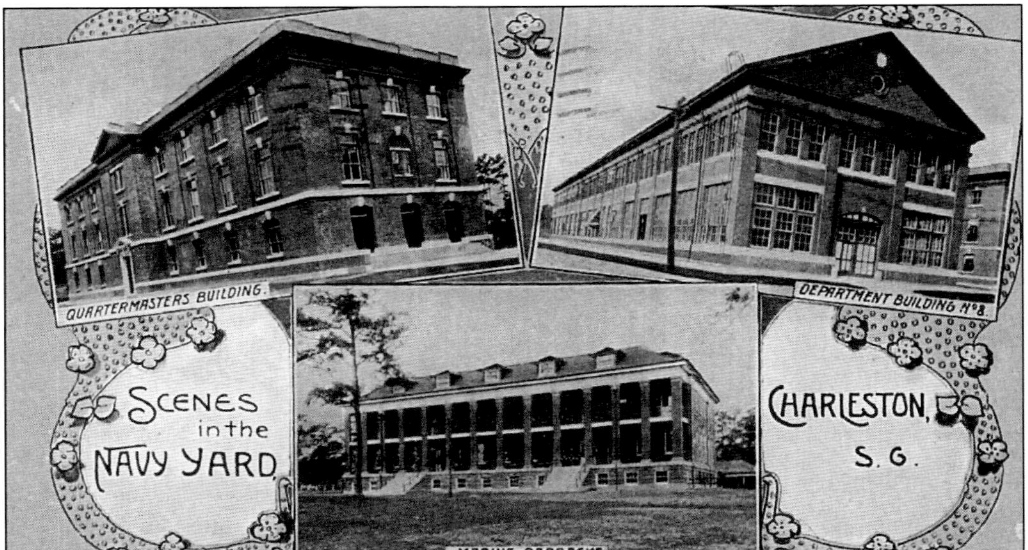


SCENES IN THE NAVY YARD, CHARLESTON, S.C. (Color Lithography, Curt Teich Co.,#A-23603, Chicago. IL; c. 1909.) In 1900 the 56th Congress authorized the secretary of the Navy to investigate the relocation of the Port Royal Naval Station to a new site on the Cooper River near Charleston, thus providing a wider and deeper harbor. By August 12, 1901, the U.S. Navy had taken formal possession of the lands constituting the Navy Yard. Most of the yard's principal edifices were built between 1901 and 1909.

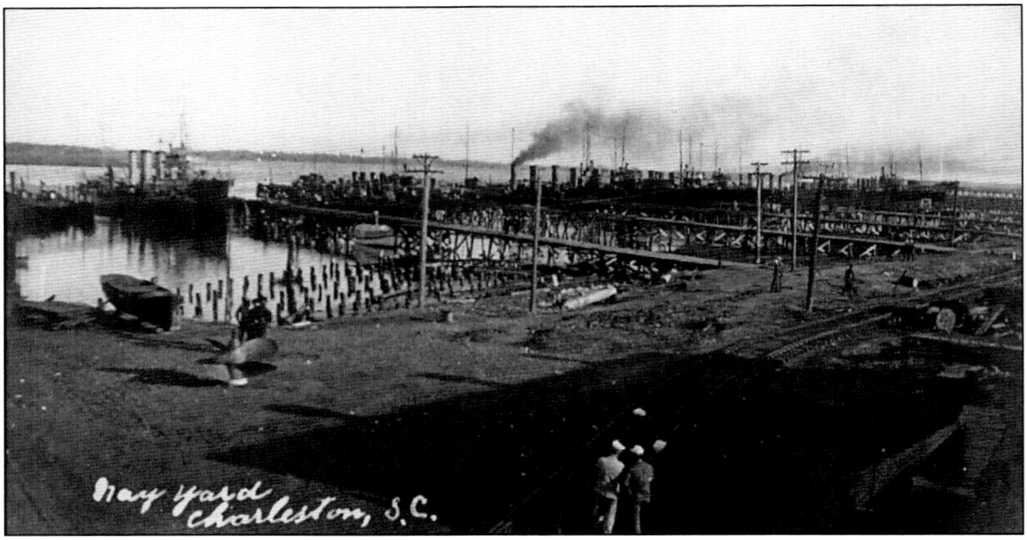


NAVY YARD, CHARLESTON, S.C. (Photoprint, 3½" X 5½"; c. 1912.) Located 6.5 miles north of the Battery, the 2,250-acre purchase for the Navy Yard included lands which had been Chicora Park, as well as the plantations known as Marshlands, Retreat, Long Point, and The Groves. The price was approximately $49 per acre. This photoprint does not frame a well-defined single subject but selects a general back-lot view.

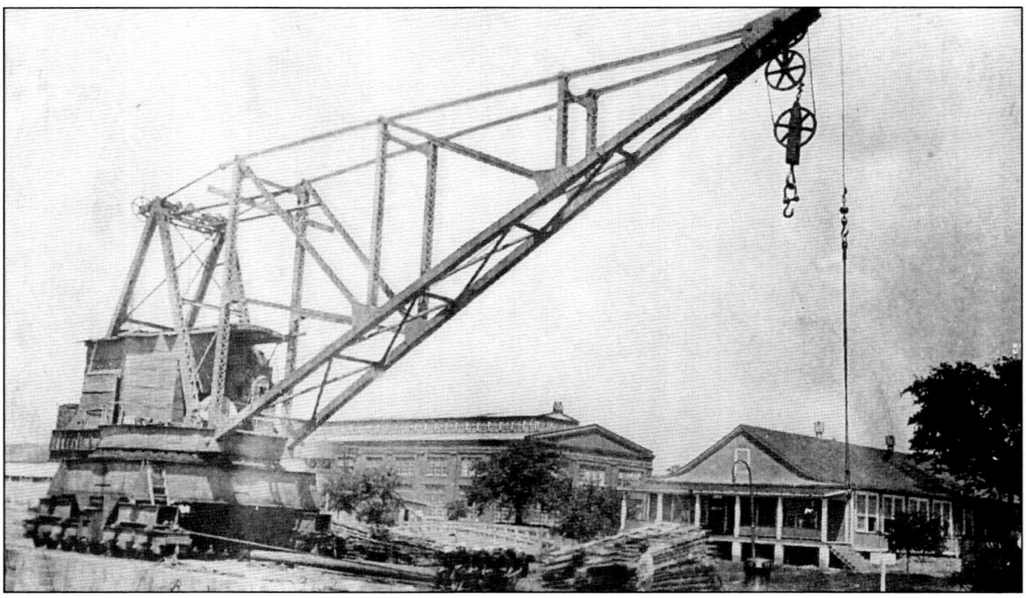

[CRANE AT THE NAVY YARD.] (Photoprint; *c.* 1919.) W. Hugh Harkey Jr., in his book *Greetings from Charleston* (1994), has summarized the impact of the Navy Yard and World War I on the economy of Charleston. When the war started, the yard was employing 1,240 civilians; before it ended, the number had reached to 5,000. Eighteen ships were built, and near the end of the war, the yard's annual payroll exceeded $9,000,000. Equipment like the heavy-duty crane seen here carried on the work of the yard as it continued to build vessels for several years after the war. While this amateur snapshot defines the crane quite sharply, the sailors seated beneath it, center, are almost lost.

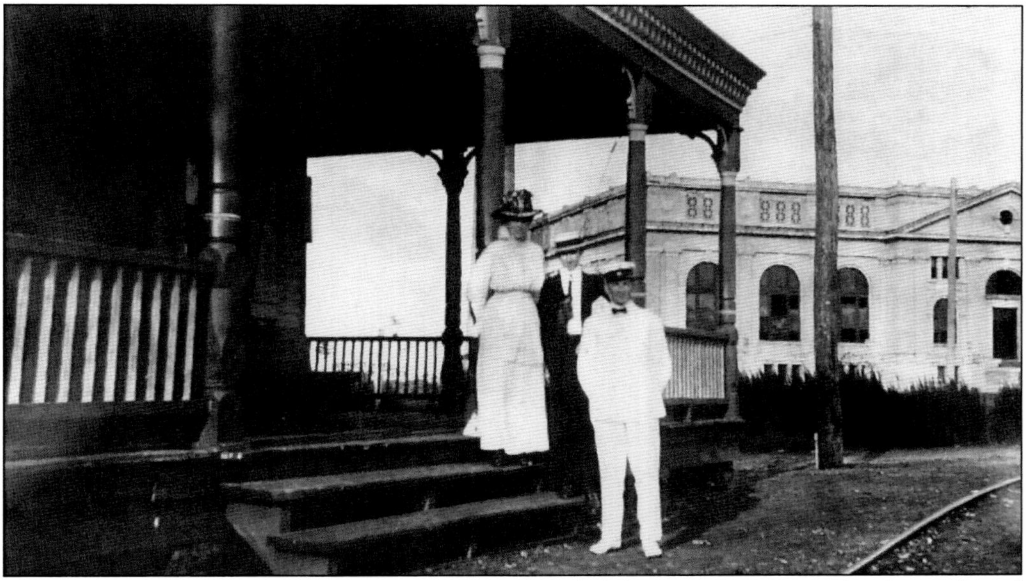

[CHARLESTON, S.C.,YEOMAN BLOXHAM, NAVY YARD.] (Photoprint; *c.* 1918.) This informal portrait of Yeoman Harry H. Bloxham, perhaps with his wife, Eva, made in the yard on July 8, 1916, is a candid, amateur one with a fresh spirit to it.

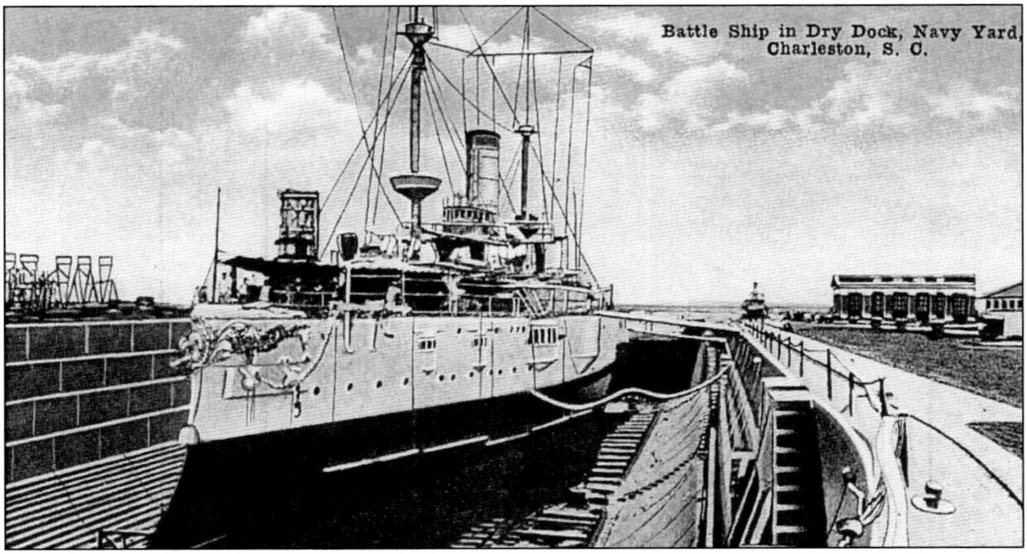


BATTLE SHIP IN DRY DOCK, NAVY YARD, CHARLESTON, S.C. (Color Lithography, E.C. Kropp Co., #8551-N, Milwaukee, WI; *c.* 1918.) The printed note on the back of this card informs the viewer that the yard, "most beautifully located on the Cooper River," could be reached by the Meeting Street or Navy Yard car and that the government had expended "millions of dollars on its dry dock, buildings and officers' quarters." The 575-foot-long dry dock—using 250,000 feet of Winnsboro (South Carolina) Gray granite—was completed in 1909, and work was begun on vessels of the fleet. Considered one of the finest in the East, it was large enough to take destroyer-cruiser class ships. The fact that the note also mentions the presence of the cruiser *Olympia*, Admiral Dewey's famous flagship of Manila Bay, may date this card from the years 1914–1915, when the cruiser was tied up or in dry dock at the yard.

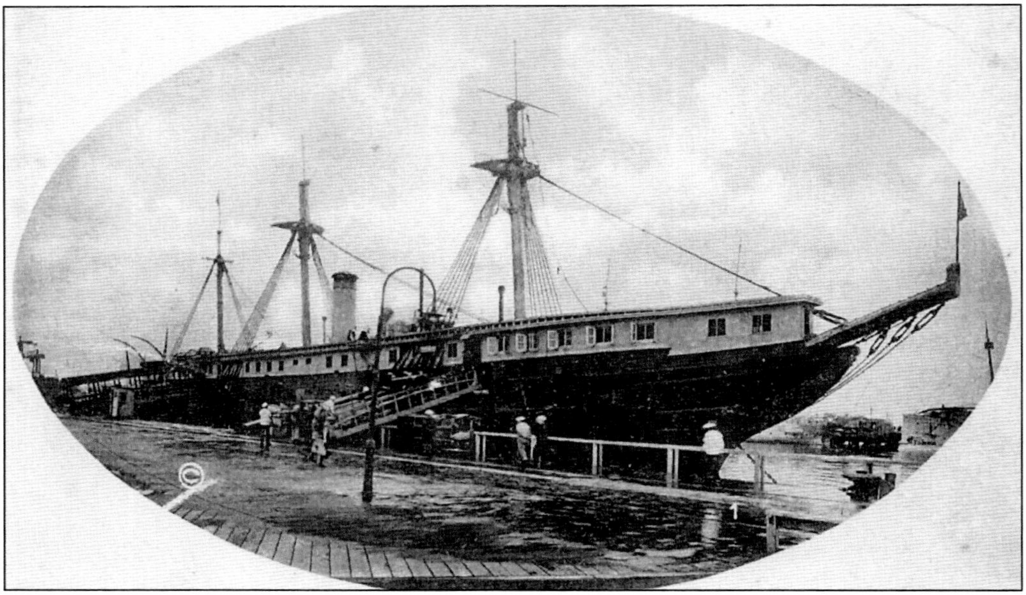

U.S. NAVAL TRAINING CAMP, CHARLESTON, S.C. (Receiving Ship *Hartford*). (Collotype, Albertype Co., Brooklyn, NY; *c.* 1918.) The old frigate *Hartford* was of particular interest to the visitor to the Navy Yard. Used as part of the training camp set up at the yard during World War I, it had been the Federal flagship of Commodore Farragut in the Battle of Mobile Bay in August 1864.

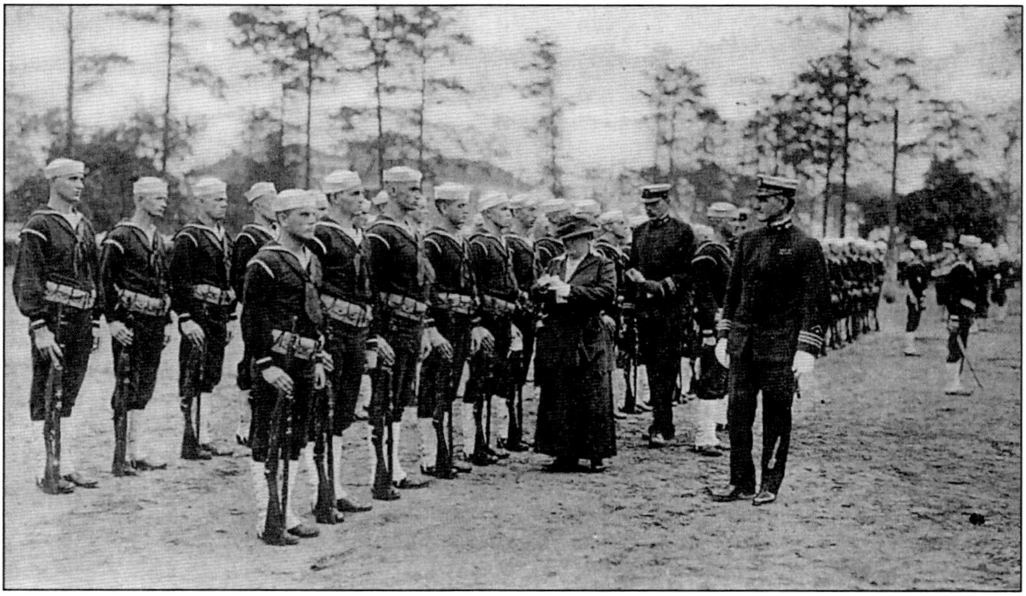

U.S. NAVAL TRAINING CAMP, CHARLESTON, S.C. (Collotype, Albertype Co., Brooklyn, NY; *c.* 1918.) Camp Begley was established at the Navy Yard in 1917. The second commandant was Commander Mark St. Clair Ellis. Jim McNeil, in his book *Charleston's Navy Yard: A Picture History* (1985), writes that Mrs. Ellis, a well-to-do woman said to be the first in America to earn a mining degree, was especially popular with the men. As she is shown doing here, she often passed out awards to athletic contest winners.

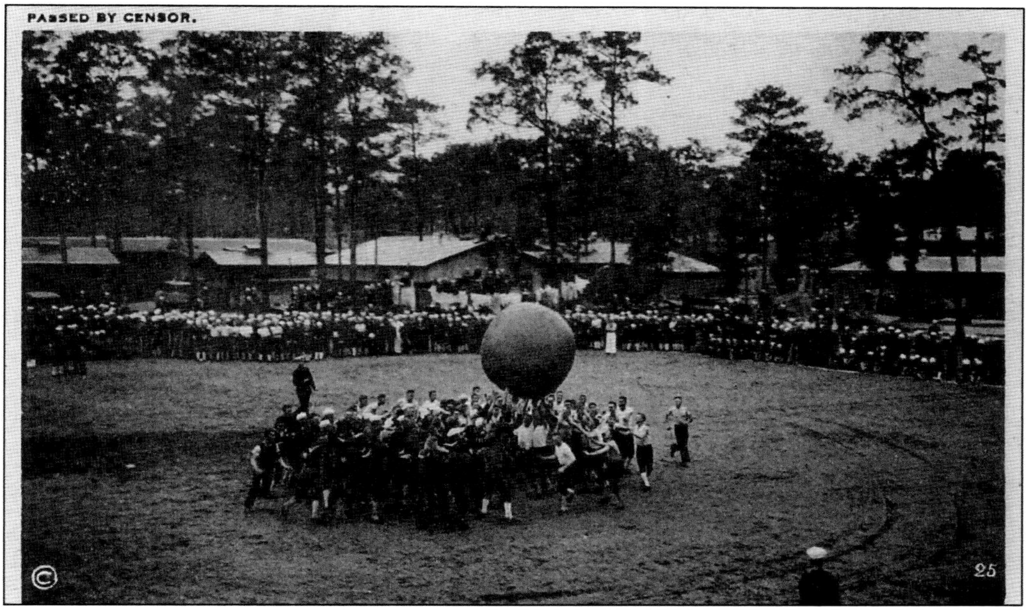


U.S. NAVAL TRAINING CAMP, CHARLESTON, S.C. (Collotype, Albertype Co., Brooklyn, NY; c. 1918.) The views on this page represent a twenty-two-card set which could be purchased in booklet form and which showed not only the physical layout and facilities of the camp, but also the range of training exercises, competitive drills, athletic events, and off-hour activities that engaged the men, shown here in a duck ball contest. The phrase "Passed by Censor" which appeared on each of the cards in this set reflects their war-time origins.

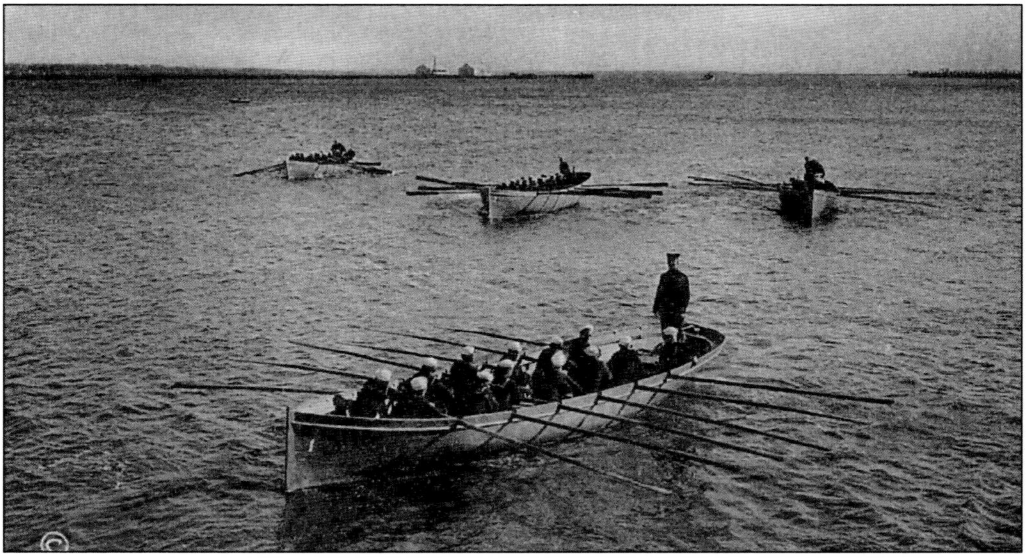

U.S. NAVAL TRAINING CAMP, CHARLESTON, S.C. (Collotype, Albertype Co., Brooklyn, NY; c. 1918.) Camp Begley provided basic training for up to five thousand men at a time, with an emphasis upon "modern methods of training suited to the modern man." "We want you to learn how to defend yourself with a rifle, the bayonet, and the pistol," Ellis declared in his "Commander's Policy." "We want you to learn how to row a boat and how to swim and play baseball and football." Here some enlistees have been photographed during boat drill.

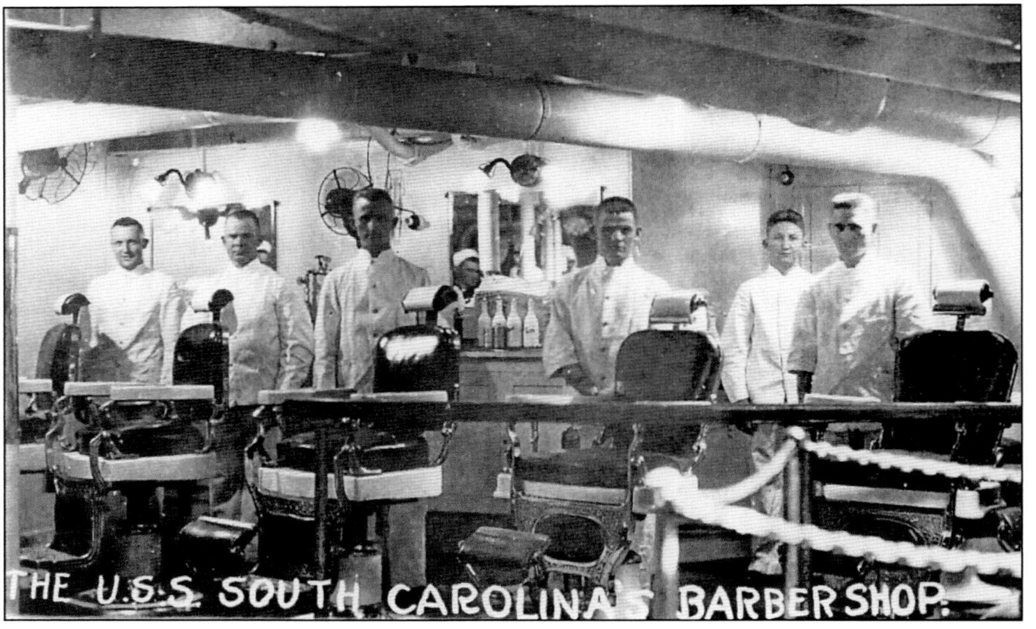


USS SOUTH CAROLINA, THE BARBER SHOP. (Photoprint; *c.* 1918.) This undated photoprint showing Navy barbers lined up at their duty station provides a rare record of an essential part of the routine on board the USS *South Carolina*.

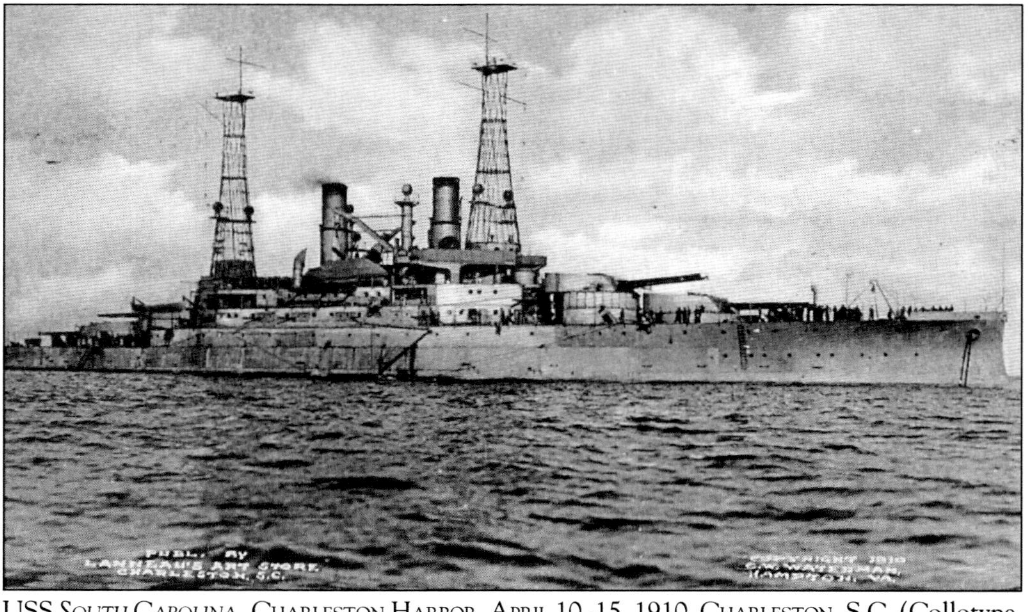

USS SOUTH CAROLINA, CHARLESTON HARBOR, APRIL 10–15, 1910, CHARLESTON, S.C. (Collotype, Albertype Co., Brooklyn, NY, cp. O.W. Waterman, Hampton, VA; 1910.) Lanneau's Art Store, one of Charleston's best-known and longest-lived photographic establishments, published and marketed this formal postcard of the USS *South Carolina*, taken in the harbor in April 1910. Completed in December 1909 at a cost of $6,683,874, the ship had a length of 453 feet, a speed of 19.5 knots, and a crew of 805 men and also carried eight 12-inch guns and twenty-two 3-inch guns.

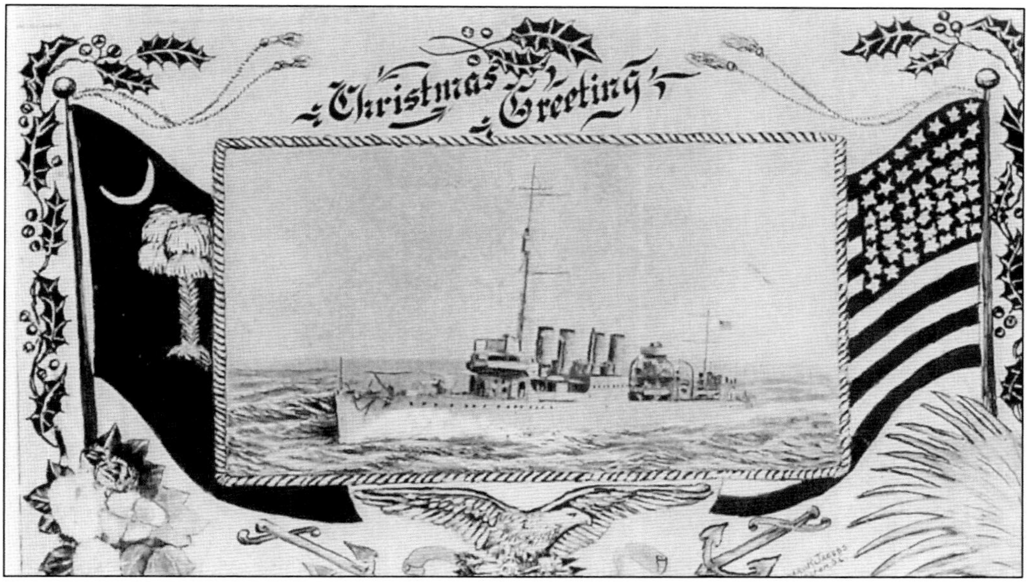


CHRISTMAS GREETINGS, USS *CHARLESTON*. (Photoprint, Howard Jacobs, Charleston, SC; c. 1918.) The United States Protected Cruiser *Charleston*, shown here on a card issued as a Christmas greeting, was the second of that name in the American Navy. The ship was christened and launched at Newport News, Virginia, on January 23, 1904. The occasion of the cruiser's visit to "our own glorious harbor" in early January 1906, for the purpose of receiving the silver service prepared for her, was characterized by editor James C. Hemphill as "one of the most interesting and historic incidents in the life of this city." This unique card was probably designed by a sailor on board the *Charleston* and created so that his shipmates could send a special Christmas card to their friends and relatives.

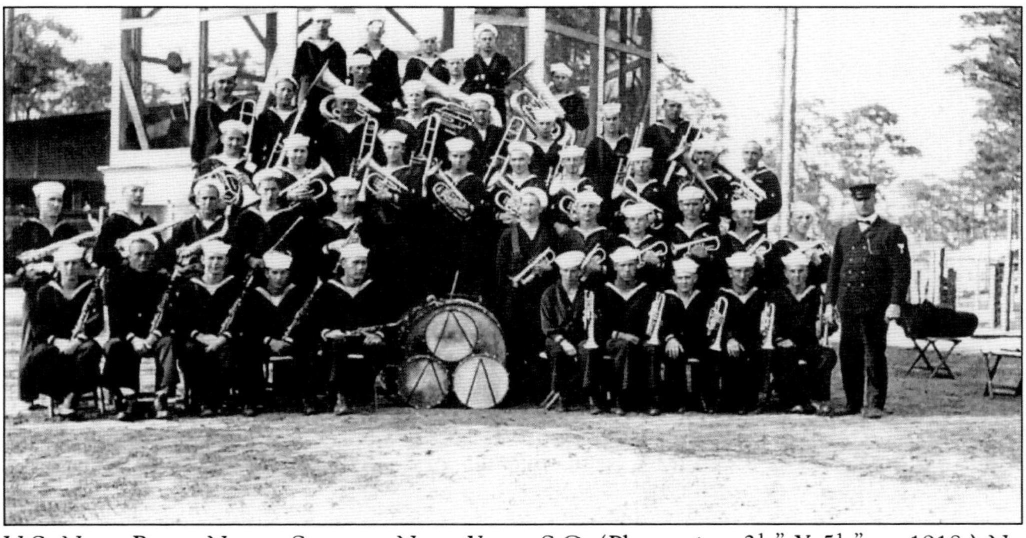

U.S. NAVY BAND, NAVAL STATION, NAVY YARD, S.C. (Photoprint, 3½" X 5½"; c. 1918.) No military post would be complete without its band. This limited-production photograph of the Navy Yard's forty-five-piece band was probably made by a Naval photographer between 1918 and 1922. Examples of this type are occasionally found in public and private collections, but only one copy of this card has been found.

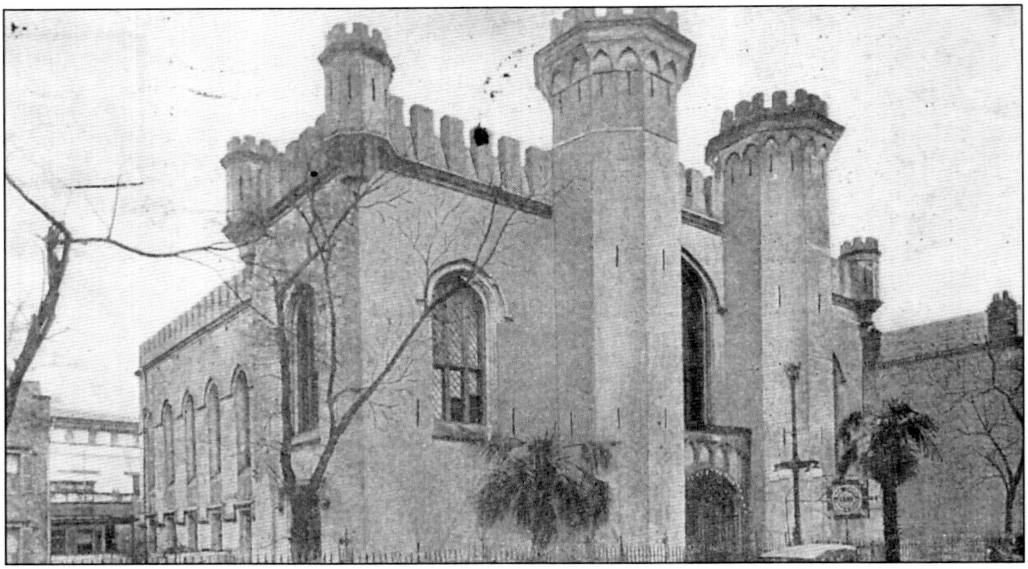

RED CIRCLE CLUB, CHARLESTON, S.C. (WAR COMMUNITY SERVICE). (Color Lithography, 3 1/2" X 5 1/2"; 1919.) The German Artillery Hall once stood at 65 Wentworth, between King and Meeting Streets. Erected in 1845, it served as the military hall for the Fourth Brigade of the Second Division, South Carolina Militia. During World War I it functioned as the Red Circle Club of the War Camp Community Service. On the back of this card, the sender says, "This is where we write letters, get our meals, etc. while in Charleston. It's an old armory." It was demolished in 1930.

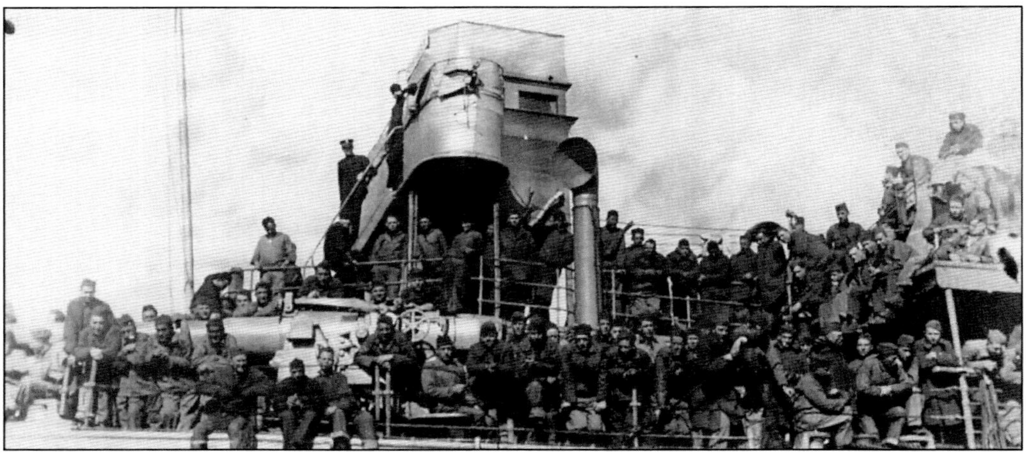

[HOMEWARD BOUND, USS *POWHATAN*.] (Photoprint, 3 1/2" X 5 1/2"; 1919.) "Homeward bound, USS *Powhatan*" reads an almost illegible note at the top of this card, showing members of the 120th Infantry Division leaving St. Nazaire, France, for Charleston at the end of World War I. The postcard here is one of a set, with other views showing the welcome ship USS *McColl* greeting a transport, and crowds cheering the docking of the USS *Powhatan*. "The Charleston companies were among the overseas soldiers who were landed in the spring of 1919 at the new Port Terminals near North Charleston," Thomas P. Lesesne would write in his *History of Charleston County South Carolina* (1931). "Many of the units in the Thirtieth (Old Hickory) and Eighty-First (Wild Cat) divisions passed through the Port Terminals. They were taken by special trains to Camp Jackson for routine preliminary to demobilization."

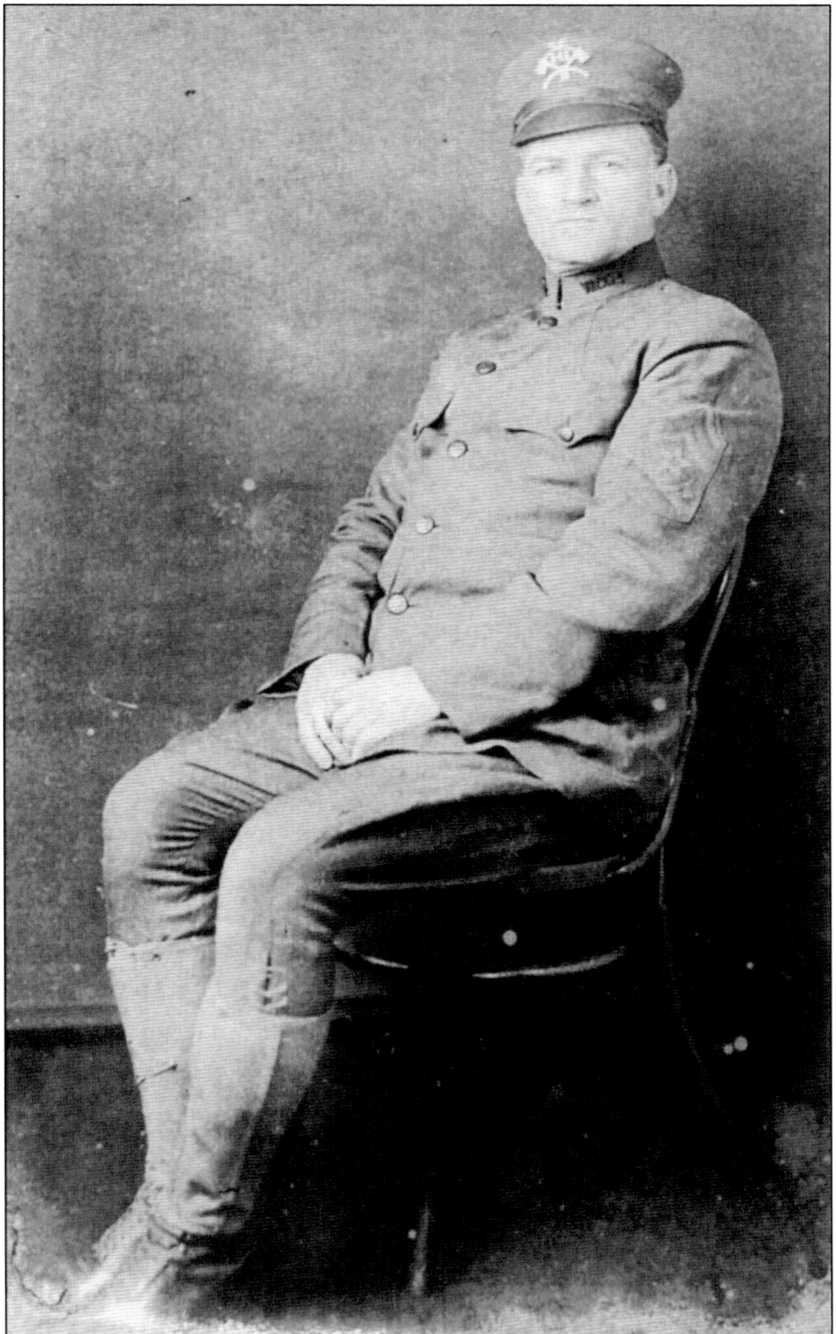

[PORTRAIT OF SERGEANT RODERICK ELLSWORTH.] (Photoprint, 5½" X 3½"; *c.* 1918.) The name "Roderick Ellsworth"—listed in the 1920 federal census as a Charleston resident—has been written on the back of this otherwise unidentified portrait of a man in uniform. The military unit represented by the metal design on Ellsworth's cap and on his sergeant's sleeve patch (S.C. 141, over crossed axes) has yet to be identified.

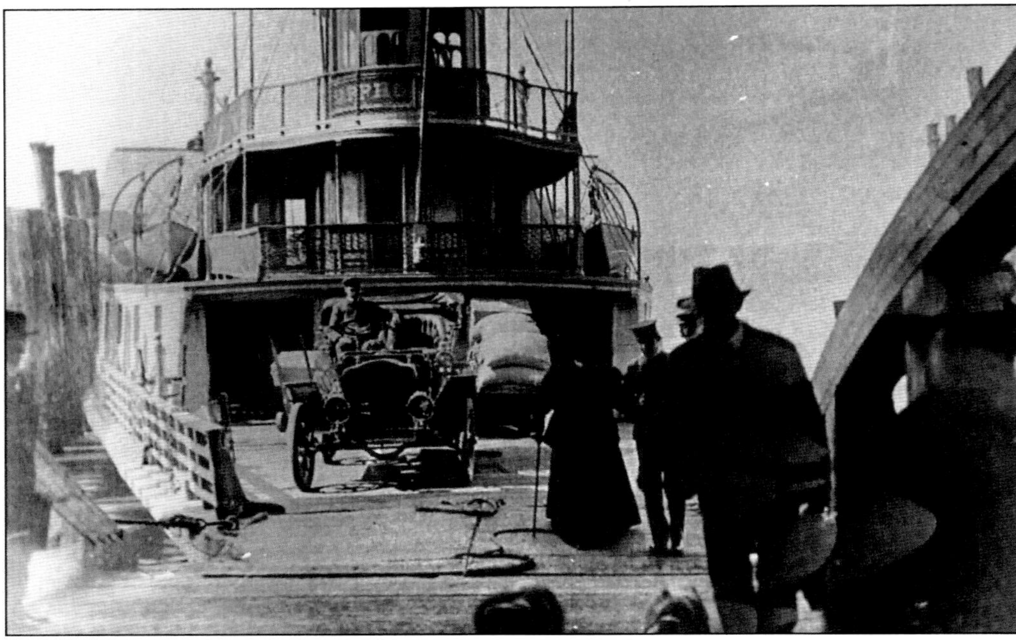

[FERRY DOCK MT. PLEASANT.] (Photoprint; *c.* 1910.) Passengers with and without vehicles here disembark from the ferry boat *Sappho* after the twenty-minute trip across Charleston Harbor to Mount Pleasant. The foot passengers might now have taken the electric train for the 9-mile ride to the Isle of Palms. The other well-known ferry which made this run was the "palatial steamer *Lawrence*" (see p. 100). The boats left the wharf at the Custom House, at the foot of Cumberland Street, almost every hour during the day and night up to midnight.

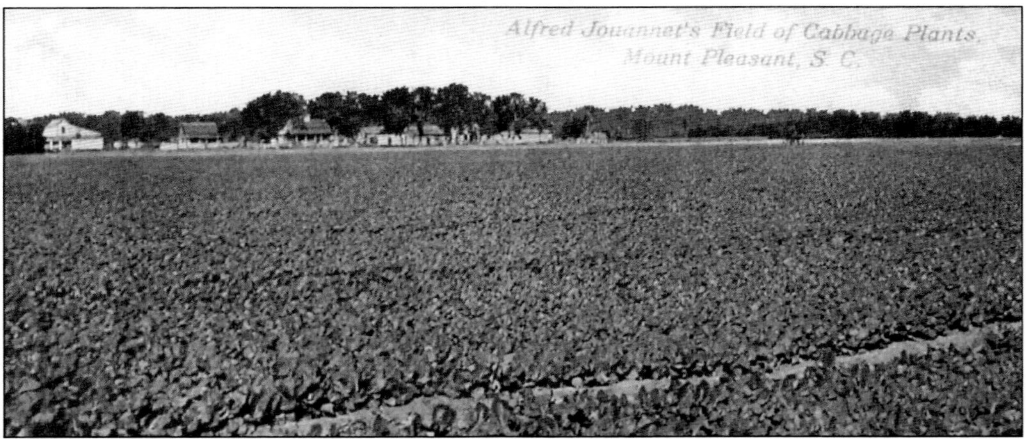


ALFRED JOUANNET'S FIELD OF CABBAGE PLANTS, MT. PLEASANT, S.C. (Color Lithography, $3^{1}/_{2}$" X $5^{1}/_{2}$", Curt Teich Co., Chicago. IL; Commercial Colortype Co., #19649, Chicago, IL, publisher; *c.* 1912.) Charles F. Kovacik in his essay "Landscapes of the East Cooper River Region" (*The Historic Landscape of Mount Pleasant: Proceedings of the First Forum on the History of Mount Pleasant*, 1993) states that fresh market vegetable cropping appeared as an economic alternative to plantation agriculture in Mount Pleasant even before the Civil War and that truck cropping later provided some relief for the farmers of the region. Cabbage plants, such as these on the Jouannet farm, contributed $150,000 to the economy of Charleston County in 1914.

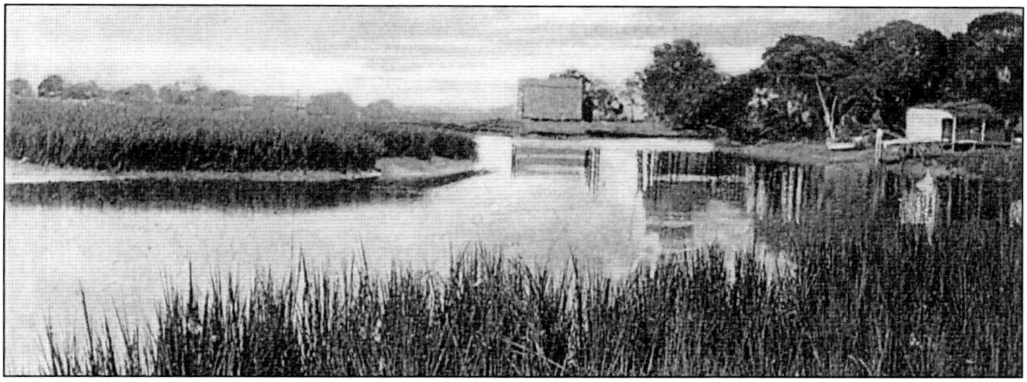

VIEW ON SHEM CREEK, NORTH, MT. PLEASANT, S.C. (Collotype, 3½" X 5½", [Knackstedt and Nather Co., Hamburg, Germany]; Rotograph Co., #91, New York, NY, importer; 1909.) Laylon Wayne Jordan in his 1993 essay "A Local Habitation and a Name: Mount Pleasant in the 1890s" (*The Historic Landscape of Mount Pleasant: Proceedings of the First Forum on the History of Mount Pleasant*, edited by Amy Thompson McCandless) has written: "The area around Shem Creek had a history of industrial activity going back to the middle of the eighteenth century. In 1889, the most important works along its banks were two saw-mills and a crate factory. . . . A yacht works was turning out pleasure craft and river freighters in 1892. Three years later, Captain Robert Magwood purchased land along Shem Creek and launched the durable Mount Pleasant Boat Building Company." This quiet view belies the activity which lined portions of the creek during this period.

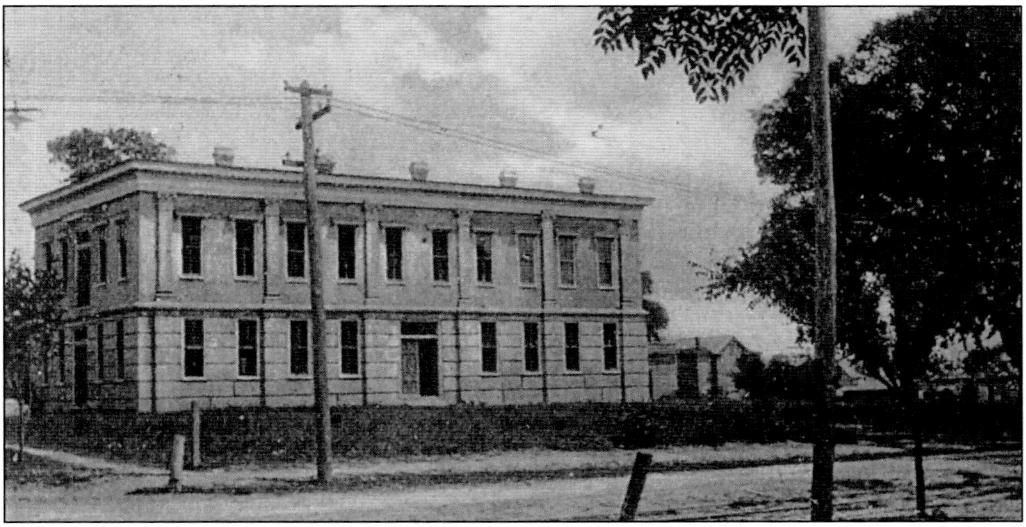

LUTHERAN THEOLOGICAL SEMINARY, MT. PLEASANT, S.C. (Collotype, 3½" X 5½", [Knackstedt and Näther Co., Hamburg, Germany]; Rotograph Co., #86, New York, NY, importer; 1911.) From 1883 to 1895 Mt. Pleasant was the county seat of Berkeley County, and the brick building above was erected in 1885 as the courthouse. After Mt. Pleasant became a part of Charleston County again, the courthouse was purchased by the Lutherans of Charleston for use as the main building of the Lutheran Theological Southern Seminary, which was relocated from Newberry in 1898. In 1911, the year this card was mailed, the seminary was removed to Columbia. Subsequently this building has served as the First Baptist Church and the Town Hall. After Hurricane Hugo in 1989, it was named the Darby Building and is currently used as a multi-purpose cultural center.

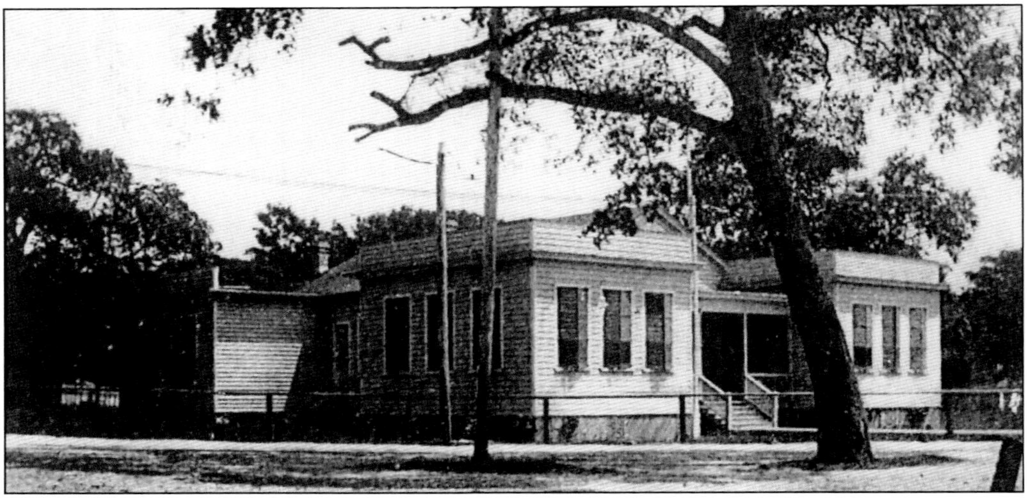

MT. PLEASANT ACADEMY, MT. PLEASANT, S.C. (Collotype, 3½" X 5½", [Knackstedt and Näther Co., Hamburg, Germany]; Rotograph Co., #85, New York, NY, importer; 1909.) Postmarked February 14, 1909, this postcard probably depicts the new building erected in 1908 as the Mount Pleasant Academy, whose history as a school can be traced back to formal incorporation in 1809. This postcard—along with the four other Knackstedt and Näther issues—came from a larger series of six to twelve images that were ordered by A.H. Patjens of Mt. Pleasant, which in a "chamber-of-commerce" style documented the town's sites of public interest.

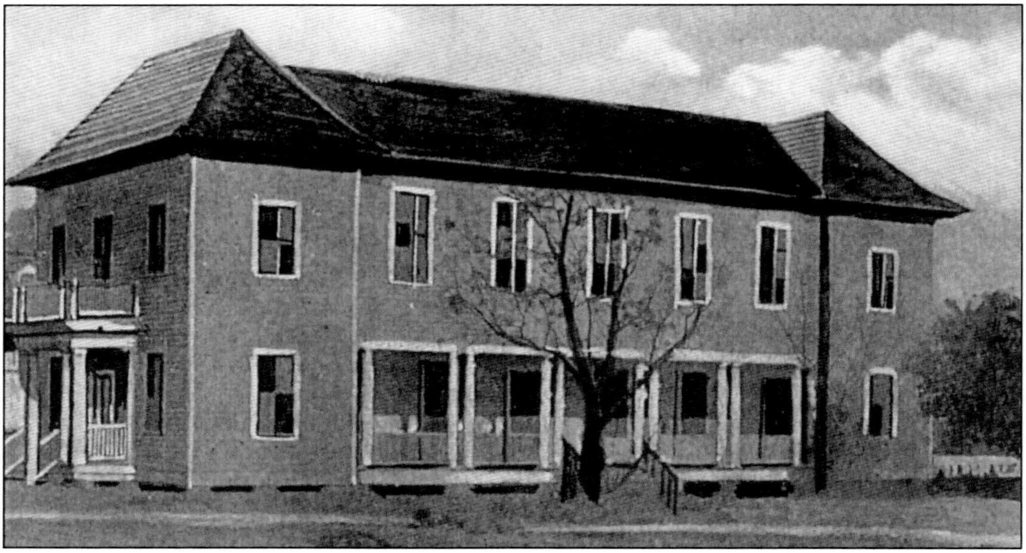

PYTHIAN HALL, MT. PLEASANT, S.C. (Collotype, 3½" X 5½", [Knackstedt and Näther Co., Hamburg, Germany]; Rotograph Co., #87, New York, NY, importer; 1909.) Pythian Hall, which once stood on the south side of King Street near the beach, was built in the late 1890s for use by the Christ Church Lodge, No. 44, Knights of Pythias. Petrona Royall McIver, in her *History of Mount Pleasant* (1960), describes it as "a large hall with Kitchen, pantry, stage and dressing room upstairs and offices, kitchen and dining room opening on to a large piazza, downstairs." When this card was mailed in 1909, the lodge had sixty-five members. Four years later the hall was destroyed by fire and never rebuilt.

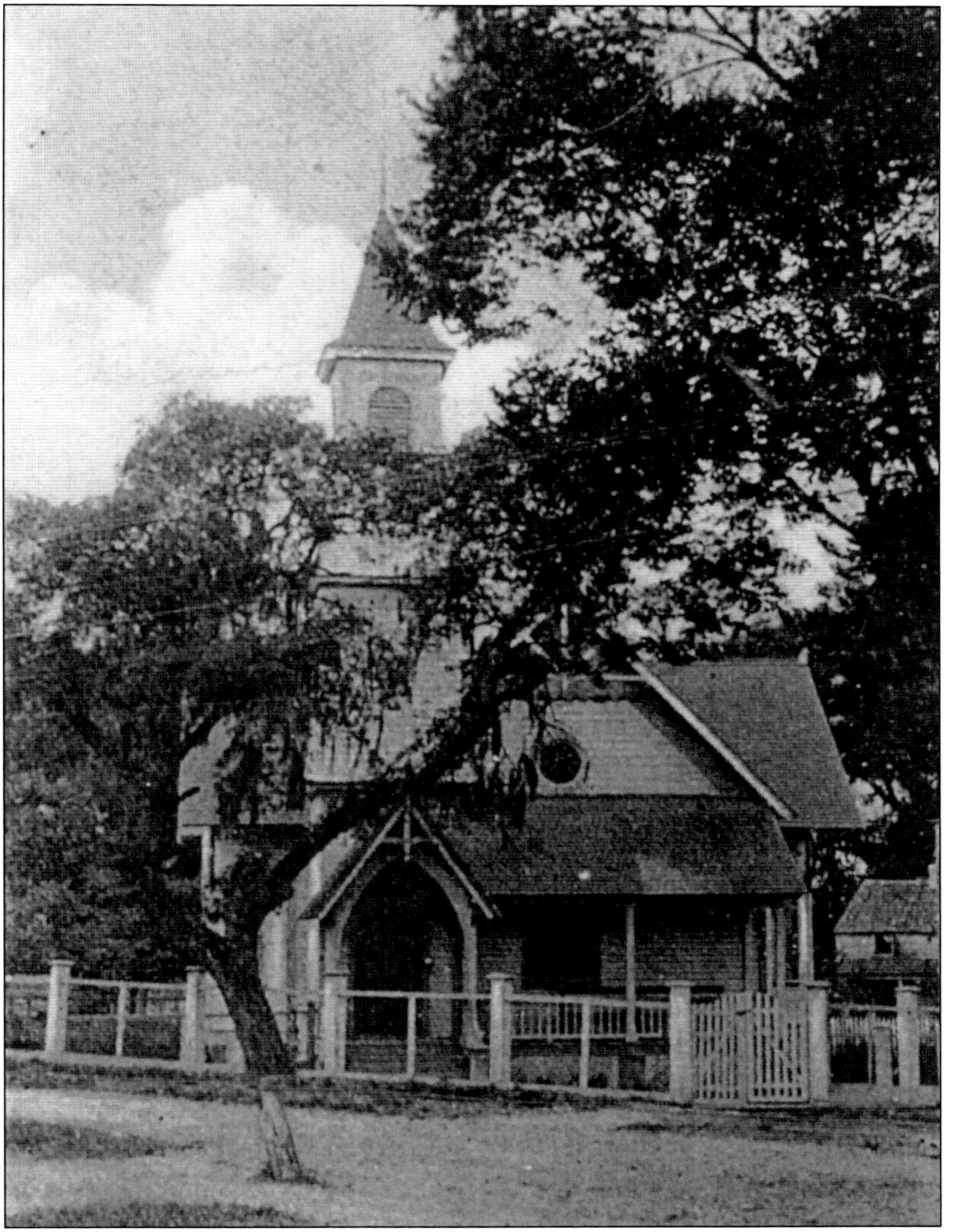

HIBBEN METHODIST CHURCH, SOUTH, MT. PLEASANT, S.C. (Collotype, 5 1/2" X 3 1/2", [Knackstedt and Näther Co., Hamburg, Germany]; Rotograph Co., #84, New York, NY, importer; 1912.) The Hibben Methodist Church, 142 Hibben Street, was erected in 1901 and served the congregation until 1958, when ground was broken for a new sanctuary on Coleman Boulevard at Brookgreen. The building was then acquired by the Seventh Day Adventists, who still use it as a gathering place.

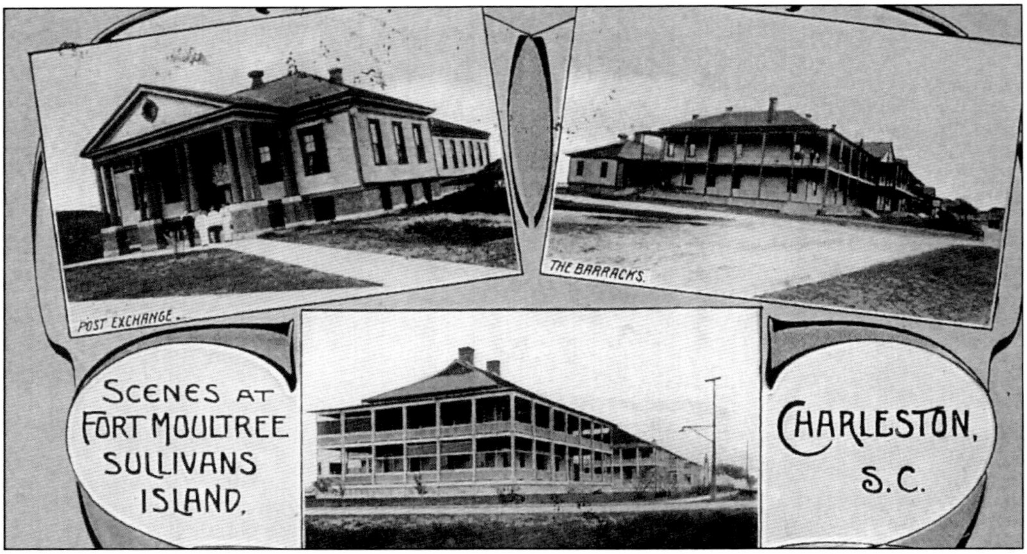


SCENES AT FORT MOULTRIE, SULLIVANS ISLAND (Color Lithography, Curt Teich Co., #A-23604, Chicago, IL; 1912.) Sullivan's Island, positioned in such a way as to be considered a key location for coastal and harbor defense, has had the presence of a military garrison since the seventeenth century. In 1896 the federal government decided that Charleston Harbor was insufficiently protected and proceeded to upgrade its defenses on the island. This development was the subject of national attention when the *New York Evening Telegraph* on August 10, 1898, ran an article about the military presence there. "It is used as a summer resort by the people of Charleston and neighboring places," wrote "L.W.," "who very often have their own pretty little cottages. . . . but the most interesting features of the island are its fortifications." This card shows the post exchange, enlisted men's barracks, and officers' quarters at Fort Moultrie.

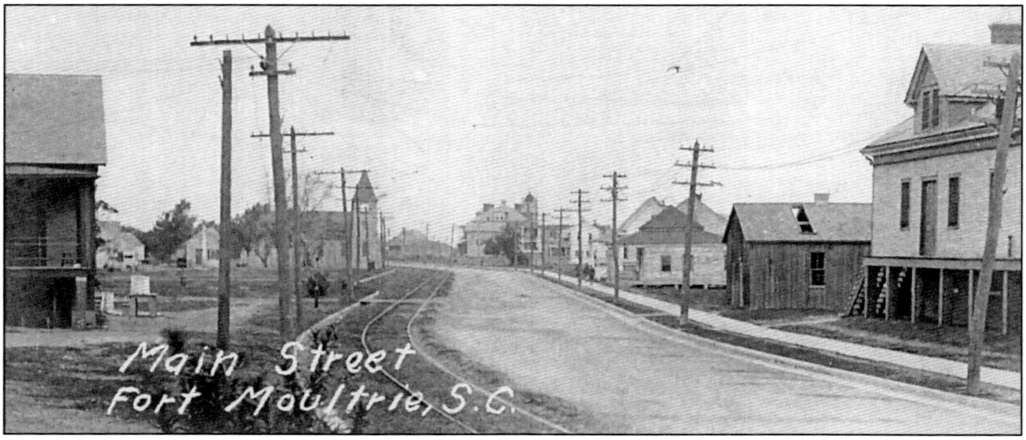


MAIN STREET, FORT MOULTRIE, S.C. (Photoprint, 3½" X 5½"; c. 1918.) "Moultrieville," reads the description in a 1911 Atlantic Coast Line Railroad tourist brochure and rate schedule, "is more of a military reservation than a residence for Summer visitors, Fort Moultrie being situated here, but it is nevertheless an attraction to them on account of parades, the music, the barracks and the numerous attractions incident to an up-to-date military post and fortification." This rare view shows the tracks of the "electric train" from which passengers could enjoy "a panorama of intense interest in the passing of Forts Moultrie, Gadsden and Johnson, with their big coast-defense disappearing guns in full view."

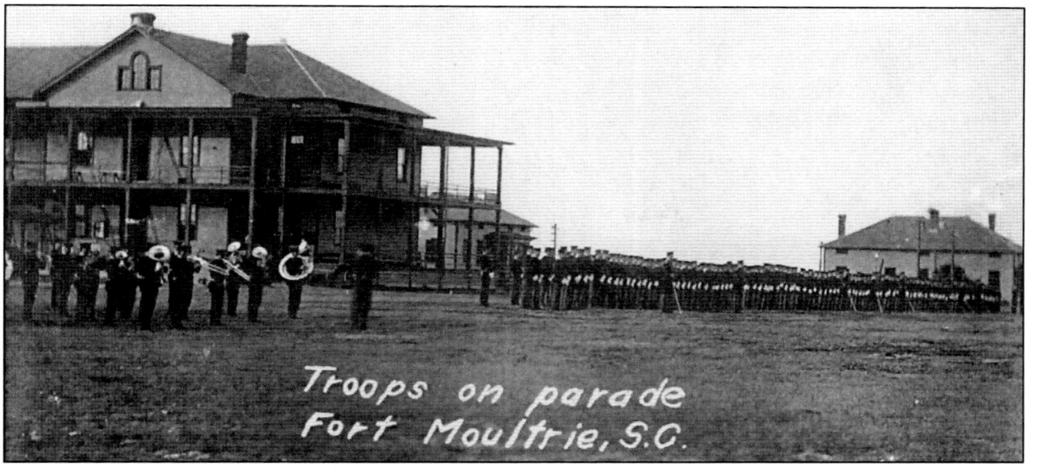


TROOPS ON PARADE, FORT MOULTRIE, S.C. (Photoprint, 3 1/2" X 5 1/2"; c. 1918.) An article in the *News and Courier* of October 14, 1898, revealed that the federal government had completed the construction of three batteries on Sullivan's Island, including the remodeling of Fort Moultrie. It was reported that battalion parade and review were held daily at 8:30 am, but because that was an inconvenient hour for spectators to view the proceedings, arrangements were to be made to hold the parades in the middle of the afternoon at least three days a week. The First Artillery Band was present at these exercises, adding to "the martial beauty of the scene." The picture here, though taken years later, illustrates this account.

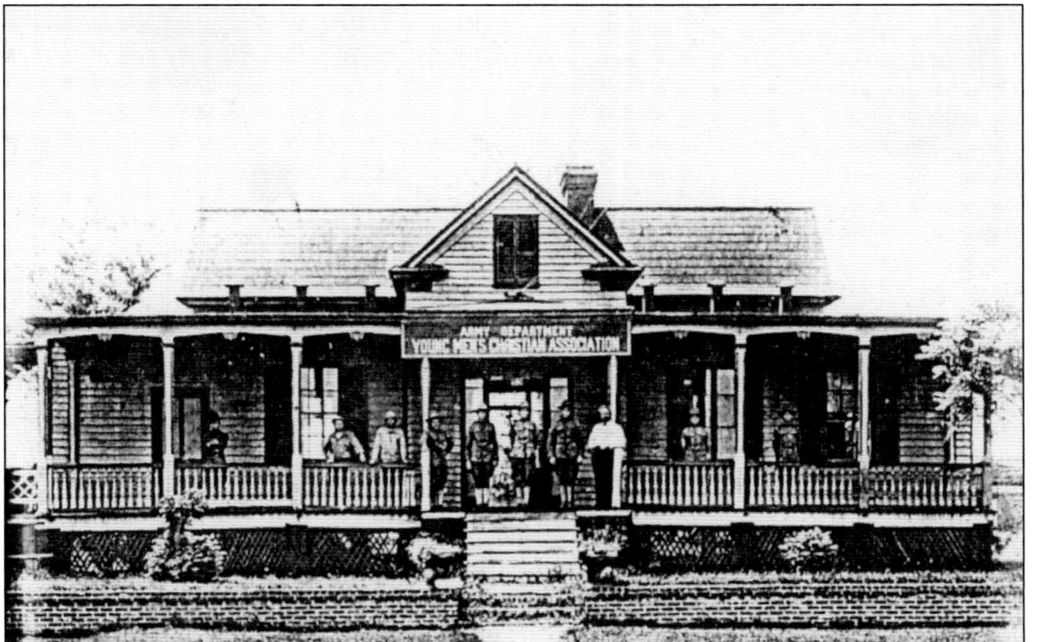


[Y.M.C.A., FORT MOULTRIE, S.C.] (Photoprint; c. 1915.) A photoprint probably made before World War I documents the presence and scope of a unit of the YMCA at Fort Moultrie. Only one card of this image and of the next one have been uncovered.

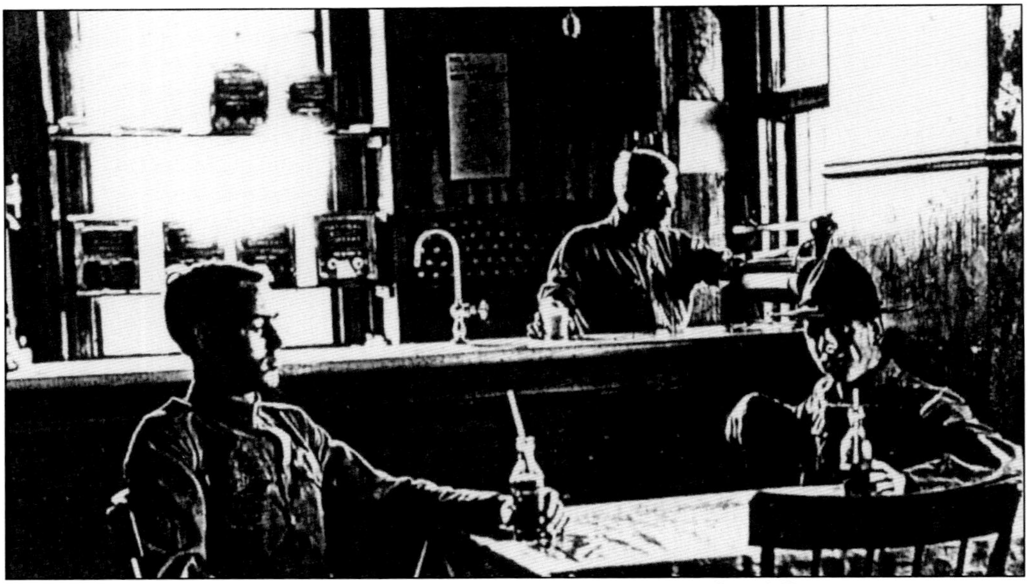

[INTERIOR OF POST CANTEEN, FORT MOULTRIE, S.C.] (Photoprint, 3 1/2" X 5 1/2"; c. 1915.) This scarce interior view showing army personnel relaxing near the soda fountain in the canteen at Fort Moultrie was taken about 1915.

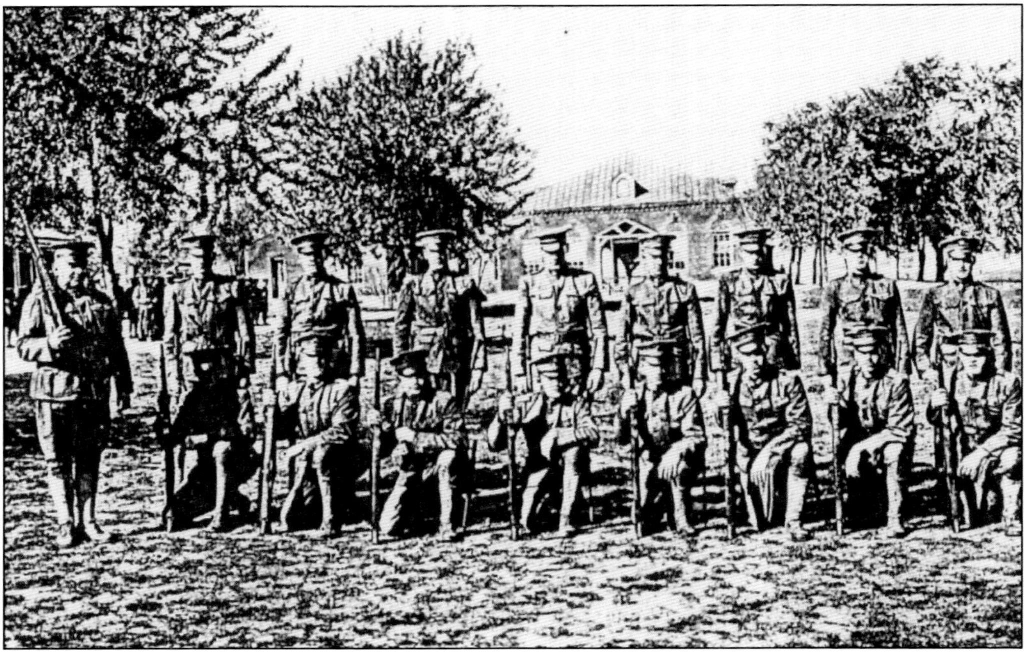

[RIFLE SQUAD, FORT MOULTRIE, S.C.] (Photoprint; c. 1915.) In turn-of-the-century newspaper accounts of garrison life at Fort Moultrie, the public was informed that drills were held regularly, not only with the big guns, but with small arms and in field work as well. The 1911 illustrated Atlantic Coast Line Railroad tourist brochure and rate schedule would later boast that "since the Spanish-American War the batteries have been modernized and Fort Moultrie of the present day is one of the largest and strongest United States Coast defense fortifications."

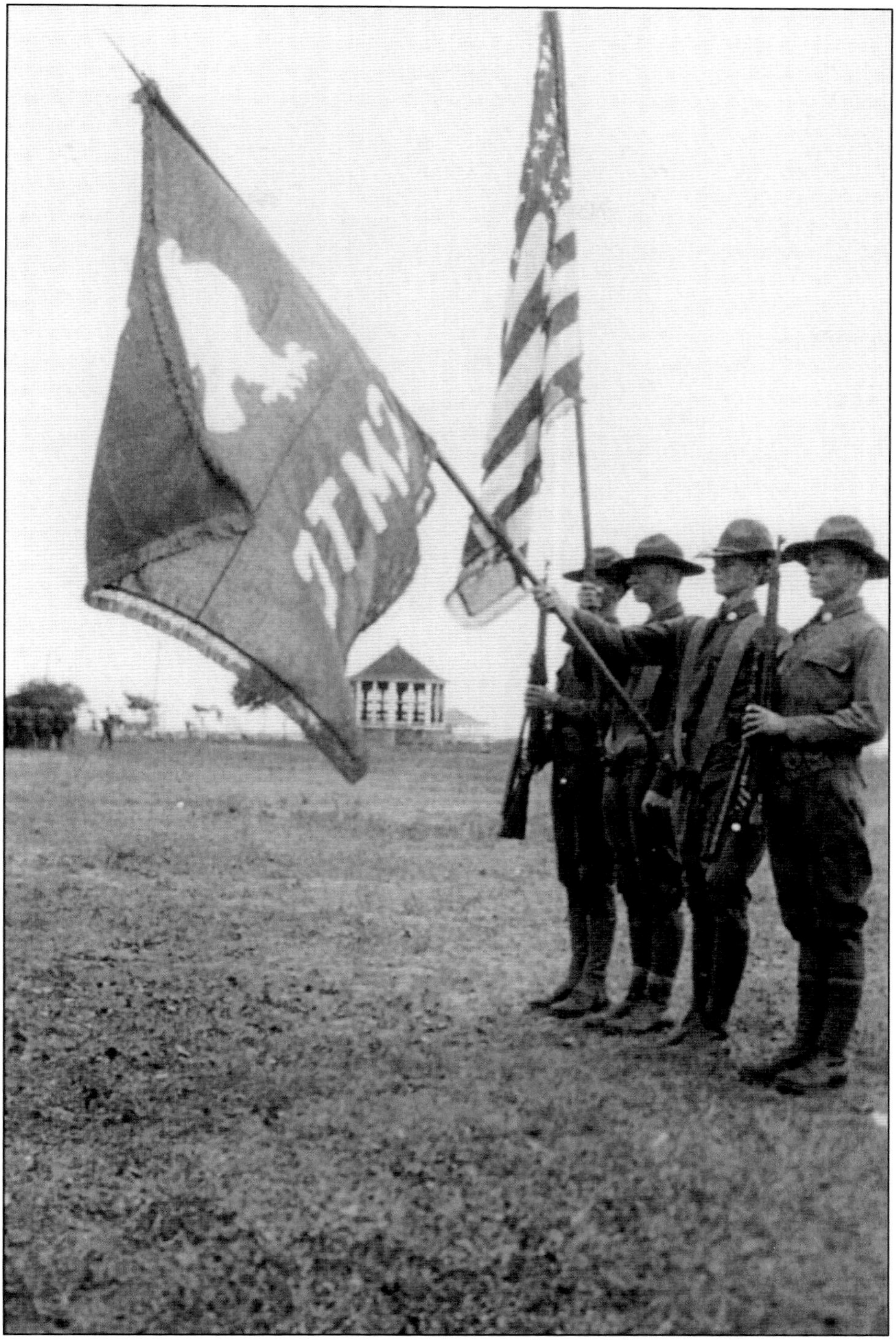

[COLOR GUARD, SULLIVANS ISLAND, S.C.] (Photoprint, 5 1/2" X 3 1/2"; *c.* 1917.) In this photoprint which probably dates from sometime during World War I, a color guard performs its routine drill on the parade ground at Fort Moultrie. These cards were made for public relations purposes and sold to recruits and visitors to the fort and can be found in private collections.

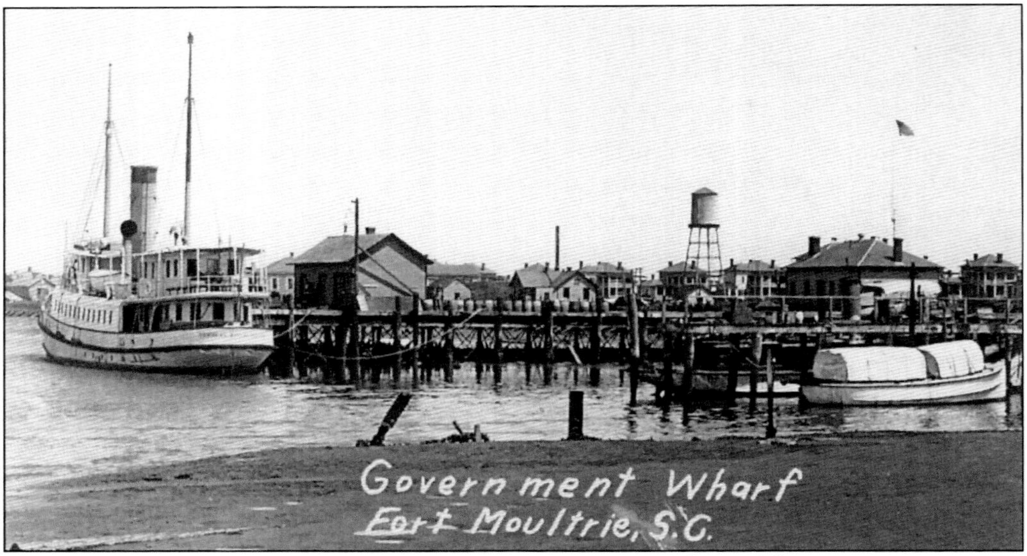


GOVERNMENT WHARF, FORT MOULTRIE, S.C. (Photoprint, 3½" X 5½"; *c.* 1918.) This rare photoprint of the government wharf at Fort Moultrie was sent by one Private Ernest E. Standish, who identified himself as being a member of the 78th Company, C.A.C. (Coastal Artillery Corps?). The boat to the left may be the *General Weeks*, one of the government steamers which ferried personnel between Charleston and Fort Moultrie around this time.

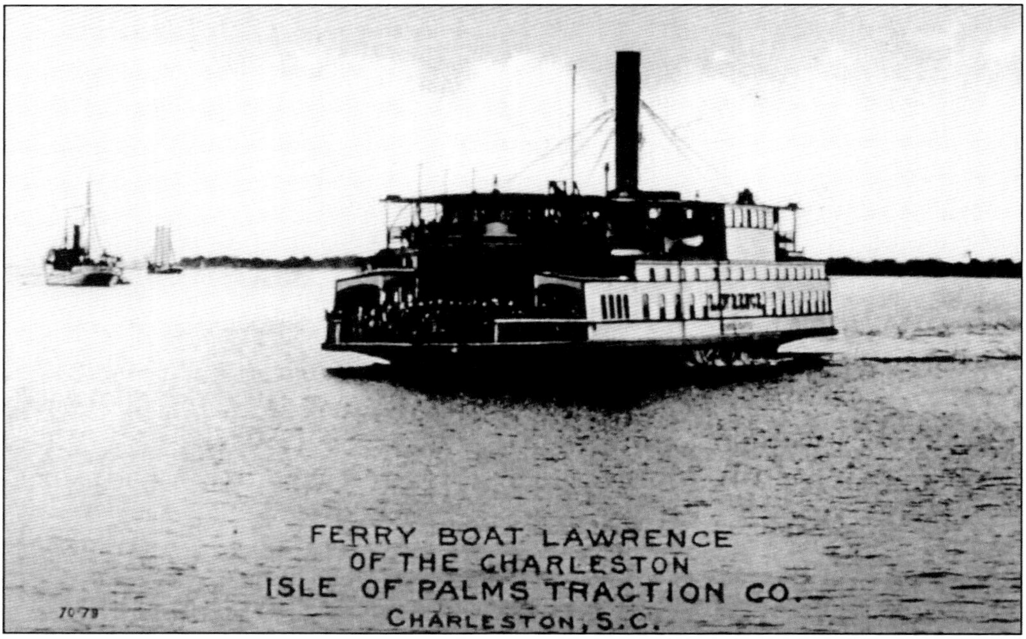


FERRY BOAT LAWRENCE OF THE CHARLESTON-ISLE OF PALMS TRACTION CO., CHARLESTON, S.C. (Color Lithography, Souvenir Post Card Co., #7079, New York, NY; 1913.) The ferryboat was the transportation link between Charleston and the Isle of Palms when this card was sent on June 27, 1913. It was mailed by H.L. Watson, who wrote to his mother in Greenwood that he "Came over on this boat. Got here at midnight. Pretty tired." Watson (1876–1956) became the well-known owner and editor of the *Greenwood Index-Journal*.

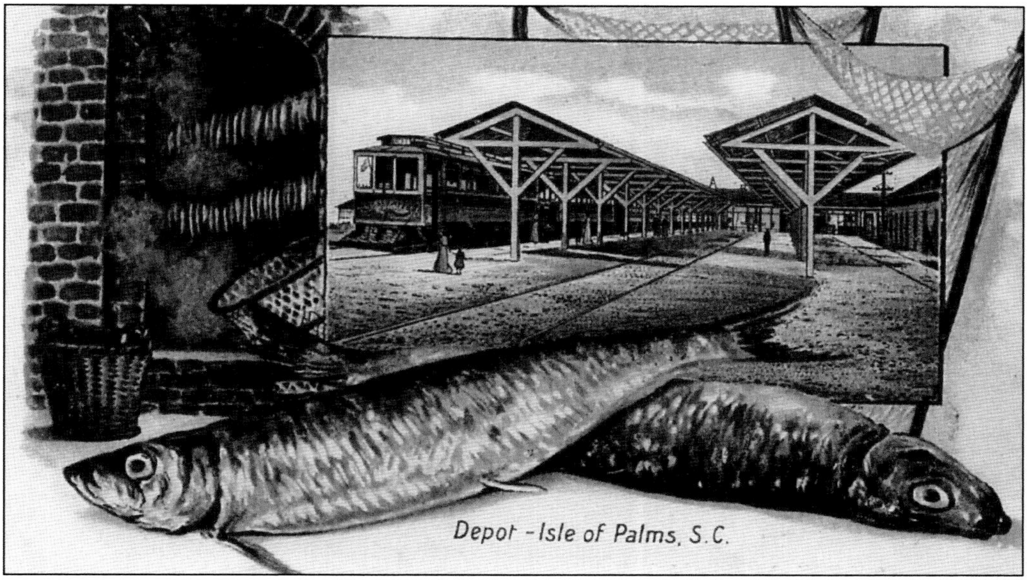


DEPOT, ISLE OF PALMS, S.C. (Embossed Color Lithography, [Rosenblatt Lithograph Institute, #13287, Frankfurt, Germany]; *c.* 1907.) *Progressive Charleston*, a promotional booklet published in 1903, speaks of the Isle of Palms on Sullivan's Island as "The Only Resort of Its Kind On the South Atlantic Coast," refers to its transportation to and from Charleston as being furnished by "the finest electric trolley service of its kind in the country," and mentions its "large cafe, affording all the delicacies in season." The Rosenblatt Lithograph Institute—printer of several types of view-cards—continued its older "Gruss aus" ("Greetings from") cards, artistically arranging illustrations of sea shells and fish around the photographs. These higher-priced issues were not banned by the tariffs and were popular at fashionable hotels.

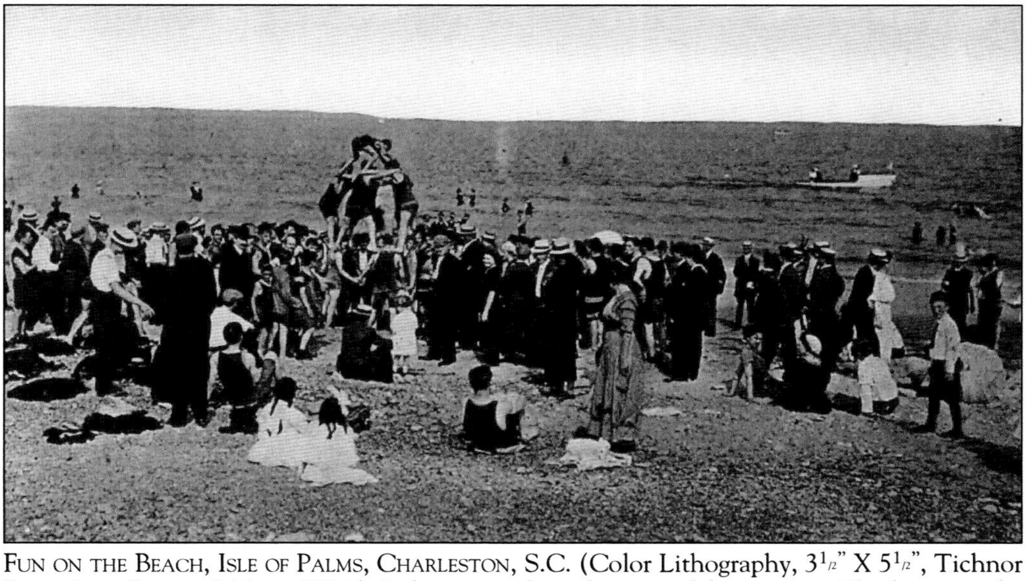

FUN ON THE BEACH, ISLE OF PALMS, CHARLESTON, S.C. (Color Lithography, 3½" X 5½", Tichnor Bros., Inc., Boston, MA; *c.* 1914.) At least as early as the turn of the century, Charleston spoke proudly of the beach on the Isle of Palms as the best on the entire Atlantic coast, with the finest surf in the country (*Charleston and Vicinity—Illustrated*, 1901).

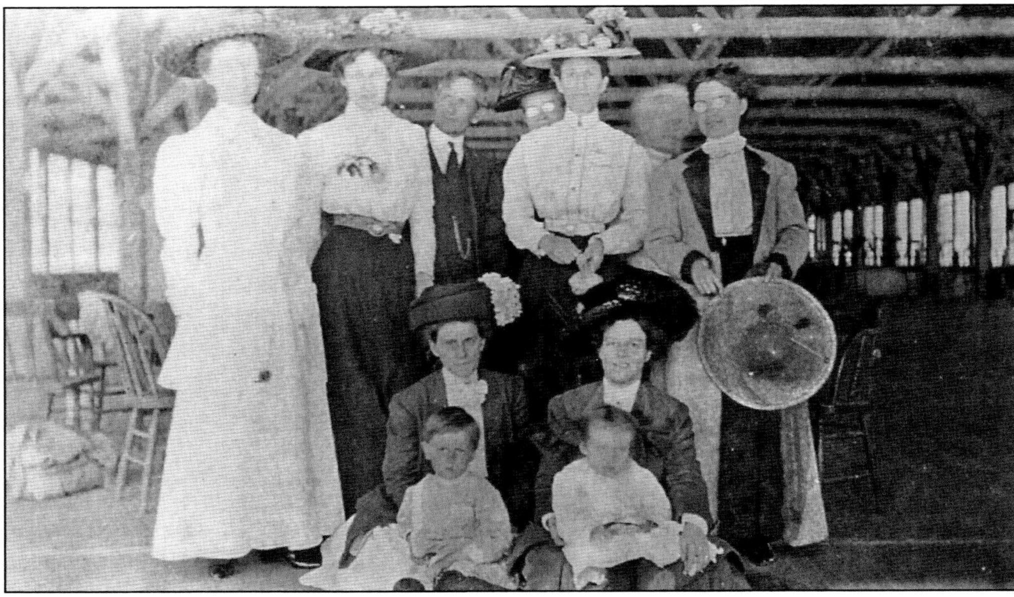

[GAMMAGE FAMILY PORTRAIT, ISLE OF PALMS.] (Photoprint; *c.* 1912.) The undated message penciled on the back of this amateur photoprint picturing members of Charlotte Gammage's family and friends in the pavilion reads: "Taken on the Isle of Palms—when Nell was here. Do notice how Br. O. is making eyes at her." An article on the opening of the Isle of Palms, "formerly Long Island," in the *News and Courier*, August 15, 1898, declared that for those who did not care to go into the water, there was "ample shelter from the sun and rain in the pavilion with over a thousand comfortable chairs for them to rest on at their leisure, and varied refreshments at command, at all times under the same roof."

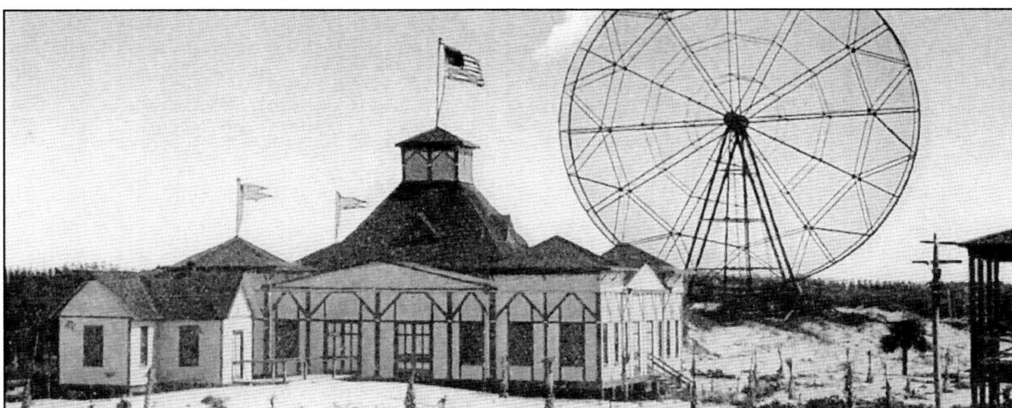

ISLE OF PALMS, CHARLESTON, S.C. (Color Lithography, 3 1/2" X 5 1/2", McGown-Silsby Lithographic Co., New York, NY; *c.* 1914.) In a news article entitled "Coney Island of the South," which appeared in the *News and Courier* on October 14, 1898, it was announced that the Charleston and Seashore Railway Company had purchased the Ferris wheel from Atlantic City and the steeplechase and electric carousel from Coney Island. The work of breaking ground for the foundations of these attractions was begun the same day. The Ferris wheel, which had to be taken apart and shipped by rail, was "the first ever brought South except the one which was seen in Atlanta at the last Exposition there [1895]." It was expected to be in operation by the first week of that November.

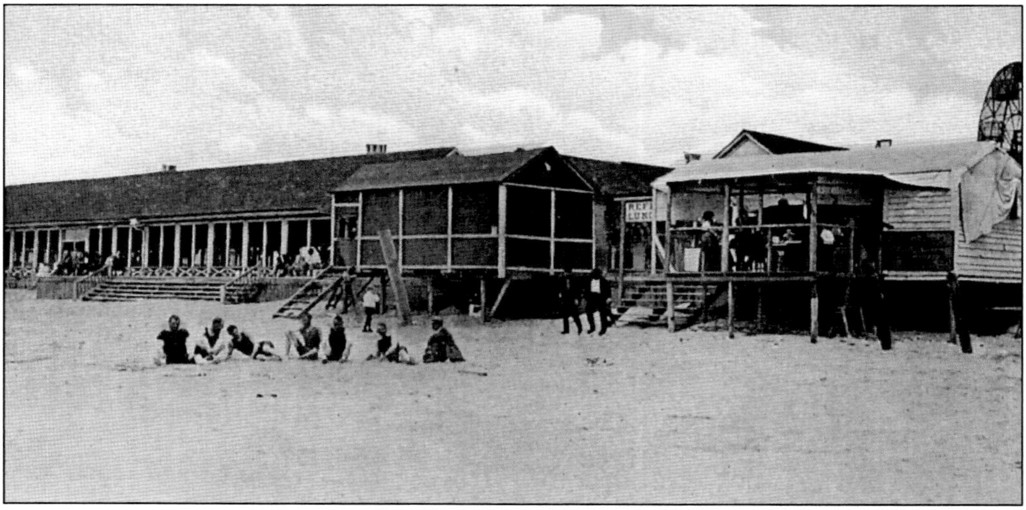

THE PAVILION, ISLE OF PALMS, S.C. (Color Lithography, 3½" X 5½", Curt Teich Co., #A23588, Chicago, IL; *c.* 1910.) The Pavilion at the Isle of Palms was considered one of the "handsomest" in the South, according to the Atlantic Coast Line Railroad booklet issued in 1911. There were "excellently arranged sets of dressing rooms for bathers and every convenience known to a first-class seashore resort." Dances were held in the Pavilion, with music furnished by military bands and "the strictest decorum . . . maintained by the management of the resort."

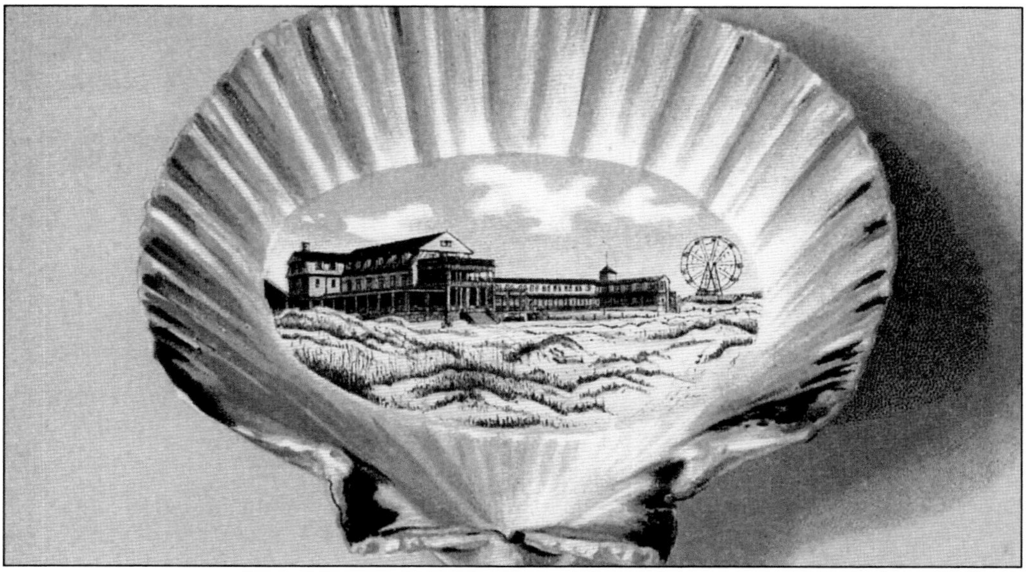

HOTEL SEASHORE, ISLE OF PALMS, S.C. (Embossed Color Lithography, 3½" X 5½", [Rosenblatt Lithograph Institute, #13286, Frankfurt, Germany]; *c.* 1908.) *Progressive Charleston* (1903) mentions "an excellent hotel" on the Isle of Palms and claims that, in addition to bathing, the amusements there were many and varied and included "dancing and concerts, boating, fishing and love-making by moonlight." Eight years later the Atlantic Coast Line Railroad would advertise the Seashore Hotel as "beautiful, well appointed, well kept," facing "one of the finest beaches on the Atlantic Ocean" and offering from its verandas views of the ships in Charleston's harbor as they passed and repassed.

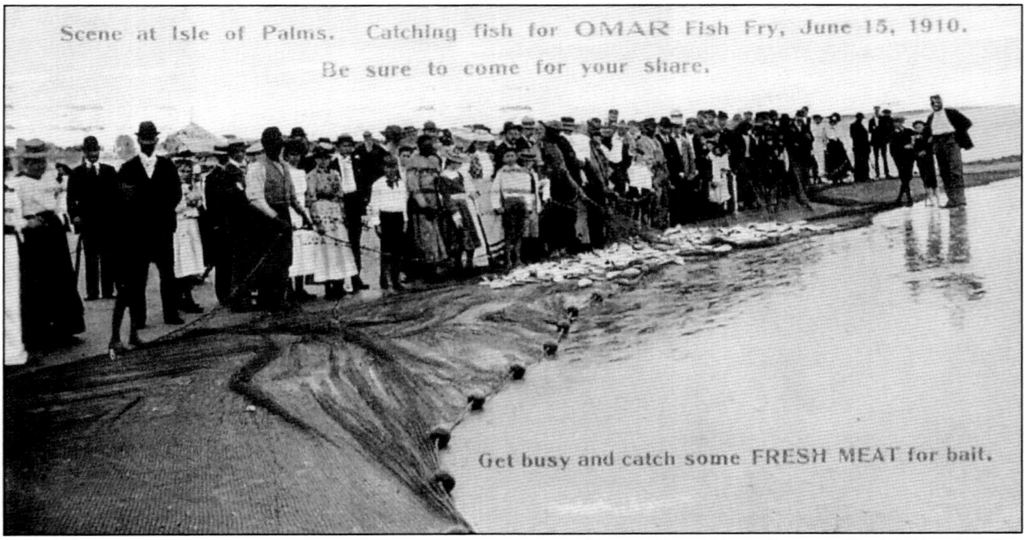


SCENE AT THE ISLE OF PALMS, CATCHING FISH FOR OMAR FISH FRY, JUNE 15, 1910. (Color Lithography, 3 1/2" X 5 1/2", [German Printer Unknown], Paul C. Koeber, New York, NY, importer; 1910.) The Omar Temple used this standard seining shot on the Isle of Palms as a mail-out providing notice for their events on June 15, 1910. It is postmarked May 18, 1910 and addressed to "Hon. M.L. Smith, Camden, S.C."

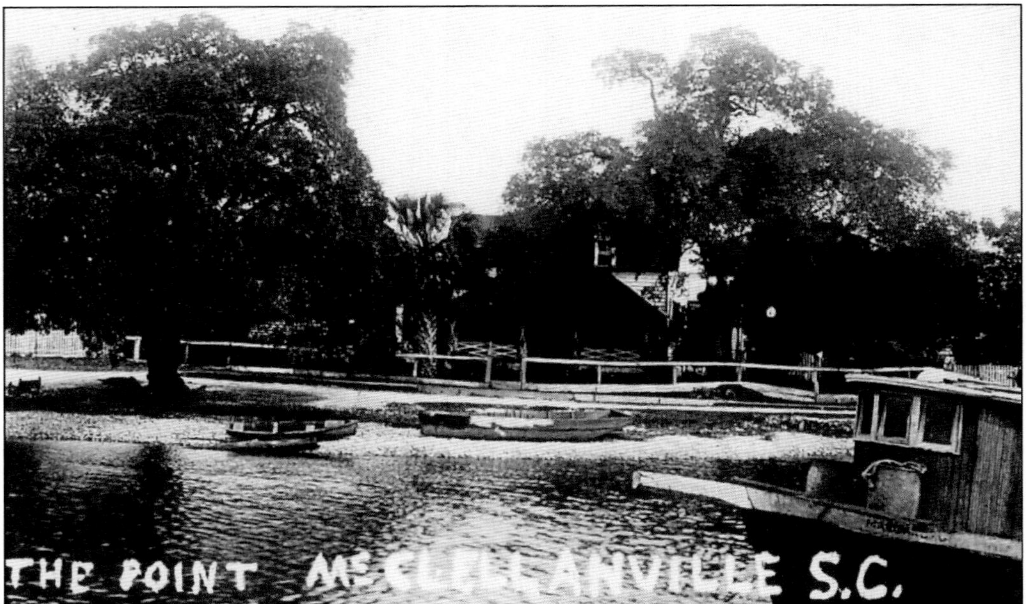


THE POINT, MCCLELLANVILLE, S.C. (Photoprint; *c.* 1910.) William P. Baldwin, in his 1984 book *The Visible Village: A McClellanville Scrapbook 1860–1945*, identified this photograph as the home of R.T. Morrison II. Baldwin speaks of the tranquillity and beauty of this isolated, self-sufficient fishing village located 40 miles north of Charleston. He quotes the Reverend John L. Girardeau (1825–1898): "McClellanville is very much like heaven. It is hard to get to, but when you get there you don't want to leave." Cards from this small, isolated town were limited in number and are very difficult to find.

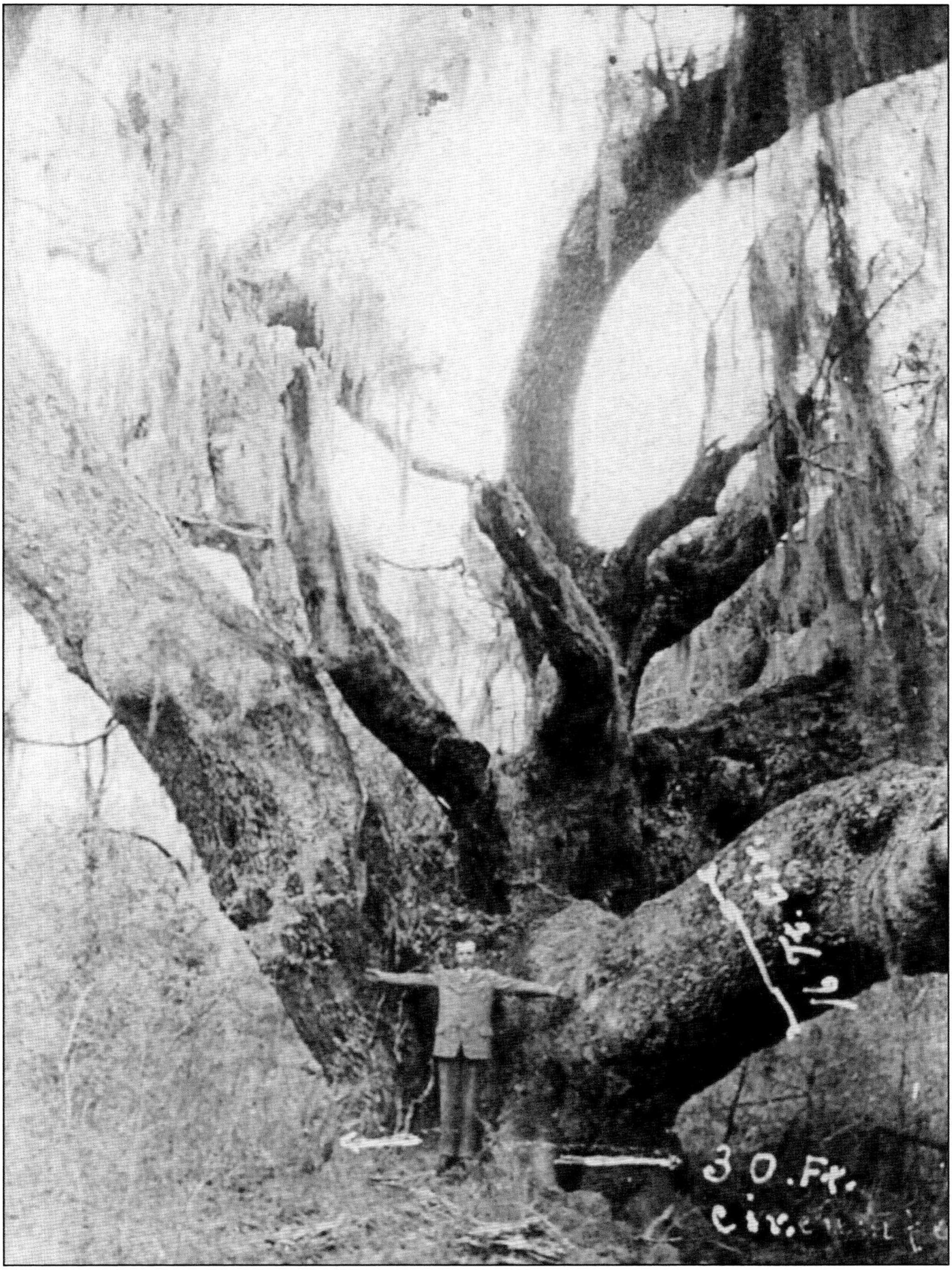


MAMMOTH OAK NEAR MCCLELLANVILLE, S.C. (Photoprint, 5½" X 3½"; c. 1910.) Baldwin includes in his book on McClellanville an undated picture of a dying Peachtree Oak, claimed to be the largest in the state. A circumference of 30 feet is indicated for the oak featured on this amateur photoprint card, identified as one near the town. Postcards with superimposed details were made in small numbers for local tourists and are occasionally found in local collections.

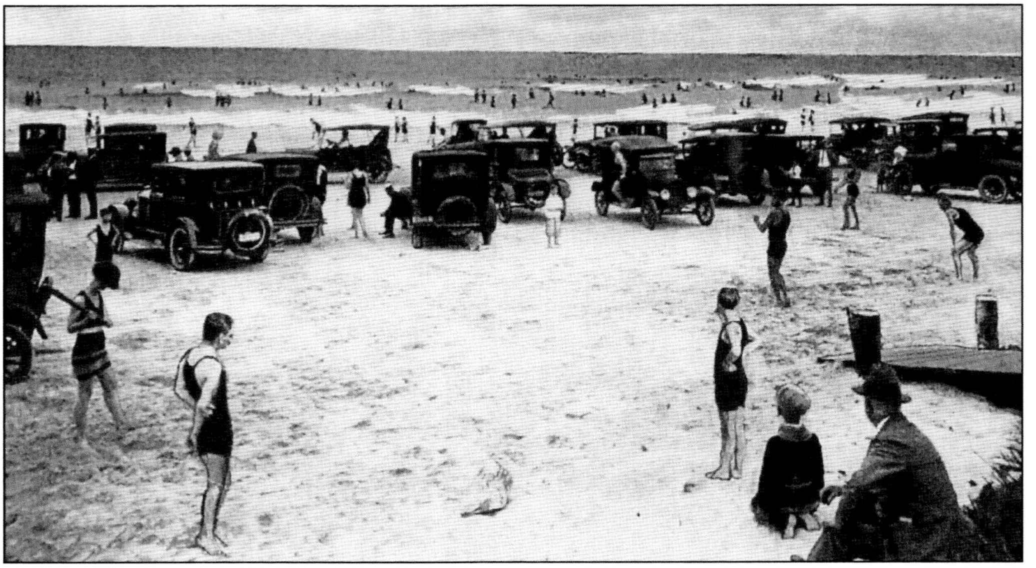

THE BATHING BEACH, FOLLY BEACH, S.C. (Color Lithography, Tichnor Bros., Inc., #126519, Boston, MA; *c.* 1930.) By 1930, when this card was mailed, the automobile had become the principal means of covering the 12-mile distance from Charleston to Folly's "beautiful 10-mile stretch of beach," which the local tourist brochures would promote as "one of the finest bathing beaches in America." This Tichnor Brothers' inexpensive postcard exemplified the quality of most domestic-issue view-cards produced for both local and national discount stores.

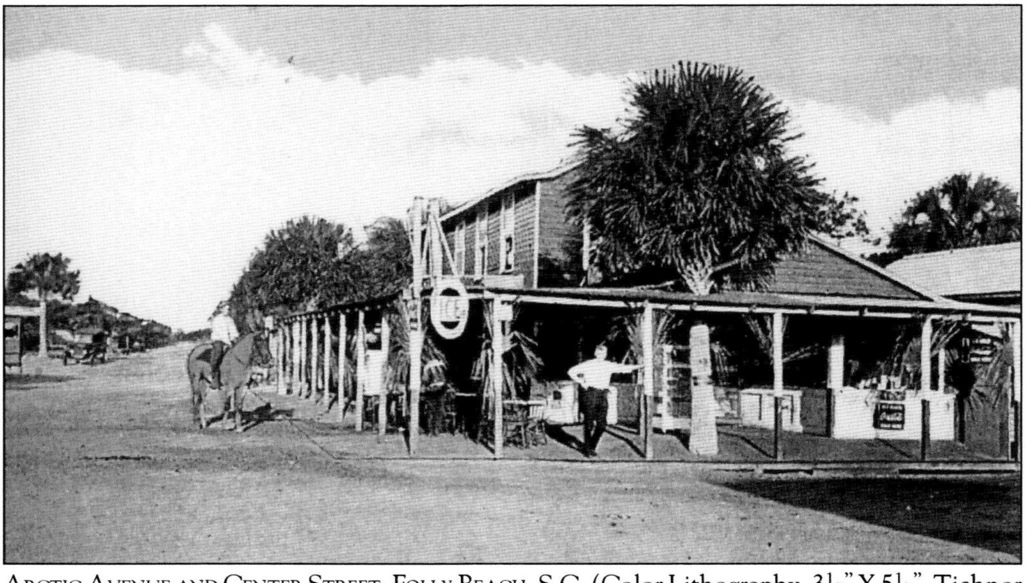

ARCTIC AVENUE AND CENTER STREET, FOLLY BEACH, S.C. (Color Lithography, 3 1/2" X 5 1/2", Tichnor Bros., Inc., #126529, Boston, MA; 1922.) This "downtown" view of Folly Beach suggests not only something of the informal twentieth-century architectural style and leisure pursuits of the place, but also the possible origin of its name. "Folly" as it applies to the island may have arisen out of the old pirate practice of referring to the Carolina Sea Islands as "Follies," as that term was used in English to mean "dense foliage" or a "clump of fir trees on a hill." Many specimens of Lowcountry trees and shrubs grow in the island's interior, as seen here.

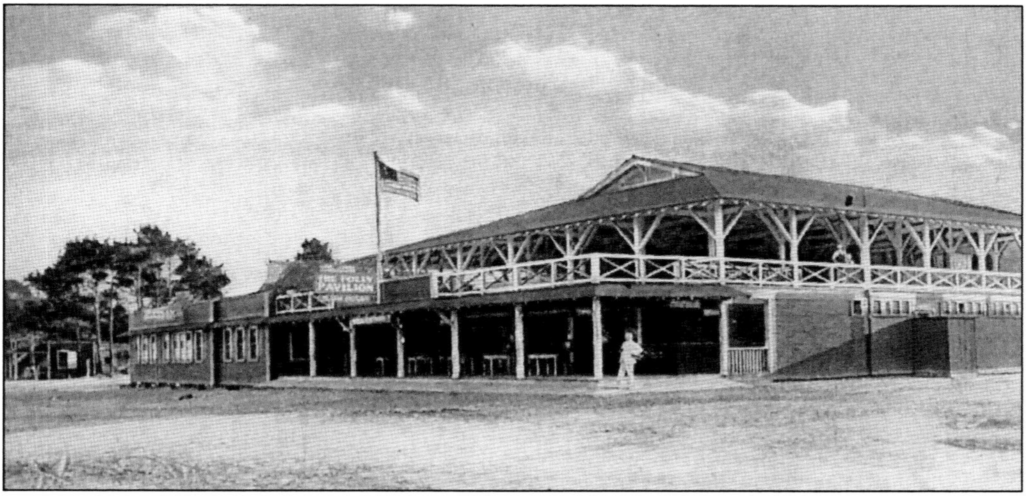


THE FOLLY PAVILION, FOLLY BEACH, S.C. (Color Lithography, 3½" X 5½", Tichnor Bros., #126523, Boston, MA; *c.* 1925.) This quiet, perhaps off-season, view of the large, simple, functional Folly Pavilion nevertheless conveys something of the truth of the claim Folly would later make that it was one of two of the "only truly public beaches in the entire region." Folly Beach—lacking the public transportation system developed for the Isle of Palms' beaches—developed later in the 1920s and only began to be documented by the common beach postcards in the mid-to-late 1920s.

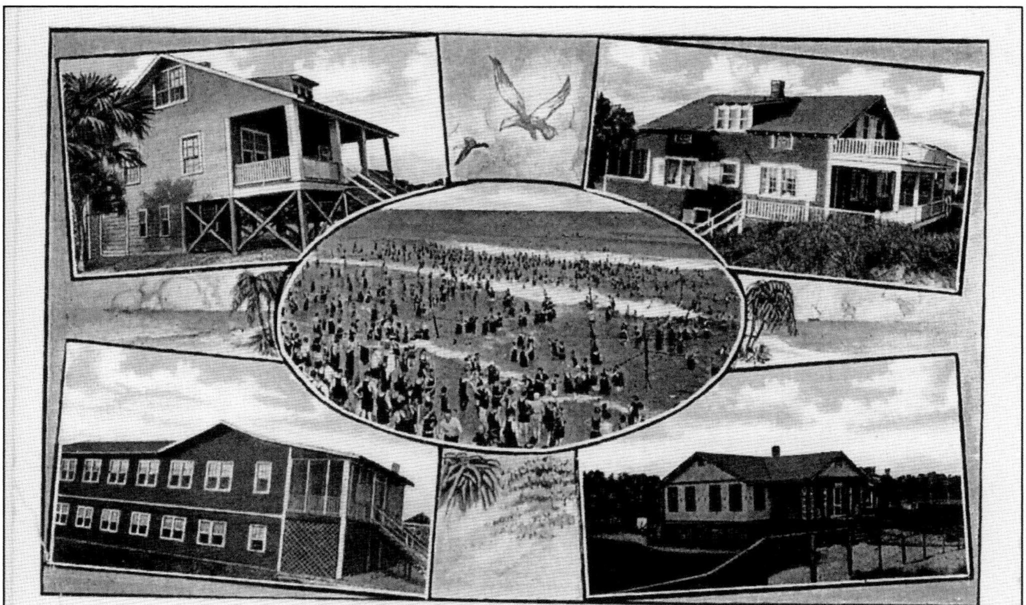


BEAUTIFUL CONSTRUCTED HOMES AT FOLLY BEACH, S.C. (Color Lithography, Tichnor Bros., #126525, Boston, MA; *c.* 1925.) The promotion of Folly Beach as a good investment for either a permanent or seasonal residence seems to be the principal focus of this multi-image card, probably published in the late 1920s. The homes and bungalows were nestled upon and among the hills between the ocean to the south and east, Lighthouse Creek on the north, and the Folly River on the west.

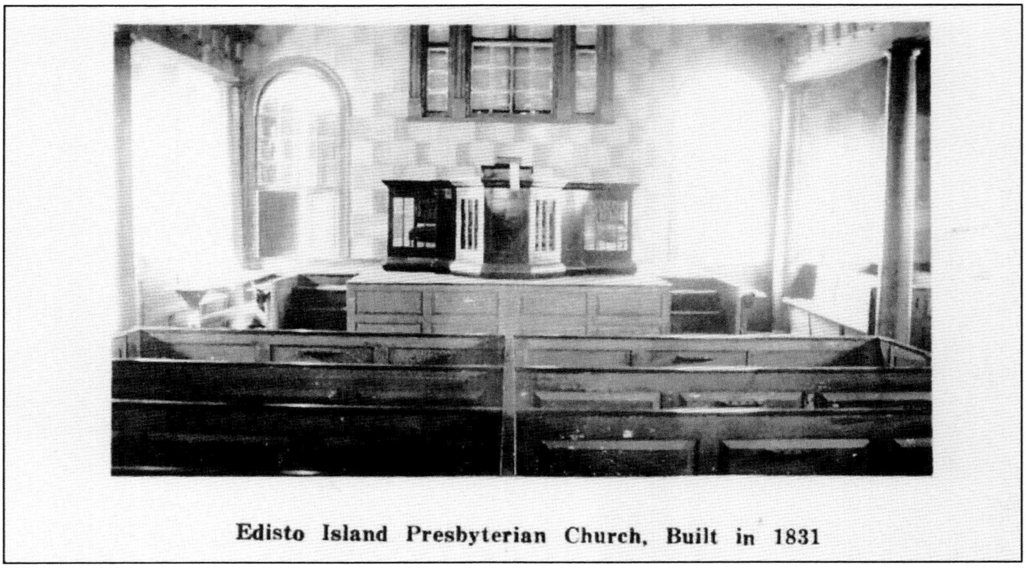


EDISTO ISLAND, PRESBYTERIAN CHURCH, BUILT IN 1831. (Photoprint, 3½" X 5½"; *c.* 1925.) "Forty miles southwest of Charleston . . . within the arms of two tidal rivers, lies a fabulous Island," Nell S. Graydon writes at the beginning of her *Tales of Edisto* (1955). The "oldest uninterrupted Presbyterian organization in South Carolina" was founded on Edisto between 1686 and 1710. It is unusual to discover an interior view of a small rural church.

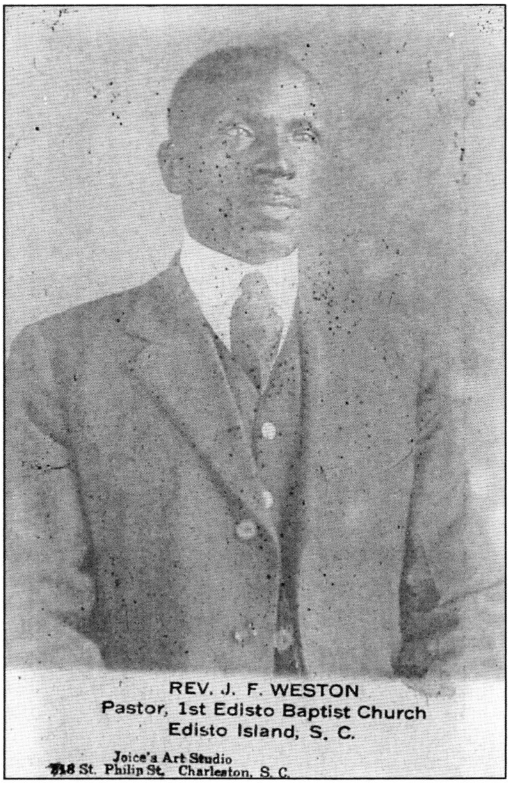


REV. J.F. WESTON, PASTOR, 1ST EDISTO BAPTIST CHURCH, EDISTO ISLAND, S.C. (Photoprint, 5½" X 3½", Joice's [sic] Art Studio, Charleston, SC; *c.* 1921.) This postcard portrait of the Reverend J.F. Weston of the First Edisto Baptist Church was made about 1921, when black photographer Garfield Joyce was operating his studio at 218 St. Philip Street in Charleston. Two years later Joyce moved his place of business to King Street, and by the end of the decade he was no longer in Charleston. This is the only example of Joyce's photography uncovered in the postcard format during this research.

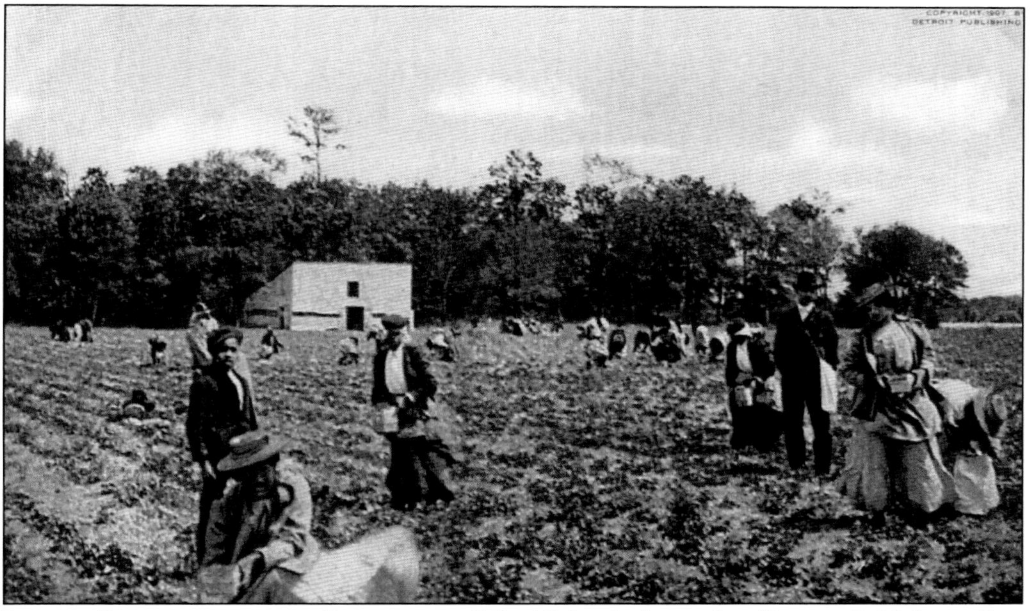

PICKING STRAWBERRIES NEAR CHARLESTON, S.C. (Color Lithography, Detroit Publishing Co., #11543, Detroit, MI; cp. 1907.) Strawberries have long been one of the principal small farm-to-market crops produced in the Charleston area. This view of children working side by side with adults was a common one in a period and region not yet subject or sensitive to considerations of child labor as a social or legal issue. This is one of a series of seventeen cards, among the largest units the Detroit Publishing Company ever produced for South Carolina.

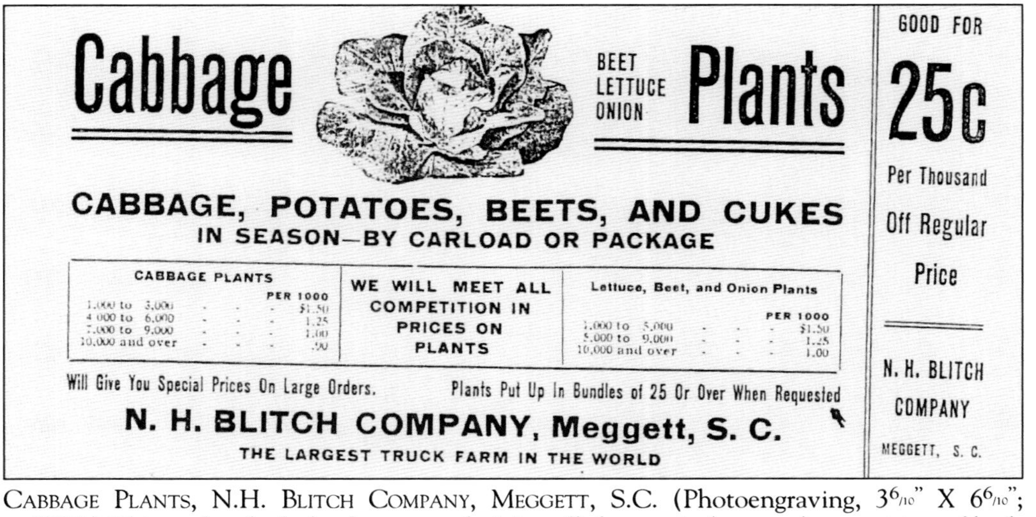


CABBAGE PLANTS, N.H. BLITCH COMPANY, MEGGETT, S.C. (Photoengraving, $3^{6/10}$" X $6^{6/10}$"; c. 1906.) This undated wholesale rate card giving all the particulars on the provision of both setting plants and harvested produce was sent to W.B. Boyle in Sumter by the N.H. Blitch Company of Meggett, which claimed to be "the largest truck farm in the world." Meggett became known as the center of truck farming in Charleston County. This seldom-seen advertising card was produced by a local printer.

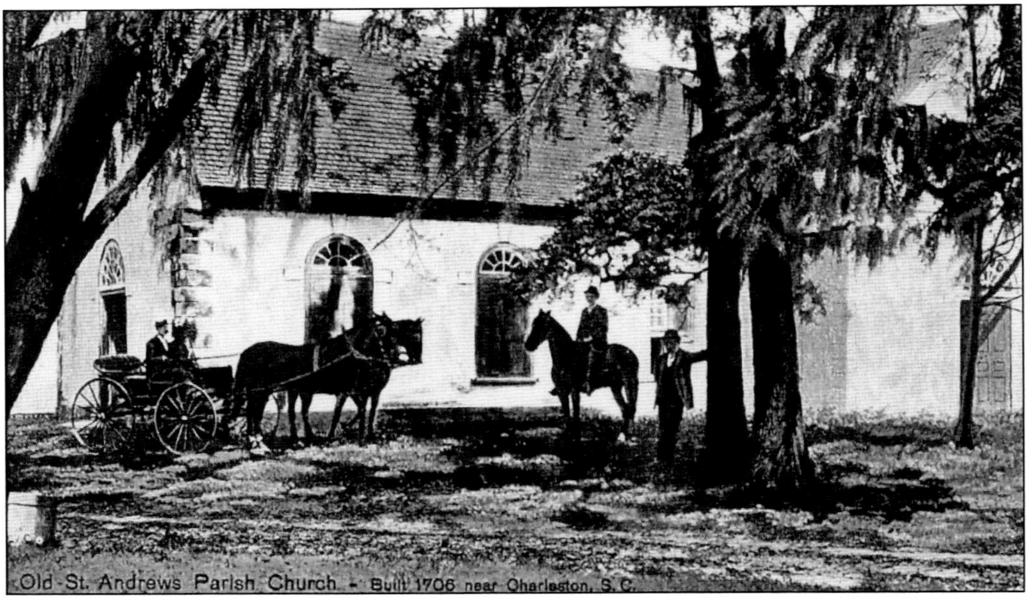


OLD ST. ANDREWS PARISH CHURCH . . . CHARLESTON, S.C. (Color Lithography, 3 1/2" X 5 1/2", [Louis Glaser, Leipzig, Germany]; Hugh C. Leighton, #26354, Portland, ME, importer; *c.* 1907.) The construction of Old St. Andrew's Episcopal Church, 2604 Ashley River Road, began in 1706. According to Mary Moore Jacoby's notations in her book *The Churches of Charleston and the Lowcountry* (1994), its walls are "the oldest examples of Anglican architecture in South Carolina." Between 1891 and 1955 the church was dormant, except for occasional services.

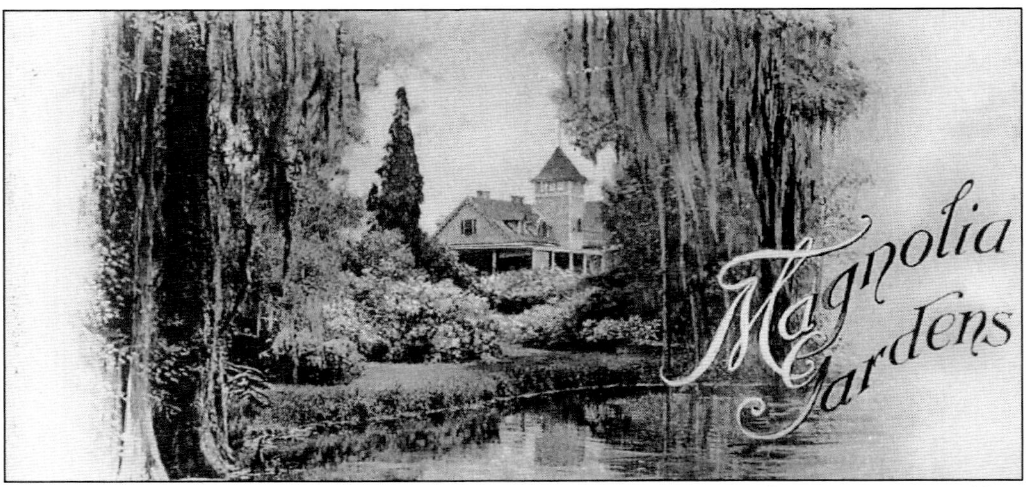


MAGNOLIA GARDENS, CHARLESTON, S.C. (Hand-Colored Collotype, Albertype Co., Brooklyn, NY; *c.* 1920.) Seen across the lake and through the moss-hung trees, on the cover card of a twelve-card booklet of hand-colored images of Magnolia Gardens, is the Magnolia Plantation House. Actually the third structure to occupy this site, it is the original Summerville cottage, with later additions, of the Reverend John Grimke-Drayton, who established the gardens. In 1870 he had it floated to Magnolia on barges and mounted upon the foundations of the second manor house, which Sherman had burned in 1865. The Gardens have long been famous for their many rare trees and shrubs, with forests of camellias of all varieties and azaleas in many colors.

# *Two*

# Berkeley County

Picture postcards from Berkeley County for this period are scarce. But the few that have surfaced in the course of extensive investigations for this project nevertheless provide the basic clues to its identity. The county is one whose social, economic, religious, and architectural roots have been defined by a long history of plantation development, especially that of rice cultivation. The handful of cards representing this county reflect the beauty and richness of the land, the strength and tenacity of an agrarian people, and the simplicity and elegance of the English church tradition. Interested persons may turn to p. 93 to see what the Berkeley County Court House looked like between 1885 and 1895, when Mount Pleasant was the county seat.

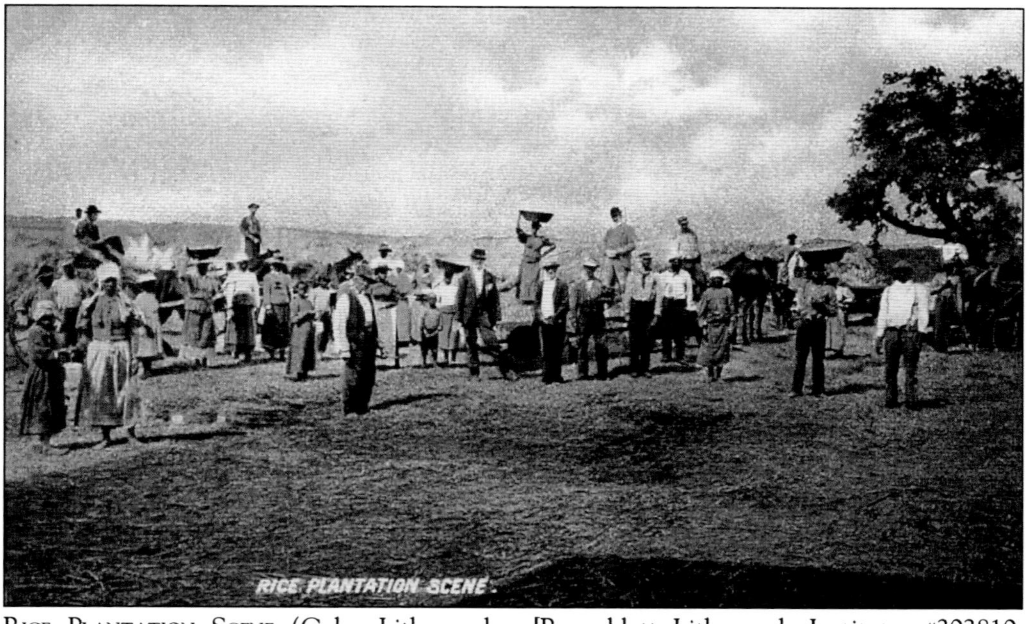


Rice Plantation Scene (Color Lithography, [Rosenblatt Lithograph Institute, #202810, Frankfurt, Germany]; 1909.) "The rice plantation flourished in South Carolina for two hundred years—from the 1690's to the final devastation by the hurricane of 1911," historian George C. Rogers Jr. has written. Berkeley County took the leading part in the early production of rice in the province. Even at the turn of this century, Berkeley still had 9,212 acres under cultivation, producing nearly six million pounds of rice in 1900, according to Robert P. Stockton (*Historic Resources of Berkeley County South Carolina*, 1990). This rice plantation scene shows how labor-intensive the growing of the crop was, and who bore the principal burden of it.

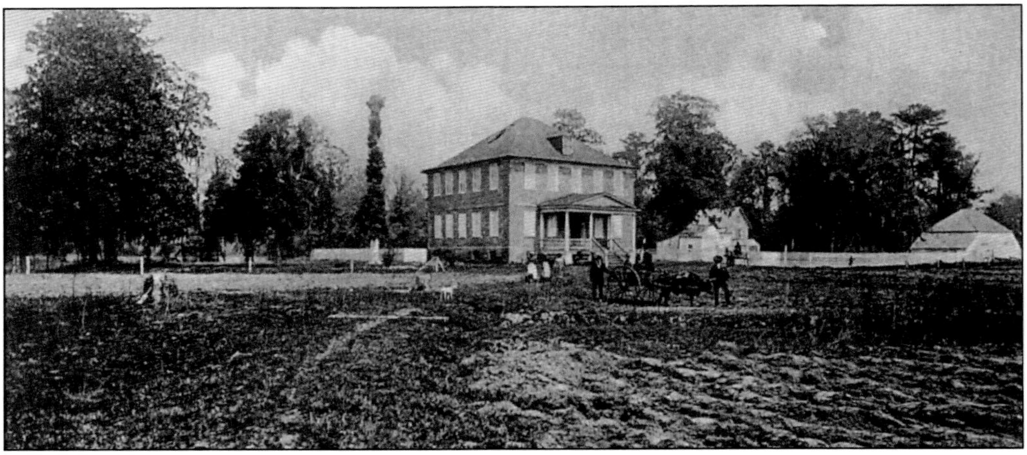

INGLESIDE HOUSE, INGLESIDE, S.C. (Collotype, 3½" X 5½", [Trenkler & Co., #80859, Leipzig, Germany]; G.G. Lange, K.L.V. Schwalbach, Germany, exporters; American Historical Art Publishers, NY, importers; 1909.) Ingleside House was a pre-Revolutionary home once located some 8 miles from Summerville and fronting on the Southern Railroad tracks. Located in the historic and highly desirable St. James Goose Creek section of Berkeley County, it was situated on an extensive tract known for its fine rice fields. The late Katherine D.M. Simons (1890–1969), in her book *Historic Spots Near Summerville* (*c.* 1924), refers to this house as "The Hayes," identifies its first owner as John Parker, and says that it "was burned not many years ago."

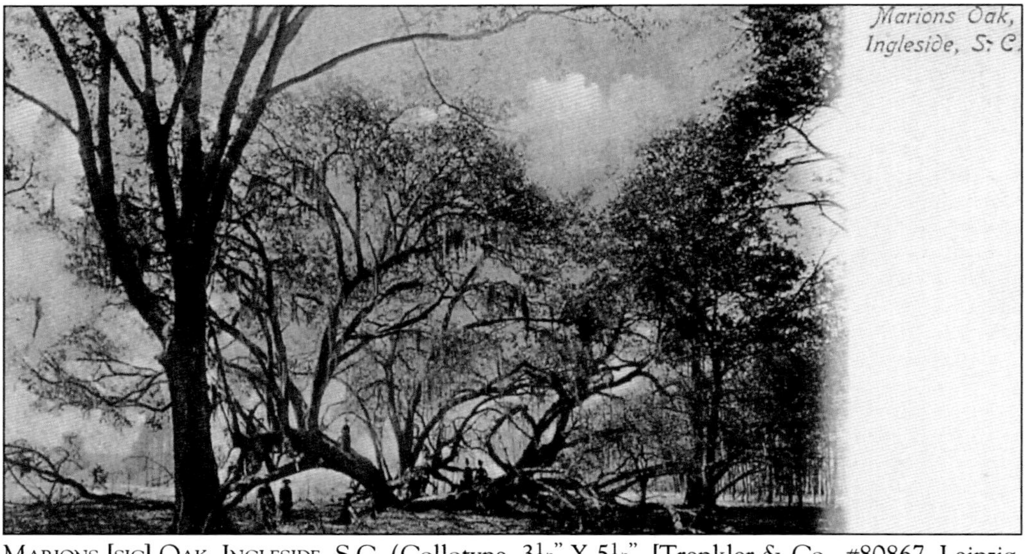


MARIONS [SIC] OAK, INGLESIDE, S.C. (Collotype, 3½" X 5½", [Trenkler & Co., #80867, Leipzig, Germany]; G.G. Lange, K.L.V. Schwalbach & Co., Germany, exporters; American Historical Art Publishers, NY, importers; *c.* 1908.) Marion's Oak at Ingleside, in this view, seems to invest the place with an eerie sense of beauty and to dwarf the inhabitants who nonetheless cling to it and linger around it. Katherine Simons locates the giant oak, "now split in three," as between the ruins of the old Colonial house and the railroad track. She acknowledges that this tree had many rivals in lower South Carolina for the honor of being identified as "Marion's Oak," the scene of his historic sweet potato banquet in the Revolution. But she concludes that this is probably the old tree that "saw them dine."

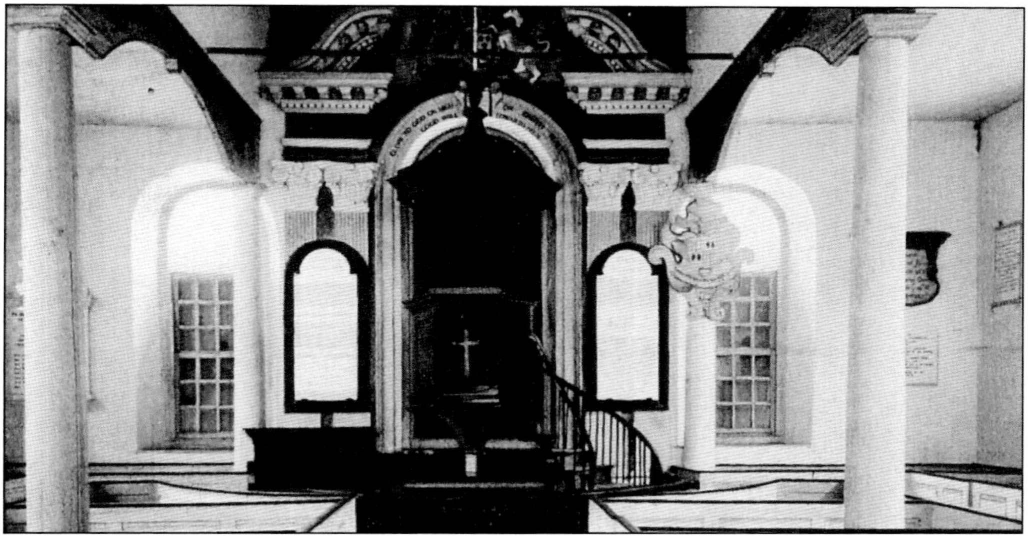

INTERIOR OF GOOSE CREEK CHURCH . . . NEAR CHARLESTON, S.C. (Color Lithography, 3½" X 5½", Gray Lithographic Co., N.Y., NY; *c.* 1908.) Inside St. James's Church, back of the chancel and supported by four Corinthian pilasters, can be seen the Royal Arms of Great Britain from the time of Queen Anne. Made of stucco and brilliantly colored, this adornment may have saved the church from destruction by the British during the Revolution. The aisles are paved with flagstones, and a gallery is built over the entrance. There are twenty-four pews of the old square box pattern.

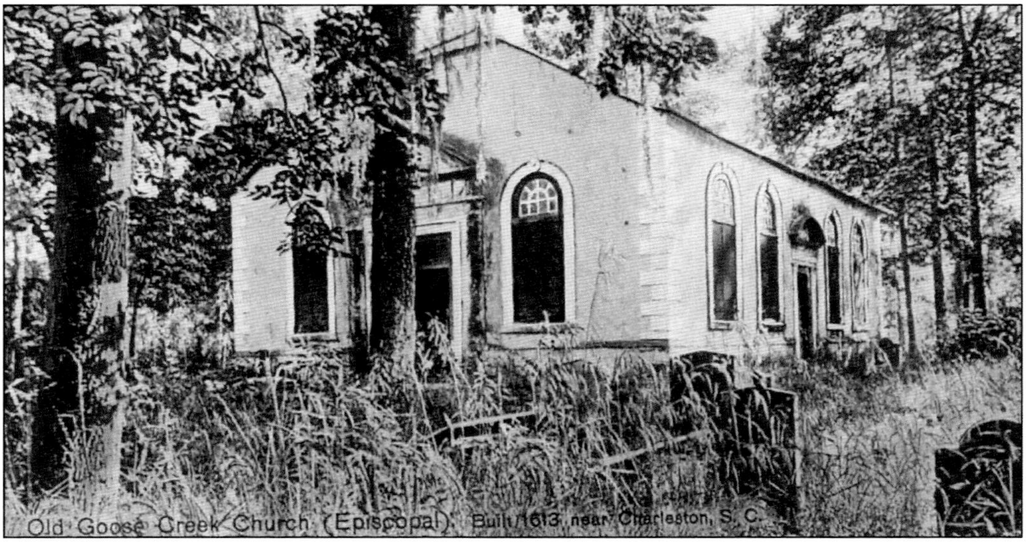


OLD GOOSE CREEK CHURCH (EPISCOPAL) BUILT 1718 NEAR CHARLESTON, S.C. (Color Lithography, 3½" X 5½", [Louis Glaser Co., Leipzig, Germany]; Hugh C. Leighton, #26355, Portland, ME, importer; 1908.) The St. James Goose Creek Episcopal Church, some 10 miles east of Summerville, was one of the original ten parishes established in South Carolina by the church act of 1706. The slate-roofed, 50-by-40-foot brick sanctuary is the oldest Anglican church building still standing outside of Charleston. A National Historic Landmark, it is considered architecturally one of the finest churches in the Lowcountry. The sender of this card remarks, "In this church yard my Grand Father is buried."

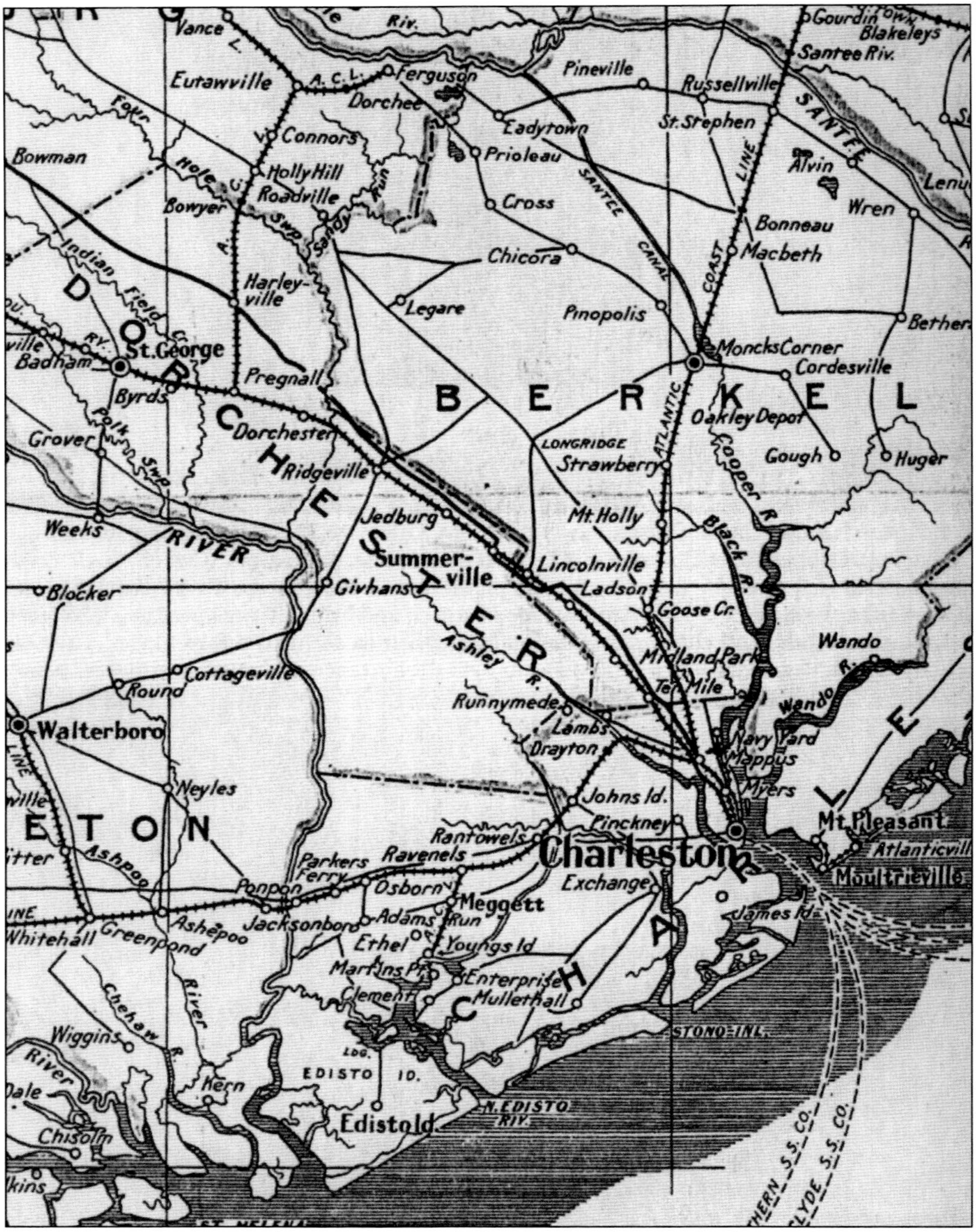


Regional County Map. The sections of Berkeley and Dorchester which include Goose Creek, Summerville, and St. George are shown on this 1913 map of North and South Carolina published by the National Survey Company of Portland, Maine. Also worth noting are the several railroads—especially the Southern Rail Road which ran northwest from Charleston through St. George.

# *Three*

# DORCHESTER COUNTY

An old center of agrarian culture, Dorchester County, some 613 square miles in area, was established in 1897 from portions of Colleton and Berkeley Counties. Its rich old rural tradition is reflected in many of the images here, which nevertheless focus upon the county's two principal towns, Summerville and St. George.

According to Katherine Simons, Summerville was given its name by planters from Dorchester and thereabouts, "who, in the summer, moved their families from the lowlands by the river to a higher, drier, and notoriously healthy spot in the pineland." But the town's golden age as a winter resort is the one that the viewer will discover here, when, between 1890 and 1920, the town blossomed as a health spa and rural retreat which still could capitalize on its proximity to Charleston.

St. George, closer to the outer edges of the county, is the westernmost place covered by this book. And it is fitting that the volume should conclude with images of loaded cotton wagons in town and religious camp grounds down the road. For the mix of town and country, of land and buildings and community—old and new, of labor and faith, and of hardship and beauty, is one which will also characterize the images of the state and the experience of South Carolinians beyond the peculiar glories of Charleston, Berkeley, and Dorchester.

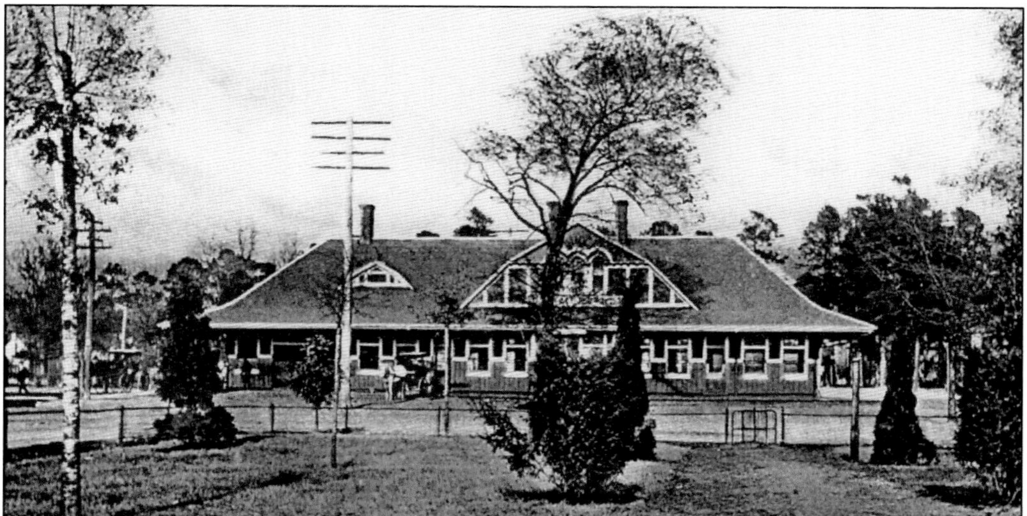

SOUTHERN R.R. STATION, SUMMERVILLE, S.C. (Color Lithography, 3½" X 5½", [Alfred Schulze, Berlin Germany]; American News Co., #A3237, New York, NY, importer; *c.* 1906.) Many visitors to Summerville would have traveled by rail and arrived at its Southern Railway's passenger station, an illustration of which was included as a completed project in the promotional booklet *Designs from the Work of Frank P. Milburn*, published by the architect in Columbia in 1903. The station was demolished in the 1950s.

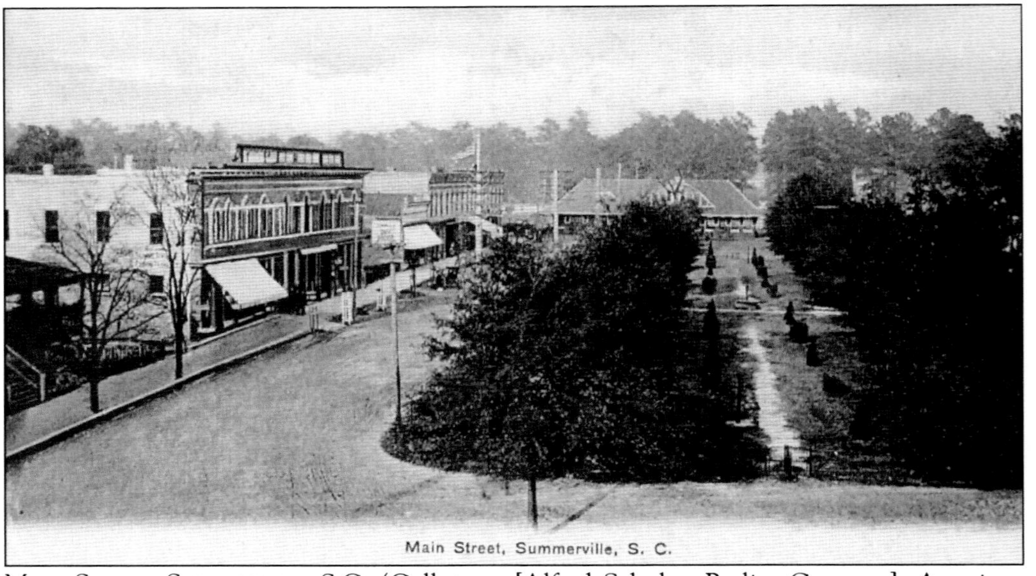


MAIN STREET, SUMMERVILLE, S.C. (Collotype, [Alfred Schulze, Berlin, Germany]; American News Co., #A3237, New York, NY, importer; 1907.) This postcard view of Summerville's Main Street, probably taken from the bell tower on top of the three-story town hall (built in 1892), shows the Summerville Furniture Company (to the left, with the awning) and the railway passenger station in the center beyond the trees.

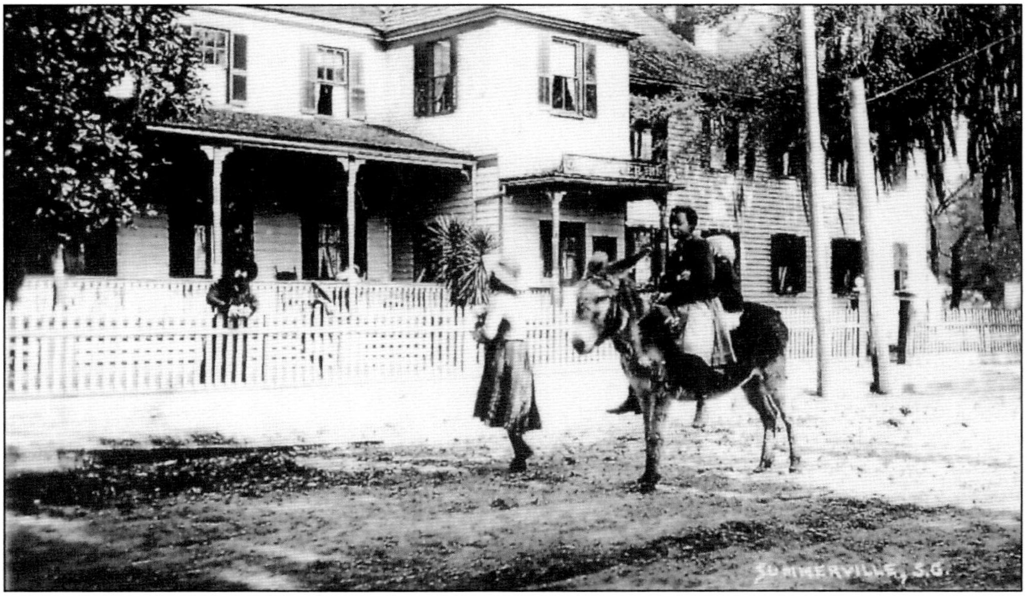


DORCHESTER INN. (Photoprint, 3½" X 5½", Harris Photo Post Card Co., Pittston, PA; 1909.) "This is where we are staying," writes a child on the reverse of a card sent on January 13, 1909, to a Sunday school teacher back in Montclair, New Jersey. This amateur photoprint reflects the residential quietness and neighborliness of the modest Dorchester Inn on Sumter Avenue. It began as the Dorchester Hotel, then became the Dorchester Inn, and finally, in 1912, the Carolina Inn. It was demolished in the 1960s. Harris was a small mail-order company that probably placed classified ads in various national trade and general publications.

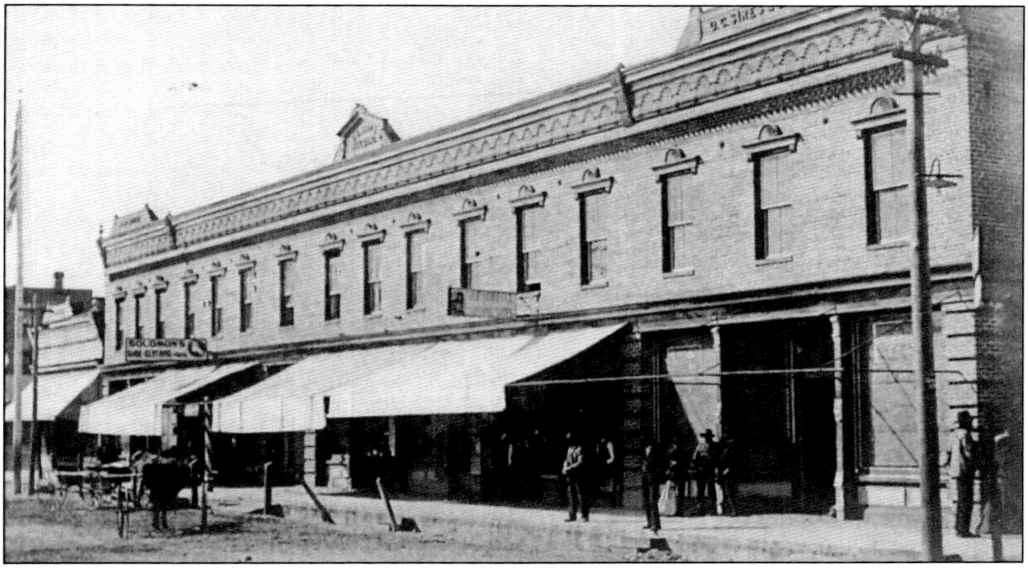

Sires Clothing & Shoes Co., Summerville, S.C. (Photoprint, 3½" X 5½"; *c.* 1907.) Sires and Brothers may have issued this card, which bears their name and shows their establishment most prominently here among the storefronts in this view of Summerville's main business block, which may have included a bank, a pharmacy, and a grocery store. The name "Solomon's" appears on a sign to the left, and the presence of a flag at the far left may indicate the location of the post office. Rare photoprint cards of this type are found occasionally.

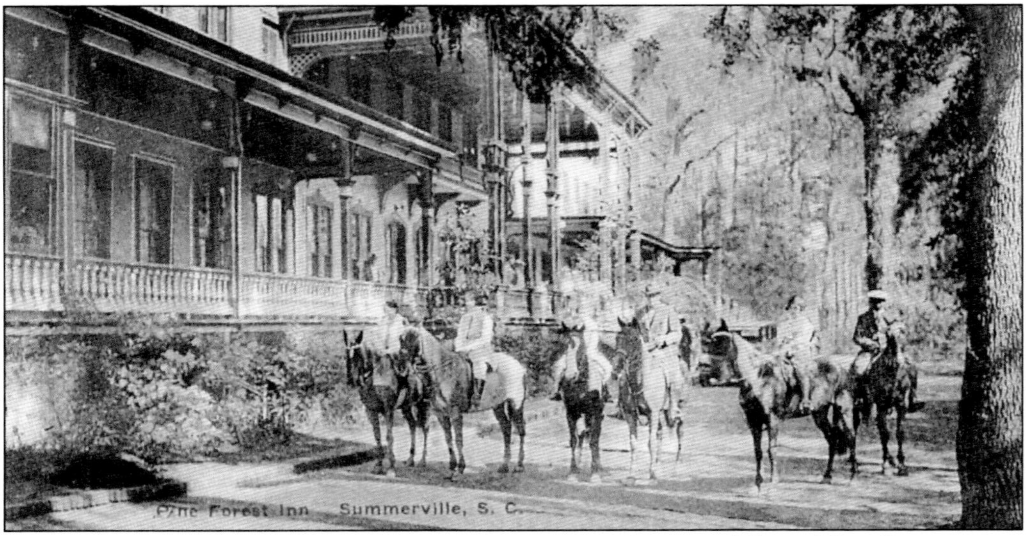


Pine Forest Inn, Summerville, S.C. (Hand-Colored Collotype, 3½" X 5½", Albertype Co., Brooklyn, NY; *c.* 1920.) In its inaugural issue of May 15, 1892, an illustrated monthly magazine published in Summerville called *The Pine Forest_Echo* featured an article on "The Palace in the Pines" and described the Pine Forest Inn's 225-foot-long grand piazza, which fronted nearly south and provided a sweeping view of the dense pine forest. Horseback riding was a favorite amusement, as good horses were easily obtainable. The inn had opened in 1891 under the ownership of Captain Frederick W. Wagener, the Charleston merchant of German descent who figured so prominently in the region's business and cultural affairs.

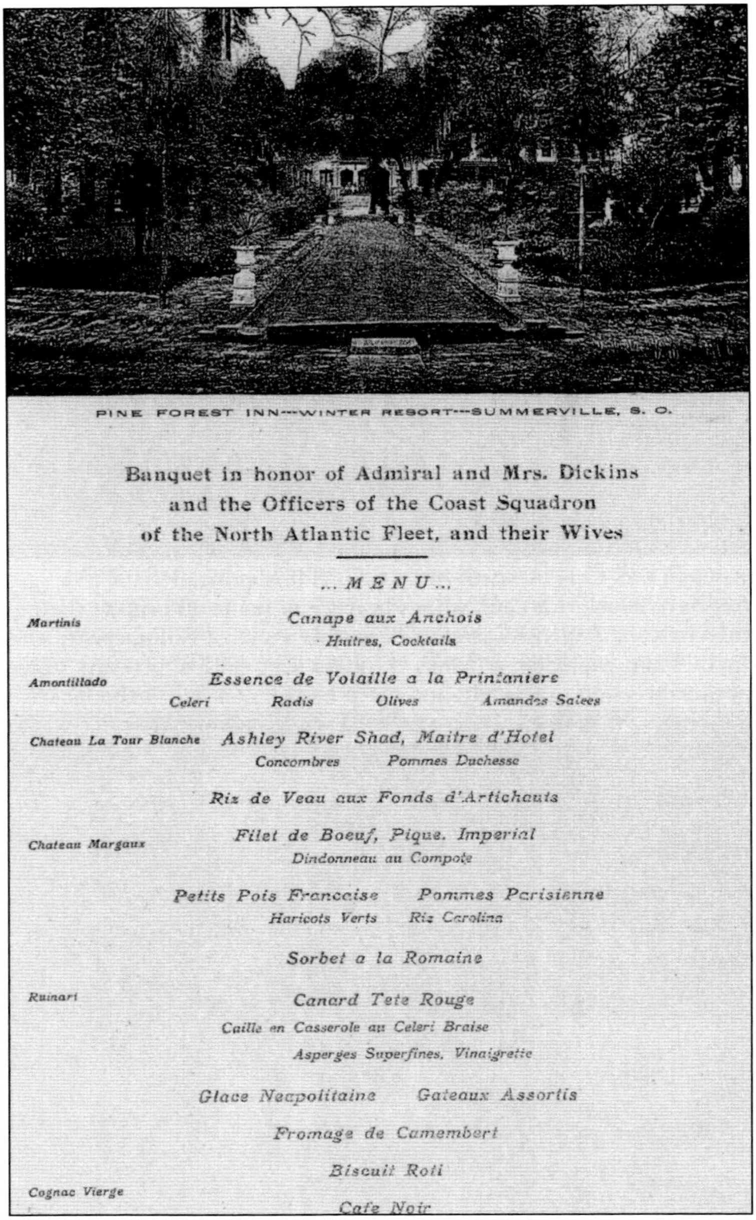

PINE FOREST INN—WINTER RESORT—SUMMERVILLE, S. C.

Banquet in honor of Admiral and Mrs. Dickins
and the Officers of the Coast Squadron
of the North Atlantic Fleet, and their Wives

...MENU...

*Martinis* — *Canape aux Anchois*
*Huitres, Cocktails*

*Amontillado* — *Essence de Volaille a la Printaniere*
*Celeri* *Radis* *Olives* *Amandes Salees*

*Chateau La Tour Blanche* — *Ashley River Shad, Maitre d'Hotel*
*Concombres* *Pommes Duchesse*

*Riz de Veau aux Fonds d'Artichauts*

*Chateau Margaux* — *Filet de Boeuf, Pique, Imperial*
*Dindonneau au Compote*

*Petits Pois Francaise* *Pommes Parisienne*
*Haricots Verts* *Riz Carolina*

*Sorbet a la Romaine*

*Ruinart* — *Canard Tete Rouge*
*Caille en Casserole au Celeri Braise*
*Asperges Superfines, Vinaigrette*

*Glace Neapolitaine* *Gateaux Assortis*

*Fromage de Camembert*

*Biscuit Roti*

*Cognac Vierge* — *Cafe Noir*

PINE FOREST INN—WINTER RESORT—SUMMERVILLE, S.C. (MENU, FEBRUARY 3RD, 1906). (Color Lithography, 10 1/8" X 5 1/2", [Ainslie & Grabow Press, Swampscott, MA]; 1906.) The Pine Forest Inn was the setting for a party of about one hundred at a special banquet on February 3, 1906, hosted by Captain Wagener, honoring Admiral and Mrs. Dickins. Commander of the Coast Squadron, Admiral Dickins had established his headquarters at Charleston that winter. Menu cards—such as this one printed by a national resort, hotel, and steamship line stationery supplier—were produced with blank menu sections and a standard view of the resort and were sold in bulk volume. The patrons could write a note to family or friends on the tear-off postcards while waiting for the meal. Many of the mailed cards have been found, but few have been located with the menu attached.

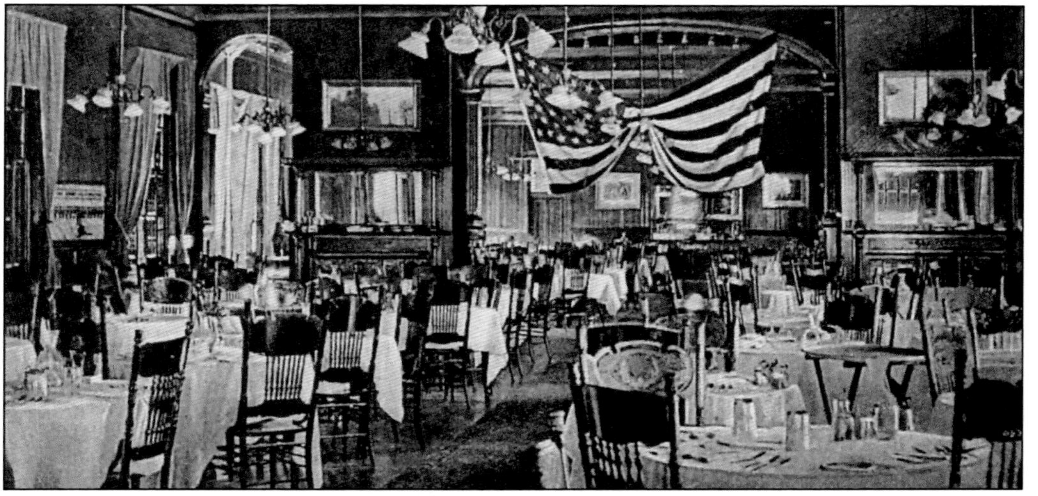

MAIN DINING ROOM, PINE FOREST INN, SUMMERVILLE, S.C. (Sepia Collotype, 3½" X 5½", [Stengel and Co., #96390, Dresden, Germany]; 1908.) The presence of the flag in this view of the main dining room of the Pine Forest Inn may represent special decorations installed for a party of visiting military or political dignitaries. With the wealth and prestige behind it of Captain Wagener, who had been the key leader and private financial backer of the exposition of 1901–1902, the inn became a turn-of-the-century Lowcountry showplace and retreat where state visitors were entertained. It had been built to a design by S.A. Woods, a New York architect who was an expert in planning such hotels.

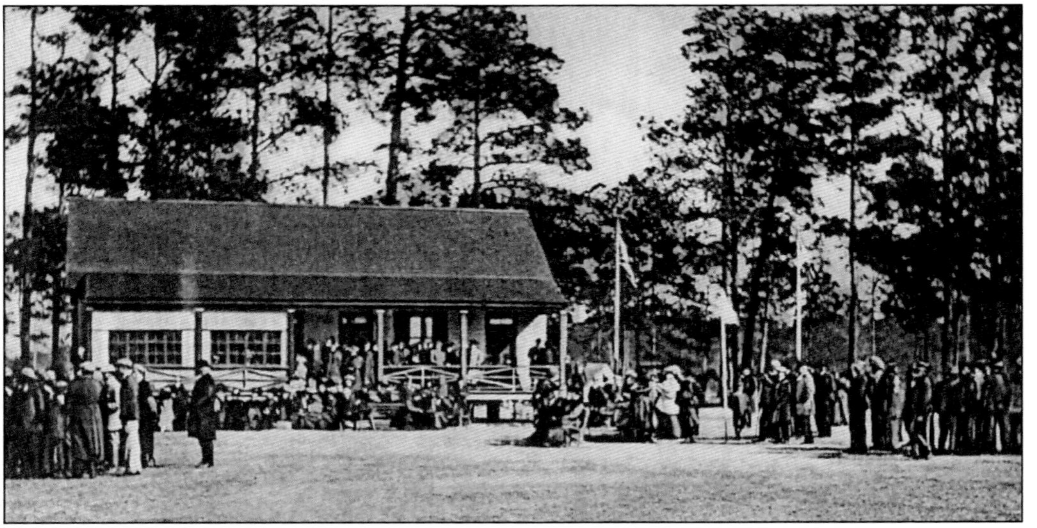

AT FINISH OF A GOLF EVENT, PINE FOREST INN, SUMMERVILLE, S.C. (Hand-Colored Collotype, 3½" X 5½", [Stengel and Co., #96387, Dresden, Germany]; *c.* 1908.) The December 1900 article in *The Exposition* mentions the Pine Forest Golf Links as among the best in the country. Six years later a full-page illustrated ad in the Charleston *City Directory* would carry a paragraph explaining that "the former excellent golf links" had been extended to an eighteen-hole course, that artificial bunkers had been added and "the hazards difficult enough to be interesting." The turf was "the finest in the South," and "a good club-house—less than a mile from the inn—was situated on the first tee, commanding a view of the entire course." The links were to be in the charge of a professional instructor, and tournaments would be a feature during the season.

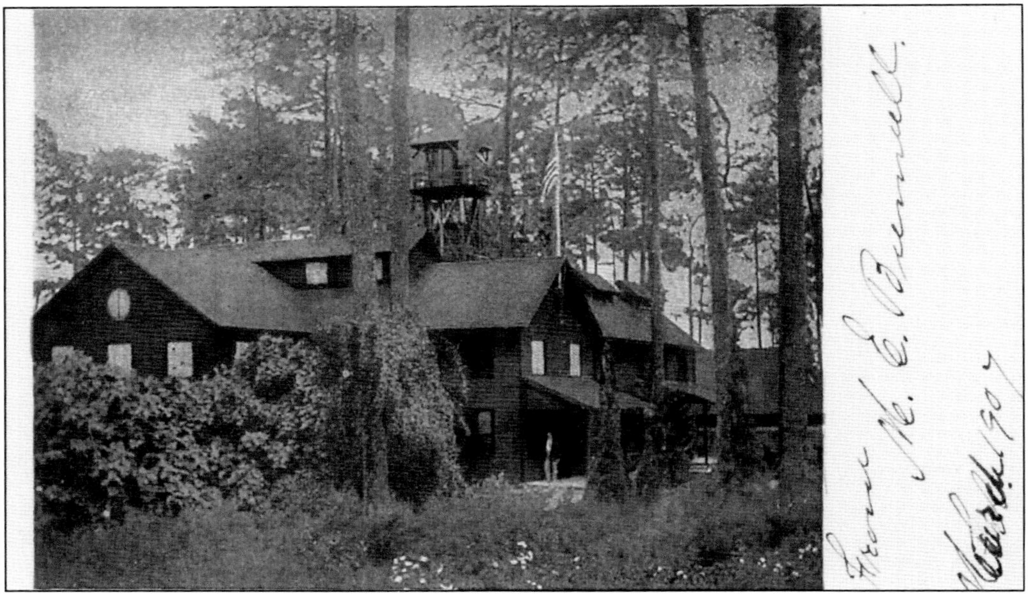

TEA FACTORY AT PINEHURST TEA GARDENS, SUMMERVILLE, SOUTH CAROLINA. (Color Lithography, 3½" X 5½", [Ainslie & Grabow Press, Swampscott, MA]; 1907.) The Pinehurst Tea Farm was established by Connecticut native Charles Upham Shepard on 500 acres of land purchased in 1888–1889 from descendants of the Middleton family. Shepard died in 1915 and, according to the late historian Legare Walker Sr., the buildings and all of the machinery used in the process of drying and manufacturing tea were destroyed in 1919.

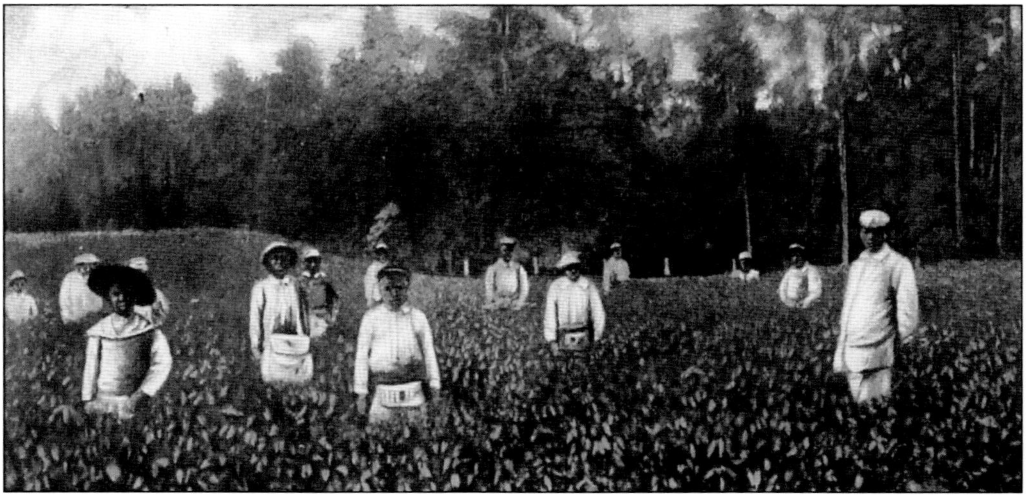

PICKERS IN A TEA FIELD AT PINEHURST TEA FARM, SUMMERVILLE, S.C. (Color Lithograph, 3½" X 5½", [Trenkler, #7092, Leipzig, Germany]; 1912.) According to the January 1901 issue of *The Exposition*, the visitor to Pinehurst could see—in addition to the machinery required for the manufacture of black and green tea, including that which had been substituted for manual labor in the curing of black tea—"a well trained body of colored children who pluck the tea-leaf, and the school, where they receive, gratuitously, a thorough education at such seasons as they are not occupied in field work." The plucking and manufacturing process lasted from May through September. This card is postmarked March 29, 1912.

TEA LEAVES AND FLOWERS AT PINEHURST TEA GARDEN, SUMMERVILLE, SOUTH CAROLINA. (Color Lithography, [Ainslie & Grabow Press, Swampscott, MA]; *c.* 1906.) Dr. Shepard's Pinehurst was claimed as the first place in the United States where tea was cultivated and manufactured for commercial use. And while tea leaves and flowers were featured on this early advertising card, Shepard established gardens which grew many other species of rare and exotic plants, shrubs, and trees.

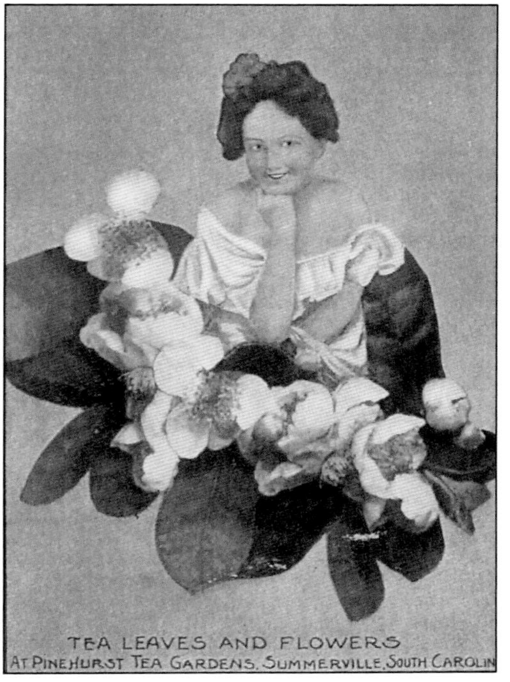


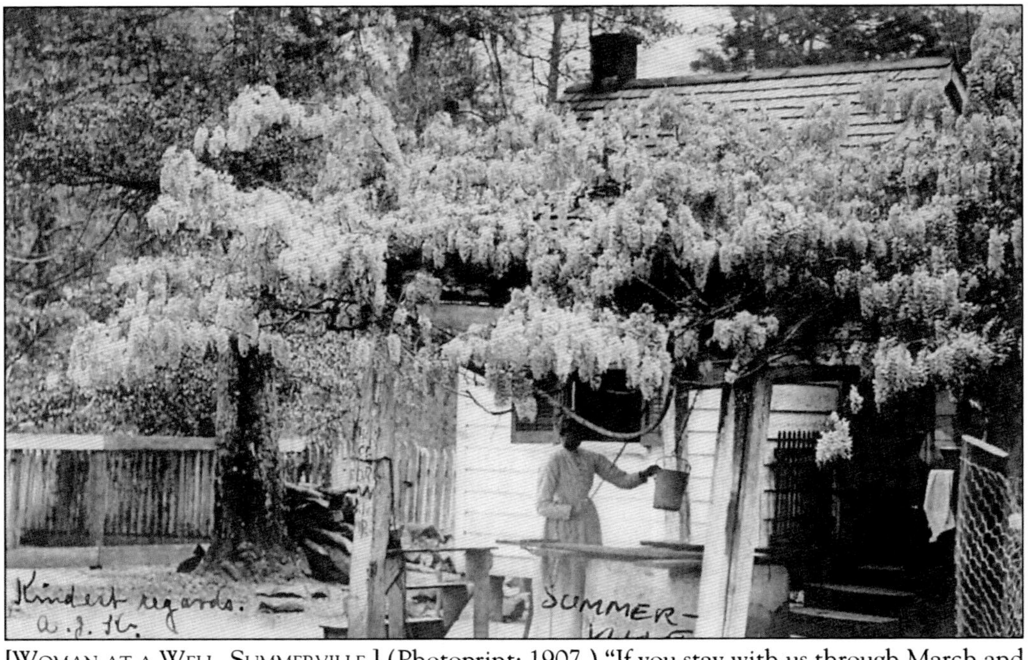


[WOMAN AT A WELL, SUMMERVILLE.] (Photoprint; 1907.) "If you stay with us through March and April," Katherine Simons once wrote, "you will see [Summerville] and its environs bloom into a floral fair." This spontaneous portrait of a woman at a well behind a modest dwelling enveloped by wisteria was mailed from Summerville in April 1907.

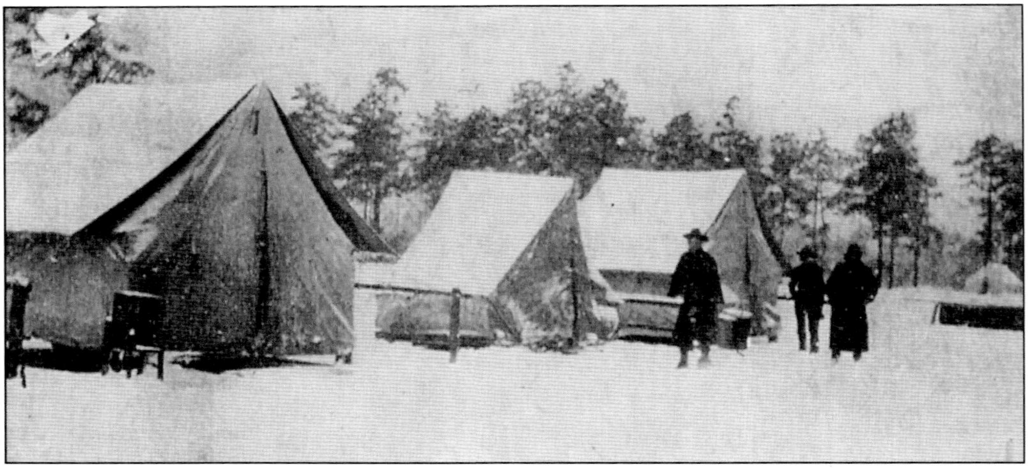

OFFICERS QUARTERS, CAMP MARION, 1899, SUMMERVILLE, S.C. (Halftone, 3 1/2" X 5 1/2", McIntyre Dry Goods Co., Putnam, CT; Major A.D. McIntyre, photographer; *c.* 1902.) The two postcards on this page, among the earliest and rarest photographic finds associated with this project, are the only known surviving images which document the existence at Summerville of the encampment established there to prepare cavalry troops—up to about five thousand men—for duty in Cuba and Puerto Rico during the Spanish-American War. By November 10, 1898, Camp Marion had been named and set up on gently sloping ground among the pines at a spot known as Gadsden's Farm, about one mile from the depot of the South Carolina and Georgia Railroad and within view of the Pine Forest Inn. Thomas P. Lesesne claims that two regiments and a battalion were trained here. This small, unique postcard set was published by a veteran of this war and printed by his hometown press.

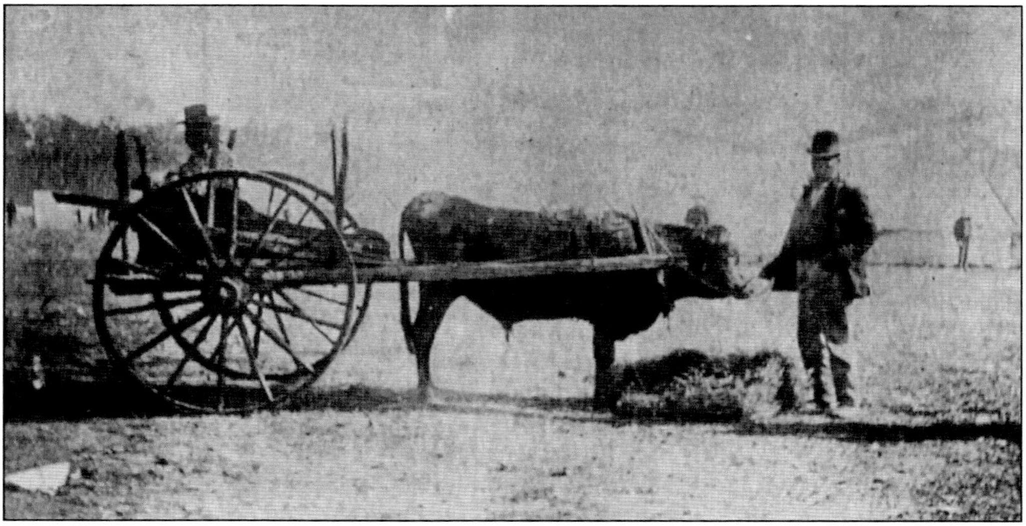

CAMP FOLLOWERS, CAMP MARION, 1899, SUMMERVILLE, S.C. (Halftone, 3 1/2" X 5 1/2", McIntyre Dry Goods Co., Putnam, CT; Major A.D. McIntyre, photographer; *c.* 1902.) About the time this photograph of camp followers was made in Summerville, Booker T. Washington wrote, in *The Future of the American Negro* (1900), "From the results of the war with Spain let us learn this . . . that no nation can disregard the interest of any portion of its members without that nation becoming weak and corrupt. . . . From this spectacle I pray God that America will learn a lesson in respect to the ten million Negroes in this country."

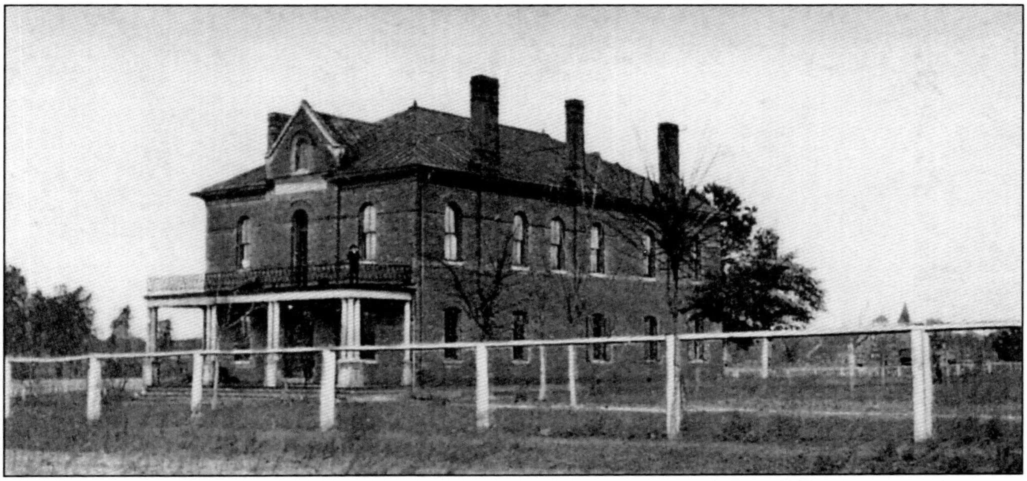

THE COURT-HOUSE, ST. GEORGE, S.C. (Hand-Colored Collotype, 3½" X 5½"; 1910.) In elections held in 1897, St. George's (spelled with the 's at that time) won out over Summerville and Ridgeville as the county seat of the newly constituted Dorchester County. The old two-story county courthouse (*c.* 1898) was originally designed as two separate units, one over the other. The ground floor consisted of county offices for daily business, while the upper floor—accessible only by outside steps on the backside—was the courtroom facility, which had a central door opening on to a porch in the front. After several remodeling jobs, a new courthouse was built on another site in 1966 and this edifice demolished. This rare card is dated "9/14/10." Small-town cards like this one are hard to find.

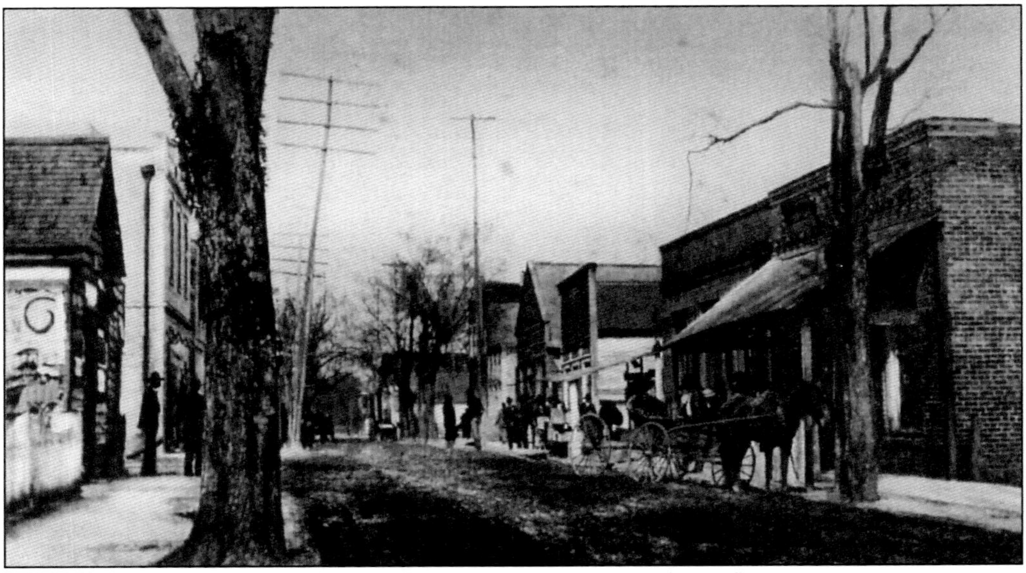

MAIN STREET, ST. GEORGE, S.C. (Hand-Colored Collotype, 3½" X 5½"; *c.* 1907.) St. George's—a name derived from the dual facts that its first settler had been James George (1789–1867) and that it was located in the parish of St. George's Dorchester—was incorporated in 1874, when the town was still in Colleton County. In her brief "History of St. George" in *Days of Dorchester* (*c.* 1970), Mrs. Harry Behling states that one of the principal roads through town was not paved until 1930, and that until then "one of the favorite Fourth of July events was horse racing down main street."

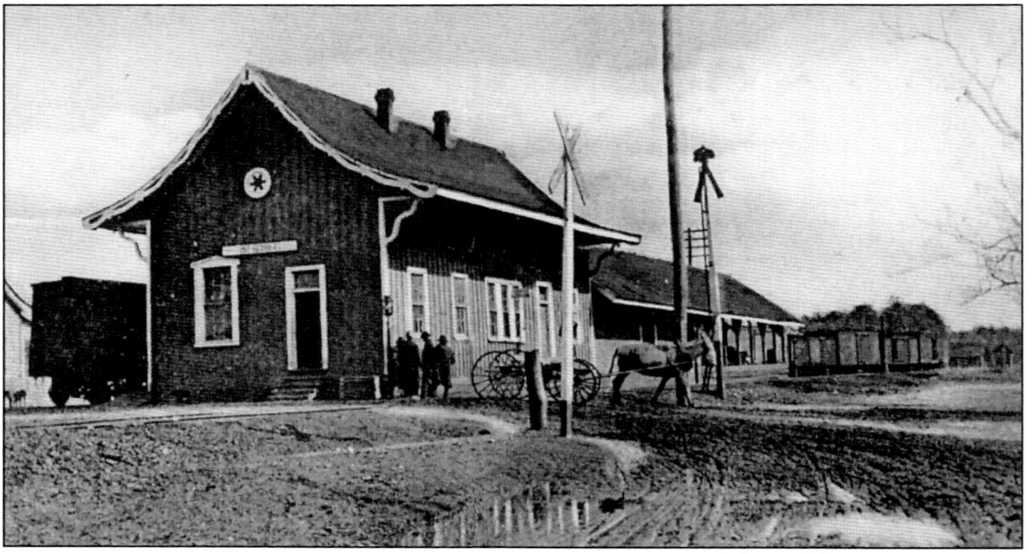

S.R.R. STATION, ST. GEORGE, S.C. (Hand-Colored Collotype, $3^{1/2}$" X $5^{1/2}$"; *c.* 1907.) Local historian Mrs. Behling reveals that St. George was "an important watering station on the railroad line" from Charleston to Hamburg. At the time this card was produced, the horse and wagon still combined with the railroad to provide the basic means of transportation in the rural precincts of South Carolina, as the picture here showing the Southern Rail Road's old passenger station demonstrates. The station was removed in 1981 for use as a lake house. This 1907 view partly blocks the freight station and boxcars (left background) where the merchants received their large cargo deliveries such as automobiles, equipment, furniture, etc.

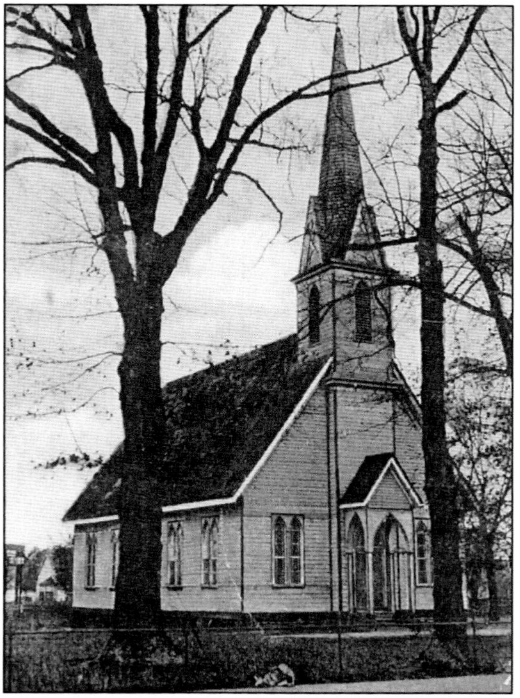

METHODIST CHURCH, ST. GEORGE, S.C. (Hand-Colored Collotype, $3^{1/2}$" X $5^{1/2}$"; *c.* 1907.) The first sanctuary of the St. George Methodist Episcopal Church South, pictured here, was built in the late 1850s on an acre of land donated by Mr. James George, the first settler of St. George. It was destroyed by fire just after services on March 3, 1918. This excellent, hand-colored card—like many others across the state—was sold by jobbers for the Paul E. Trouche Company, a Charleston retail and wholesale stationery supply firm, which imported cards for a vast array of rural merchants during the central period (1906–1912) of the golden era of postcards.

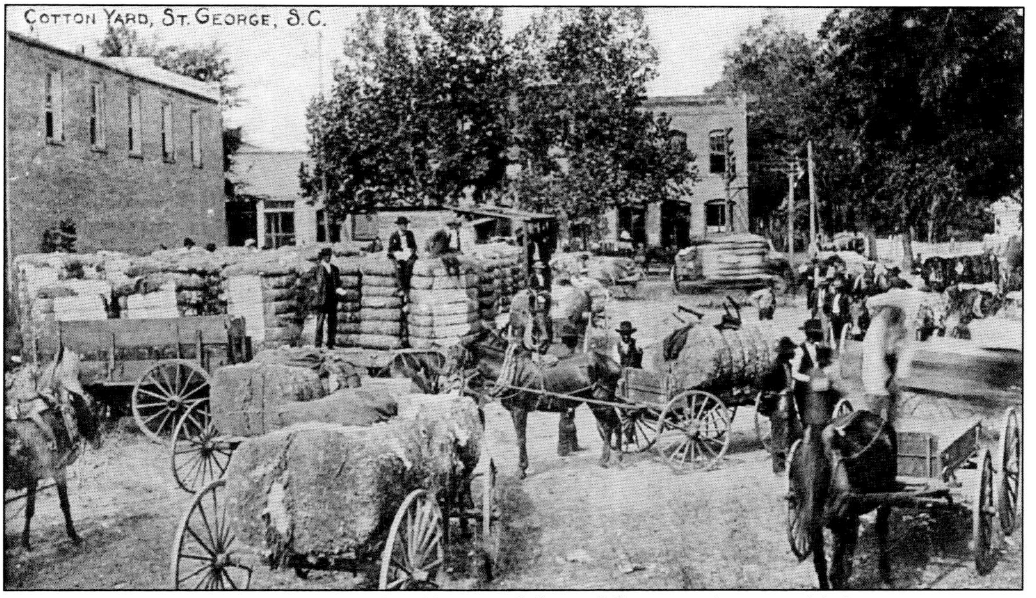


COTTON YARD, ST. GEORGE, S.C. (Halftone, 3½" X 5½", United Art Publishing Co., Series #163, New York, NY; 1911.) Pictures of loaded wagons in a cotton yard or near a town gin commonly appeared on South Carolina postcards of the era. This one is a particularly appropriate concluding set piece to that of the Cotton Palace at the exposition of 1901–1902 featured near the beginning of the book. Farmers around St. George had the special incentive of close proximity—50 miles—to a city which claimed to be a major port for the handling of the commodity directly with the European markets. In 1909, Charleston had done $16,544,057 worth of business in cotton.

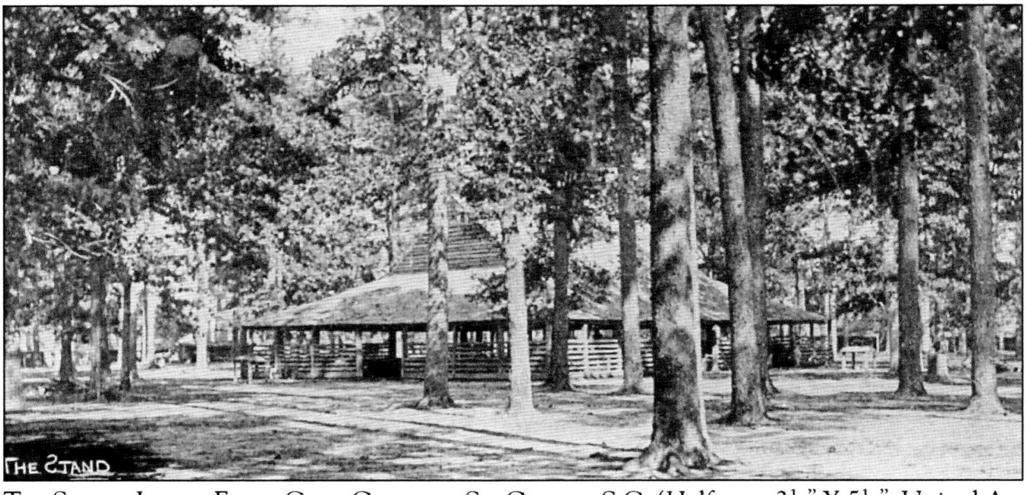


THE STAND, INDIAN FIELDS CAMP GROUNDS, ST. GEORGE, S.C. (Halftone, 3½" X 5½", United Art Publishing Co., Series #163, New York, NY; 1911.) The Indian Fields Camp Ground, located on Highway 15 about 4 miles north of St. George, has been one of the area's principal landmarks since its establishment sometime before Bishop Asbury preached there in 1801. Shown here, on a card postmarked September 13, 1911, is The Stand, the rustic tabernacle built in 1848 which is encircled by dozens of numbered wooden "tents" which house communicants during the week-long camp meeting held each fall.

# Appendix: Data on Postcard Publishers

**Albertype Co.**: See sample card on page 4.

**The Detroit Publishing Co.**, Detroit, MI, obtained the rights to "Photochrom," an "asphaltum" process using ten-color continuous-tone negative plates without halftone screens in 1897 and began printing postcards in 1898. The earliest South Carolina issues have a cp. 1900. Using a postcard-size negative plate, the images had fine details and were printed on a coated-paper stock which preserved its mint-like condition for almost a century.

**Louis Glaser Co.**, Leipzig, Germany [pre-1898] processes included both collotype and chromo-halftone lithography and are found as early as 1906 in South Carolina.

**E.C. Kropp Co.**, Milwaukee, WI [1898], importer and printer of most processes, began producing a limited number of South Carolina cards in 1907.

**Hugh C. Leighton Co.**, Portland, ME [pre-1898], an importer, distributed a large series of thirty-five Charleston images made by the Louis Glaser Company beginning in 1906. Leighton had a 30-million stock available. The 1909 tariff forced Leighton and Valentine and Sons to merge with a domestic printer to accept new contracts and continue reprinting cards from past contracts.

**Knackstedt and Nather Co.**, Hamburg, Germany [pre-1898] [Rotograph Co., New York, NY, importer], printed collotypes and [lithographic] chromo-collotypes to produce a thirty-title Charleston series beginning in 1905 with terms of $5 per 1,000 for collotypes, $10 per 1,000 for color lithographs. The tariff closed the Rotograph Co.'s import view-card business.

**The McGown-Silsby Lithographic Co.**, New York, NY [*c.* 1911] began printing its postcards after the protectionist Payne-Aldrich 1909 tariff act placed taxes on the common import view-card trade, thus eliminating foreign competition.

**Rosenblatt Lithographic Institute**, Franfurt, Germany [pre-1898], produced illustrations of sea shells and fish around small photographs. For Charleston it made a thirty-image view-card series which began distribution in 1907.

**Stengel and Co.**, Dresden, Germany [pre-1898] specialized in collotypes and chromo-collotype lithography view-cards. In 1907 it assumed some of Charleston's Paul E. Trouche Company printing contracts for South Carolina cards.

**The Curt Teich Co.**, Chicago, IL [pre-1904]—one of the most prominent national postcard companies after the 1909 tariff—was competitive with a five-color lithographic view-card production having terms of $6.50 a thousand for 3, 000 cards per subject. South Carolina's Teich cards became more plentiful after 1909.

**Tichnor Bros. Inc.**, Boston, MA, expanded its production after the tariff and produced inexpensive domestic issues for South Carolina about 1910.

**Trenkler & Co.**, Leipzig, Germany [pre-1898], processes included collotypes and chromo-halftone lithography. A five-color lithographic image had a 5,000 minimum purchase for $40 per picture. South Carolina Trenkler cards are found as early as 1906.

**Raphael Tuck & Sons**, London, Great Britain [1898]—art publishers to Their Majesties the King and Queen and the largest postcard publisher in England—subcontracted some of its international lithographic view-card contracts to Louis Glaser with its South Carolina distribution beginning in 1906.

**United Art Publishing Co.**, New York, NY, *c.* 1906], was a mail-order, inexpensive view-card publisher which expanded its advertising after the tariff became effective. Its charges began at $5 per 500 and were often used by small-store merchants in South Carolina beginning in 1909.

**Valentine & Sons**, Dundee, Scotland [pre-1898], a major view-card printer, exported color lithographic view-cards to the United States with terms of $10 per 1,000. It produced a thirty-five card series for Charleston beginning in 1907. The tariff caused it to merge its United States contracts and picture archives with other domestic companies and discontinue its view-card exports to this country.

# INDEX